San Francisco's Natural History

San Francisco's Natural History

SAND DUNES TO STREETCARS

Harry G. Fuller

Nebulosa Press
2017

ISBN-13: 9781548688004
ISBN-10: 1548688002
Library of Congress Control Number: 2017911611
CreateSpace Independent Publishing Platform
North Charleston, South Carolina

The want of sufficient level space on which to found so great and growing a city, has been partially rectified, at an enormous expense, by taking building ground from the waters, and by lowering, and in many cases absolutely removing bodily the multitude of sand hills, by which the place is immediately surrounded. What with digging out and filling up, piling, capping and planking, grading and regrading the streets, and shifting, and rebuilding, and again rebuilding the houses, to suit the altered levels, millions upon millions of dollars have been spent.

–FRANK SOULE, ET AL., THE ANNALS OF SAN FRANCISCO, 1855

In this busy, moving generation, we have all known cities to cover our boyish playgrounds, we have all started for a country walk and stumbled on a new suburb; but I wonder what enchantment of the 'Arabian Nights' can have equaled this evocation of a roaring city, in a few years of a man's life, from the marshes and the blowing sand. Such swiftness of increase, as with an overgrown youth, suggests a corresponding swiftness of destruction. The sandy peninsula of San Francisco, mirroring itself on the one side in the bay, beaten on the other by the surge of the Pacific, and shaken to the heart by frequent earthquakes, seems in itself no very durable foundation.

–ROBERT L. STEVENSON, "SAN FRANCISCO
A MODERN COSMOPOLIS," 1883

She made use of the street-cars when need be, the terrible things that people scrambled for as the panic-stricken at sea scramble for the boats.

–HENRY JAMES, "THE JOLLY CORNER"

Nature's plan has evolved through millions of years while man's plans for the earth cover a short span of time and are very often both selfish and short-sighted.

–HELEN CRUICKSHANK, THOREAU'S BIRDS, 1964

Golden Gate

N
W—E
S

▲ Fort Point

Crissy Lagoon ▼

Marsh

Presidio

El Polin

▲ Mountain Lake

Lobos Creek

Seal Rocks

Lands End

Lone Mountain

Chain of Lakes

Elk Glen Lake

Sand Dunes

Twin P
▼

Laguna Honda

Pacific Ocean

Mt. Davidson 938 feet

Ocean Beach

Pine Lake
▼

Lake Merced
▼

San Francisco
before 1750

rt Mason

*Washerwoman's
Lagoon*

*North
Beach*

*Russian
Hill*

*Telegraph
Hill*

*Yerba Buena
Cove*

Laguna Salada

*Portsmouth
Square*

*Rincon
Point*

*Happy
Valley*

*China
Basin*

**Mission
Bay**

Mission Creek

**San Francisco
Bay**

*Laguna
de
Manantial
(Lake McCoppin)*

Potrero Hill

n
on

*Precita
Creek*

Islais Creek

**Hunters
Point**

*Yosemite
Creek*

**Visitacion
Valley**

Table of Contents

Introduction

The history, natural history, natural beauty and complex heritage of San Francisco will entrance and attract people as long as there are North American cities. Residents, visitors and tourists will continue to find joys, challenges and adventures in this city that rose in an historic instant from the sand dunes, the steep hills and fog-wet chaparral. This book is meant to help readers see what we and our ancestors have done to the environment in San Francisco. There were many observant and literate visitors to San Francisco Bay starting in the late eighteenth century, so we have much more information about what was here and what came later than for any other location on the Pacific coast of North America. Drawing on this rich trove of sources, I hope to give a view of the San Francisco Peninsula before colonization. Some changes were wrought by European diseases and weeds long before the first European people came to San Francisco. Then I describe what we know about changes that began with the mission and presidio. Thereafter alterations in the landscape, the wildlife and flora intensified with the Gold Rush and the rapid urbanization of what was briefly a small Mexican village at the far edge of a teetering Spanish Empire.

When dealing with plants, mammals or streams I have tried to follow the sequence of changes and events chronologically where possible. The accounts of those early visitors vary depending on the season. One may note deer hunting, another an elk hunt. Some noted the spring flowers, another the sere colors of a dry August. Some things, of course, happened without anyone taking note. When was the last wolf seen in San

Francisco? The first rat or cockroach? Fortunately there was often some-body who could recall when there were rattlesnakes on Russian Hill, fur seals in the Bay or dunes covered with blooming lupine in what became the Sunset District

My focus is the City and County of San Francisco but many changes and trends were regional. Some were felt over a wide area of California including San Francisco. Other changes affect the whole California coast-line or the Pacific Ocean off North America. From the extermination of the grizzly bear to the spread of pampas grass, San Francisco has been typical of many widespread changes.

In this age of alternative realities it should be made explicit that I tried to stick to the physical reality that can be seen, heard and touched. I did not use tweets, dreams, the voice of some deity or other specious sources.

When I write about "discovery" and naming of organisms I hope the reader understands in almost all cases the Native Americans already knew much more about the tree or bush or sea mammal than any of the early Europeans. Most white men in the eighteenth and nineteenth centuries learned little from the resident population. They often brought with them images and names from Europe. As late as the 1920s an American graduate student in biology was sent out from U.C. Berkeley to try to discover the nesting sites of Wandering Tattlers in Alaska. He failed one whole spring and summer, looking along the rocky coastline where tattlers can be seen every spring and fall. After that a fellow graduate student, in anthropol-ogy, suggested that the biologist ask the Inuit. The next season he did ask and the Inuit explained to the young man, "look above the tree line in mosquito time." Sure enough, the tattlers were breeding above the treeline on rocky slopes of Alaska's higher mountains. Back when most white men thought the best thing they could do for Native Americans was conversion to Christianity, settlement around missions or brutal extermination, there was not much attempt on the part of the arrogant and ignorant newcom-ers to learn from those who knew the land and its creatures so well. Yet, one of the first examples of a concerted effort to save the Indians' deep knowledge base happened right in San Francisco.

Ishi was the last surviving member of the Yahi tribe. At age 50 he came out of the Sierra Nevada foothills near Oroville where he was "captured" like a wild animal and put into prison for his "own protection." From 1911 until his death in 1916 Ishi spent his final years in the protection of University of California anthropologists who attempted to learn as much as they could about his tribe and their destroyed culture. Most of his final years he lived in a university building in San Francisco.

"Scientific discovery" means the species is being introduced to the systematic naming and counting system set up in Northern Europe by Linneaus and those who followed this system. Carl Linneaus began publishing information on his binomial nomenclature in 1735 and his system grew both in sophistication and acceptance among European scientists over the next decades. It is the basis of modern taxonomy. During the exploration and eventual Americanization of California, science was still largely a discipline in Protestant nations. It was still carrying the stigma in Catholic countries of having been spawned along with the Reformation. Thus the Spanish and later Mexican explorers and writers were much less likely to care about what had become standard scientific naming outside the Catholic sphere in Europe and North America.

Some historic designations are too broad or vague to necessarily refer to a single species, e.g. "scoter." In some cases, such as birds, there is a widely accepted set of name arbiters so often there is little disagreement about a species common and/or Linnean name. This is not true for all organisms and the botanists seem most prone to scientific disagreement as to naming. In all cases I have tried to hew to the most generally accepted name among American scientists. In Europe, for example, loons are still referred to as "divers." I have not included most Latin binomial species names in the text.

With bird species names I have used the custom found among many American ornithological publications: complete and specific common names are capitalized, while shorthand or incomplete names are not. To wit: California Scrub-Jay or scrub-jay, European Starling or starling.

In many of the explorers' journals and publications there are archaic spellings and for the most part I have left those. Where it seemed clear to the author what animal or plant was really meant that modern designation is included in brackets. I opted to spare you the footnotes.

In all cases I have tried for accuracy though some of the historic narratives quoted are likely inaccurate, hypothetical or based on hearsay.

There is a map immediately after this introduction which shows most of the lakes and streams that we can be sure existed around 1840. On the book's website there are numerous historical images and more maps showing alterations and early settlement locations. The website also contains complete list of animal and plant species with their scientific binomials. That URL is: https://ecowise.wordpress.com/2017/04/20/sfnh/

There is a chronology of important and crucial events in the natural history of San Francisco. I hope you find this a useful tool to follow our story. That is to be found between the map and the Preface. Nearly everything mentioned in the chronology appears again in the text where it is pertinent.

At the end, just before the Index, is a detailed Bibliography including some notes from the author. There are some federal government websites listed but many of those links may disappear because the content mentions climate change and right-wing censorship may eventually kill those web pages.

In building the Index for this book I have used only common names for plants and animals. "Brandt's Cormorant" can be found under both Brandt and cormorant.

The deepest and severest threat to the natural world today is climate change. It has and will continue to affect nearly every organism still living in the San Francisco Bay Area. Clearly our abuse of this planet is exacerbated by an ever-growing population and heedless economic exploitation of nature.

Climate change is global and will eventually be an inevitable crisis for all species on earth. In a review of several books on the subject in the "London Review of Books," critic Benjamin Kunkel gave a concise, foreboding summary of the situation as it stands:

Most of [the globe's]...population is poor by European or North American standards and doesn't constitute any automatic constituency for ecological restraint. Governments and corporations, for their part, have little incentive to slow, much less stop the general destruction. The collective activity of humanity is sapping the ecological basis of civilization—and no collective agency capable of reckoning with the fact can yet be discerned... The ecological reality, once acknowledged, can become a political imperative, leading to collective environmental decision-making where for now there is only collective vulnerability to ecological change as a consequence of collective inertia.

Science and conservation groups are involved in on-going research into the effects of climate change, invasive species and an enormous range of pollutants. Over time I can only hope we ruling primates can figure out what is inevitable and what we might do to improve our ecological situation in the twenty-first Century.

San Francisco Chronology

1578 SIR FRANCIS DRAKE LANDS in Northern California, possibly at Pt. Reyes; Drake stopped on the Farallones to collect birds' eggs and seal meat for his crew.

1603 Spanish explorer Sebastian Vizcaino sails along the California coast, discovers San Francisco Bay, charts and names the Farallon Islands.

1660 Royal Society founded in London. It promotes understanding of natural history through observation and empiricism rather than older methods based on religion or the Aristotelian beliefs.

1769 Portola Expedition first sees San Francisco Bay from land; Father Crespi part of this expedition.

1770 Pedro Fages leads land expedition to explore San Francisco Bay Area, sees Golden Gate from East Bay.

1775 Ayala expedition sails *San Carlos* into the bay, first European ship to enter San Francisco Bay. August 5. It anchors at Sausalito. Ayala maps bay and names Alcatraz Island.

1776 DeAnza Expedition camps near Mountain Lake. Founding of San Francisco Presidio and Mission Dolores.

1784 Captain Cook's journal published in England, publicizes wealth of fur-bearing sea mammals along northern Pacific coast of America.

1785 Captain Cook sails along the Pacific coast of California; he noted the numerous sea otters, already valued for their fur.

1786 La Perouse exploration of the Pacific; lands at Monterey, first California visitors from outside Spanish Empire since Drake's visit.

1789-1791 Malespina makes exploratory expedition along Pacific coast of Americas. Political crisis in Spain prevents any publication of findings about natural history of the area.

1792 Capt. Vancouver's British expedition lands in San Francisco. Archibald Menzies is ship's surgeon & naturalist.

1796 *Otter* is the first American sailing vessel to visit California and lands at Monterey.

1805 Lewis & Clark Expedition first official presence of U.S. on Pacific coast when they reach mouth of Columbia River near today's town of Astoria, Oregon

1806 Rezanov's expedition from Russia lands in San Francisco. Beginning of a series of measles epidemics among Coastanoans.

1812 Russians found posts at Fort Ross and Bodega Bay north of San Francisco.

1816 Otto von Kotzebue commands a Russian expedition to California.

1817 Russians establish permanent hunting on Southeast Farallon Island. French expedition led by Camille de Roquefeuil arrives in California.

1820 Estimated 200,000 northern fur seals killed for their pelts.

1821 Mexico becomes independent of Spain, retains control of California.

1826 American fur trapper and explorer, Jedediah Smith, leads his party across Sierra Nevada into California.

1826-7 Capt. Beechey's British ship *The Blossom* in San Francisco Bay; Lt. George Peard part of the crew.

1827 Dr. Paul-Emile Botta visits California aboard French trading ship commanded by Captain Duhaut-Cilly.

1834 Mexico ends mission control of lands in California. All mission properties decreed to belong to the pueblo-dwelling Native Americans.

1835 British ex-patriot William Richardson settles on shore of Yerba Buena Cove, builds first house in what becomes the center of San Francisco.

1835-6 Future author, Richard Henry Dana, Jr., is a crewman aboard *Pilgrim*, a Yankee trading ship along the California coast.

1840 Russians sell Fort Ross to Jacob Sutter after fur industry collapses from over-hunting.

1841 Lt. Wilkes' U. S. Navy Expedition arrives in California.

1841-2 Hudson's Bay Company sends George Simpson to California.

1842 Goats first released onto Yerba Buena Island.

1846 Start of war between Mexico and United States.

1847 In January United States Lt. Washington Bartlett, alcade, officially changes name of town from "Yerba Buena" to "San Francisco." Sales of underwater lots begin.

1848 California becomes part of the United States at end of Mexican-American War. Discovery of Gold in on Sutter's Ranch in Sacramento River Valley starts Gold Rush and an influx of thousands of would-be millionaires.

1850 Using steam-powered machinery, bay fill becomes major engineering effort along San Francisco's waterfront.

1851 California becomes a state.

1852 First trolley line in San Francisco.

1853 U. S. Army begins building fort on Alcatraz Island.

1854 Half million seabird eggs collected on Farallones for San Francisco restaurants.

1855 *Annals of San Francisco* published.

1863 First Cliff House opens. Laguna Honda Reservoir built.

1867 Buena Vista Park created, San Francisco's first.

1869 Dynamite factory blows up in Glen Canyon. First starthistle noted in Oakland.

1874 Rancher Henry Miller rounds up twenty tule elk and protects them on his ranch, thereby saving them from extinction in California.

1876 Eucalyptus tree planted on Presidio Parade Ground; tree still lives.

1879-80 Robert Louis Stevenson in Northern California.

1881 Gathering seabird eggs on the Farallones officially banned but illicit egg-gathering continues for another 15 years.

1882 Washerwoman's Lagoon blamed for cholera and filled.

1883 U. S. Army begins widespread tree-planting in the Presidio.

1892 Surviving elephant seals found on Guadalupe Island, Mexico.

1894 San Francisco Midwinter Exposition in Golden Gate Park, including creation of Japanese Tea Garden.

1896 Sutro Baths built at Lands End. End of commercial egging on Farallones.

1906 Earthquake and fire destroy much of San Francisco.

1911 Fur Deal treaty protects sea otter for first time.

1915 Panama-Pacific Exposition along northern waterfront.

1916 American Robins begin breeding in San Francisco, formerly only a wintering bird.

1926 First Brown-headed Cowbird found laying eggs in native birds' nests in San Francisco.

1928 City purchases land for McLaren Park, named after the city's inimitable park chief, John McLaren. McLaren Park is second largest city park in San Francisco.

1932 First Mockingbird sighted in San Francisco.

1934 McLaren Park established.

1939-40 San Francisco Golden Gate Exposition held on manmade Treasure Island.

1963 Alcatraz Prison closed down.

1966 Sutro Baths burn down. Hooded Orioles noted in San Francisco for the first time.

1969 Native American activists occupy Alcatraz Island.

1974 Use of DDT outlawed in United States; leads to resurgence of Osprey, Bald Eagle and Brown Pelican populations.

1975 First modern era elephant seal pup born in California, at Ano Nuevo.

1980 First "Escape From Alcatraz" triathlon held; swimmers make it between island and shore.

1981 Gulf of Farallones National Marine Sanctuary designated.

1983 Golden Gate National Recreation Area formally dedicated shortly after Rep. Philip Burton was buried in Presidio Cemetery. Congressman Burton had personally authored and insured passage of the law creating GGNRA and six other national preserves around the county. Burton's statue is on the lawn at Fort Mason, part of the GGNRA.

1987 Single Raven's manzanita plant is found surviving in the Presidio.

1989 Loma Prieta earthquake causes fires and deaths in Marina built on bay fill.

1994 Presidio becomes part of Golden Gate National Recreation Area, itself a part of the National Park System.

1995 Large sewer pipe breaks along Lobos Creek leading to restoration of Lobos Dunes area of Presidio.

1999 Opening of Heron's Head Park.

1997 Clean-up and restoration of Crissy Field and its marshlands begin.

2005 In the Presidio the first phase of restoration of El Polin Springs and the Tennessee Hollow riparian habitat begins. This includes Inspiration Point, a serpentine bald.

Preface

No country in the world is more abundant than California, in game and fish of every description.

—L<small>A</small> P<small>EROUSE</small>, 1786

The pretty little bay of Yerba Buena, whose shores are doubtless destined, under better auspices, to be the site of a flourishing city.

—G<small>EORGE</small> S<small>IMPSON</small>, 1842

A citizen of San Francisco died insolvent to the amount of $41,000 the previous autumn. His administrators were delayed in settling his affairs, and his real estate advanced so rapidly in value meantime that after his debts were paid his heirs had a yearly income of $40,000.

—B<small>AYARD</small> T<small>AYLOR</small>, 1849

The sea-lions of the Cliff House. They are the great show of San Francisco. You take a train which pulls up the middle of the street (it killed two people the day before yesterday, being unbraked and driven regardless of the consequences), and you pull up somewhere at the back of the city on the Pacific beach. Originally the cliffs and their approaches must have been pretty, but they have been so carefully defiled with advertisements that they are now one big blistered abomination.

—RUDYARD KIPLING, 1889

SAN FRANCISCO'S LANDS END IS on the northwest edge of this storied city. Here salty winds off the Pacific corrode the branches and needles of pines and cypress trees, molding them into rounded shapes that hunker away from the sea. Here winter storms smash thunderous waves onto rocks that are the core of this peninsula. Then foam and dark Pacific water can climb up the cliffs to a height of forty feet. On mild autumn days the sun etches each rock, tree, and lupine flower in fine, bright detail. Then, despite the nearby ocean, you feel dry air suck moisture from your skin. Another summer day, when denizens of the Sacramento Valley see a temperature above 90 degrees Fahrenheit, Lands End is engulfed in salty, damp sea fog. Salt crystals gradually accrete on any smooth surface. The wind and rocks, fog and salt, sun, and porous sandy soil—these are the conditions that make this a unique habitat for the plants and animals that are tough enough. Its remoteness invites and confounds the visitor.

Follow the trail north from the intersection of Forty-eighth and Point Lobos Avenues. It follows Adolph Sutro's old street car line that closed in 1929 after more than three decades of operation. Since then, nature has camouflaged most of the structures people made. The trail, once a rail bed, offers views of the ocean. You're about two hundred feet above the sea here, and you're in the Golden Gate National Recreation Area (GGNRA). A mile on, the trail finally runs into Lincoln Park Municipal Golf Course and parking lots at the Legion of Honor.

The Pacific Ocean is mercurial, its color changing with the position of the sun, clouds, wind, currents, and its own depth. It often reflects the mood of the season. At times, it shimmers like brushed aluminum, or turns leaden gray. Midday wind drives whitecaps over the darker depths. These waves follow one another like thin lines of polished platinum, pale and hard. When the occasional sunshine is just right, the sea may look green or shine like blue vinyl. Its tones and tints in flux, the restless sea flows back and forth through the Golden Gate.

The name "Golden Gate" predates the Gold Rush and thus may refer to the blooms of the prolific California poppy. Each spring poppies would cover the unforested slopes above the sea, a gorgeous contrast to the ocean's mixed hues.

Beyond the memorial to the *USS San Francisco,* a World War II cruiser, the trail bends east. Stop here to look over the Golden Gate. Squint past the plants, ignoring that they were brought here from other parts of the earth. Notice the colors — verdure of leaves and vines, the dark gray-green of bare serpentine rock. Above the blues and greens of the waves, the offshore rocks show white streaks of seabird guano. Ravens overhead flash glossy black. Buttery blooms decorate the lupine. Red autumn leaves shimmer on the poison oak vines. A spectrum of blues and grays plays on a scrub-jay's back. In late summer comes the pale tan of the dried grasses. On a fogless night, under the wan face of the moon, the sea glints silver. These are all lasting colors, surviving from prehistoric California.

Down the slope beneath your feet are stout bushes, wind-stunted trees, bare stone where the soil covering the cliff face has slipped away. At the bottom, rocks are jumbled along the edge of the waves. You can taste the salty air. There's no real beach. It's a place where continent and ocean contend endlessly; you can hear the sounds of relentless abrasion against solid resistance. As old as the earth itself, it's an eons-old competition neither side can ultimately win..

Twisted strata of exposed serpentine show blackish-green. These metamorphic rocks have been tortured and thrust up over the ages by wrenching earthquakes. Two huge tectonic plates collide here, pushing against one another and occasionally violently shifting the very ground.

Not too far from this Lands End trail, on a promontory just north of the Sutro Baths, there's a westward view and some white shell middens, chalk-like streaks in the earth. The promontory was an outdoor dining site for generations of the Ohlone Tribe. For centuries, people plucked shellfish from the rocks below, then settled on top of the bluff to feast. You can envision them, facing the setting sun on a breezy summer afternoon, wrapped in deer skin, enjoying the tangy meal, perhaps accompanied by the sweet, tiny wild strawberries that were once so common here. All washed down with water carried from the nearby spring that now flows through the Sutro Bath ruins.

Quite a number of animals may be seen in this northwest corner of San Francisco. Western Gulls frequently soar overhead. In winter, Glaucous-winged Gulls fly by as well. A lone gull may perch on a rock pinnacle and yell at the ones passing. Brandt's Cormorants, present all year, nest on some of the offshore rocks. Cormorant cavalcades are frequent. Their feathers are two shades darker than the jagged sea stacks that poke up unevenly through the waves. In winter, you may find various scoters, loons, or large grebes grouped on the water. Small numbers of Black Oystercatchers breed on the rocks, and in spring the Pigeon Guillemots come in from the open ocean to nest in rocky clefts. Caspian, Forster, and Elegant Terns pass through, depending on the season. Their beaks will nearly always be pointed downward.

Most remarkable are the lines of Brown Pelicans, abundant from May to December. They ride the updrafts, shifting wing angles or tail-ruddering ever so slightly. Their beaks point forward until they stoop and dive into the water. The splash is prodigious. The pelican's story of near extinction and recovery is one the gripping conservation sagas of the late twentieth century. It is emblematic of the strong and inevitable imprint of humans on nature, for good and for ill. A pesticide made the shells of the birds' eggs so thin they were too fragile to incubate. Once DDT was banned, the Brown Pelican was able to reproduce normally again.

Occasionally you may glimpse a California sea lion swimming past, or spot the dorsal fins of harbor porpoises or, less frequently, a large pod of bottlenose dolphins. Each winter, northbound gray whales pass Lands End. Some pass so close they're easy to see without binoculars. A round head floating just at the surface, with two dark eyes above a soft grey nose, indicates a harbor seal. Nearby, in a tree, there may be a chattering eastern gray squirrel, a species imported from the other side of the continent.

Often a pair of ravens will soar far overhead. If the resident Red-tailed Hawk happens by, the ravens may chase it, croaking loudly. The hawk uses its superior strength and wing surface to outfly the ravens, who quickly tire of the game. Occasionally in summer, a passing Osprey will excite the ravens. The Osprey carry fish from Lake Merced across the Golden Gate, back to a nest in Marin County.

Much of what you see may seem permanent, and you may think that little has changed over the past millennia. That Marin Headland might have been coated with a green veneer of coyote bush, ceanothus, ribes vines and live oak for centuries. However, the yellow blooms in spring are often those of invasive broom plants. And when California's landscape was managed by tribes of Native Americans, the brush was regularly burned, providing better hunting and heavier acorn crops. The environment here has been deeply affected by human intervention for millennia.

Gaspar de Portola's expedition first sighted this bay in 1769. San Francisco—bay and peninsula—has changed greatly since then. In March of 1776, Juan Bautista de Anza camped at Mountain Lake and explored the south side of the Golden Gate. He found it a most fitting site for a mission, a presidio, and eventually, the city that followed. It's not just the buildings, streets, and power lines that have been put up by humans. The pines, cypresses, and eucalyptus trees were all brought here by people. Most of what was once rolling sand dunes is now paved or covered with buildings. The month of May is no longer marked by endless pale blue waves of bush lupine over the dunes. Streams that once flowed freely are now covered up. The sounds of autos and buses can be heard almost anywhere within the San Francisco city limits. But on a day with mild gusts you can still stand on this northwestern cliff above the Pacific, face into the wind, close your eyes, and hear only the sound of calling gulls, scent only salt mist, feel the vibration of the ground as waves slam into the rocks below. All this would have been familiar to the Native Americans who walked here five hundred years ago, or five thousand years before that.

CHAPTER 1

Before

The sand in those dunes originates in an unexpected place. Some of it comes from the sandstone cliffs at Fort Funston. But much of it comes from, of all places, the Sierra Nevada. During the last ice age, glaciers ground down granite rocks in the great range, and the resulting sediment was carried to the coast by great rivers that were created when the ice melted.

—GARY KAMIYA, COOL GRAY CITY OF LOVE, 2013

When the first prehistoric people trekked into South America toward the end of the Ice Age, they found a wondrous, lush continent inhabited by all manner of strange creatures, like giant ground sloths and car-sized armadillos. But these hunter-gatherers proceeded to behave like an "invasive species," with their population surging then crashing as they relentlessly depleted natural resources.

—WILL DUNHAM, REUTERS, APRIL 6, 2016

BEFORE COLONIZATION, SMALL SETTLEMENTS OR seasonal camps of Ohlone existed on Russian Hill, Telegraph Hill, Rincon Point, and in the Mission District. The Native Americans moved about as seasons affected available foods: shellfish, waterfowl, acorns, mammals, quail, strawberries, and tree fruit. The Bay Area was one of the most densely populated parts of North America before the Europeans arrived and unwittingly unleashed their deadly epidemics. The precolonial Californians changed both the habitat and the lives of the other animals in the region. From the first encounter with Bay Area nature, humans deliberately or accidentally determined who and what survived or disappeared.

Long before the first Native Americans arrived much of the western portion of the peninsula was covered by sparse vegetation and wind-sculpted sand dunes. Lake Merced was there, but its outlet to the ocean came and went depending on geological events over centuries. Trees were scarce. In protected areas and east of sheltering hills there was coastal scrub with some stunted trees, mostly coast live oak or California buckeye. There were also California laurel, madrone, and manzanita. Various willows and wax myrtle grew near the two dozen lakes and numerous freshwater streams. Tules would have crowded the shallow waters of marshes above the tide line.

The precolonial low-lying coastline of San Francisco between the Presidio and Candlestick Point would often have been marshy. Today's existing coastline bears little resemblance to what it would have looked like in 1800. Then salt marsh covered extensive portions of the old bayshore. Marshes harbored rodents, small fish, egrets, herons, bitterns. Despite all the filling, draining, and diking, the San Francisco Bay still accounts for most of the salt marsh remaining in the entire state of California. Grizzly and black bears, mountain lions and bobcats, elk and mule deer were here. Jackrabbits coursed the dunes; California ground squirrels and aplodontia lived in the coastal scrub and on sides of streams. In the air were Turkey Vultures, Red-tailed Hawks, Bald Eagles, Osprey and ravens. Every few days a gigantic California Condor would pass overhead. In the fall, shrubs and willows were teeming with warblers, flycatchers, orioles, tanagers, and vireos heading south to the tropics. Red-legged frogs lived in the lakes. Western rattlesnakes rested in the shade of manzanita and coyote brush.

One other thing we know now: the California that greeted colonizers and explorers in the late 1700s was far different than the California of just three hundred years earlier. Before 1400, the population density in California was greater than anywhere else in North America. Estimates of the precolonial population in the state as high as seven hundred thousand, mostly in the lowlands. Agriculture as we think of it was limited; there were no regimented rows of plants, no livestock in pens, no irrigation projects or canals. Those precolonial Americans managed the landscape with fire and cropping, with hunting and planting. Before colonization and European diseases arrived, the Ohlone people had voraciously hunted most large mammals into relict populations in remote places. Many larger birds had also been hunted into tiny surviving populations.

In the pages that follow, we'll trace changes that came after the post-Columbian invasions of North America by Europeans and their often unintended companions: disease, weeds, invasive animals, feral horses, free-range livestock, and more.

As colonization began in San Francisco, even modest creeks flowing in all seasons would have had runs of steelhead and coho salmon at separate times. Smelt numbers were remarkable and remarked on. In the late eighteenth century Father Junipero Serra wrote of one smelt run into shallow ocean water that lasted for 23 days. Inland tribes came to the coast to share in the bounty.

Father Crespi, a member of Portola's expedition to the San Francisco area in 1769, described Northern California before the missions were founded. His reports mention valleys crowded with large herds of pronghorn in what is now San Benito County. Deer were also abundant. In springtime, between the current locations of San Jose and Gilroy, Crespi saw thousands of geese and Sandhill Cranes. At that time cranes still nested in the Sierra every summer. In the 1820s, Jedediah Smith's party trapped beaver along the Stanislaus and Sacramento Rivers.

An important, early account of wildlife and habitat in the area was written by a Jesuit historian, Miguel Venegas. Although he never actually visited the province comprising California and Baja, he drew on the accounts of others who had explored the region, often writing questions to them to elicit as exact information as possible. He completed his 600-page manuscript in 1739 and sent it to Spain. It was revised in the 1750s by a second author, and was finally published in 1759. That's before the San Francisco Peninsula was explored and colonized by Spanish subjects. In the 1750s the revising author wrote: "In California are now found all kinds of domestick [sic] animals … they have been transported from New Spain, for horses, mules, asses [burros], oxen, sheep, hogs, and goats, and even dogs and cats have been found to thrive in this country." Horses, burros, and pigs still run wild in many parts of the western United States. Venegas described bighorn sheep, pronghorn, deer, hares, rabbits, and wild goats. He mentions very large bears near Monterey, doubtless grizzlies, and assures his readers there are plenty of snakes, scorpions, spiders, lizards, crickets, and tarantulas.

Of birds, there is an infinite variety … turtles [doves], herons, quails, pheasants [grouse], geese, ducks and pigeons. The birds of prey are vultures, hawks, falcons, ossifrages [osprey], horn-owls, ravens, and crows … with regard to night birds, there are owls and many others of a smaller kind, not seen in any other parts, nor mentioned by any naturalists [nightjars].

[A]bout the harbor of Monterey are bustards [Clapper Rails?], peacocks, geese, thrushes, swallows, sparrows, gold-finches, linnets [House Finches], quails, partridges, blackbirds, water-wagtails [shorebirds], cranes, vultures, and other birds, resembling turkey cocks … cormorants, gulls and mews … the gulls live on pilchards and other small fishes.

Venegas's description of the bird eating very small fish makes the "gull" sound more like a tern. Venegas quotes one Father Antonio de la Ascención, who made these observations of life in the Bay of San Francisco:

Here are such multitudes of fish, that with a net, which the commodore had on board, more was caught every day, than the ship's company could make use of: and these a great variety, as crabs, oysters, breams, mackerel, cod, barbels, thornbacks, etc.

The same account mentions large numbers of sardines that seasonally washed ashore, and what tasty eating they made. These fish may actually have been grunion.

Father Crespi mentions arroyos in the San Francisco Bay Area filled with live oaks and willows. He noted large thickets of blackberries and wild roses, lilies and sweet marjoram (presumably a wild mint, perhaps yerba buena). Even into the early twentieth century, dunes in western San Francisco produced a natural spring wildflower extravaganza when lupine, clarkia, buckwheat, and other low-growing plants bloomed profusely. James Roof, founder of the Tilden Park Botanical Garden in Alameda County, predicted more than a century ago, "As the years pass, people will forget that no concentrated natural flower garden in California matched the City of San Francisco."

Father Crespi said Indians fed the visitors pine nuts and acorn porridge as well as large mussels. He noted many dogs around the Ohlone villages, their only domestic animal before colonization.

Captain Jean François de La Perouse from France was the first European from outside the Spanish Empire to visit California after the founding of the missions and pueblos. In September 1786, he spent time in Monterey. About Monterey Bay he wrote: "It is impossible to describe the number of whales with which we were surrounded, or their familiarity. They spouted every half minute within pistol shot of our frigates, and caused a most annoying stench. We were unacquainted with this property in the whale, but the inhabitants informed us that the water thrown out by them is impregnated with this offensive smell." La Perouse also mentions that Mexican officials had recently realized they could profitably sell sea otter pelts in China. Thus local officials in California had been ordered to begin collecting otter skins.

Before colonization began the Ohlone and their predecessors had four main ways to change nature: fire, coppicing trees, fishing and hunting. Fire was used to protect open oak forest. The acorn crop was crucial to the

Indians. The fish runs were so great that it is not likely the Indians' catch was a major factor in the fish population. Larger prey animals from geese to elk were more intensely affected by Indians as we shall see.

CHAPTER 2

Humanity Evicts Nature

The port of San Francisco does not show itself to advantage until after the fort [Presidio] is passed, when it breaks upon the view, and forcibly presses the spectator with the magnificence of the harbour. He then beholds a broad sheet of water, sufficiently extensive to contain all the British navy.

—ARCHIBALD MENZIES, 1792–1793

IT'S ALWAYS SAN FRANCISCO BAY that first attracts the attention, imagination, greed, or admiration of the visitor. The Bay itself is a drowned estuary, a broad floodplain now inundated by the ocean. Nearby bays like Tomales and Bolinas are drowned rift valleys so they are different, narrow and steep-sided. In 1792–1793, Archibald Menzies, the medical officer for the British Expedition, headed by Captain George Vancouver, was immediately taken with the dramatic "broad sheet of water" that is the bay, described in the epigraph to this chapter. The observations by Menzies and other expedition crew are valuable as baseline information about how the area was changed over the decades that followed their visit.

During their stay in the fall of 1792, the British sailors reported a large number of waterfowl in the marsh that is now Crissy Field. Menzies describes the area between Fort Mason and Fort Point as a "low track of

Marshy Land along shore, with some Salt Water Lagoons that were supplied by the overflowings of high Tides and oozings through the Sandy
Beach: on these we saw abundance of Ducks and wild Geese."

Menzies' commander, Captain Vancouver, noted the changes in soil
between the Presidio and the mission in the village, Yerba Buena:

"This plain is by no means dead flat, but of unequal surface; the sod
is of a sandy nature and was wholly under pasture, on which were grazing
several flocks of sheep and herds of cattle. The sides of surrounding hills,
though but moderately elevated, seemed barren, or nearly so; and their sum-
mits were composed of naked, uneven rocks." Around Mission Dolores:

> The country was pleasingly diversified with hill and dale. The hills were
> at a greater distance from each other [than at the Presidio] and gave
> more extent to the plain, which is composed of soil infinitely richer than
> that of the presidio, being a mixture of sand and black vegetable mold.
> The pasture bore a more luxuriant herbage and fed a greater number
> of sheep and cattle. The barren sandy country through which we had
> passed seemed to make a natural division between the lands of the mis-
> sion and those of the presidio.

Vancouver mentions large livestock flocks. He is visiting in 1792, less than
two decades after the first colonists arrived from Mexico. Yet, already
hundreds of domestic animals are ranging across a fragile landscape.

The magnificent harbor Menzies described drew ships, speculators,
prospectors, settlers, and the attention of the whole world after gold was
discovered at Sutter's Mill in 1848. Journalist and world traveler Bayard
Taylor was sent to California to report on the Gold Rush for eastern newspapers. Here he tells us about San Francisco, less than sixty years after
Menzies noted the empty, inviting bay.

> We are in front of the entrance to San Francisco Bay. The moun-
> tains on the northern side ... come boldly down to the sea. As the
> view opens through the splendid strait, three or four miles in width,
> the island rock of Alcatraz appears, gleaming white in the distance

[that's bird-guano white]. An inward-bound ship follows close on our wake.... [T]here is a small fort [Presidio] perched among the trees on our right.... [T]he town is still concealed behind the promontory around which the bay turns to the southward, but between Alcatraz and the island of Yerba Buena, now coming into sight, I can see vessels at anchor. High through the vapor in front, and thirty miles distant, rises the peak of Monte Diablo, which overlooks everything between the Sierra Nevada and the ocean. On our left opens the bight of Sausalito, where the U.S. propeller "Massachusetts" and several other vessels are at anchor.

At last we are through the Golden Gate—fit name for such a magnificent portal to the commerce of the Pacific!... [S]outhward and westward opens the renowned harbor, crowded with the shipping of the world, mast behind mast and vessel behind vessel, the flags of all nations fluttering in the breeze! Around the curving shore of the bay and upon the sides of three hills which rise steeply from the water, the middle one receding so as to form a bold amphitheater, the town is planted and seems scarcely yet to have taken root, for tents, canvas, plank, mud and adobe houses are mingled together with the least apparent attempt at order and durability.

Today's San Francisco is defined by buildings and paved streets, but three hundred years ago, this peninsula was defined by sand and water. From bay and ocean shore to marshes and interdune lakes, the land that is now San Francisco was watery all year round. Now, the ponds in a few parks, Lake Merced, and a couple of visible creeks are just hints of what once was. In early accounts there are numerous mentions of creeks, estuaries, lakes, and marshes. Sometimes the geography is hazy and other times it seems some once-lively stream gets a single mention because it lay in the largely ignored western or southern reaches of what became San Francisco, far from the first settlements. To help visualize the location of all these prehistoric streams and extinct lakes check the map in the front of this book and the many maps on the book's website.

In the eighteenth century, the flat land east of today's Fort Point was lagoon or salt marsh. Vancouver's 1792 map shows a sand spit (or fore-dune) reaching eastward from Fort Point, closing off much of what would have been a shallow brackish lagoon. The bordering marsh opened to the bay near today's Fort Mason. It covered the area now known as Crissy Field and the Marina District. The inland extent of this shallow lagoon and marsh reached today's intersection of Lombard and Divisadero.

Much of the Marina marshland was filled using rubble from the 1906 quake. A tiny remnant of the marsh still exists in the pond at the Palace of Fine Arts. Another small piece of marsh has been restored at Crissy Lagoon in the Presidio. Flowing into that original lagoon was a spring-fed stream with three tributaries, including one born at El Polin Spring at the head of Tennessee Hollow in the Presidio. That spring was used by the Native Americans who lived nearby long before the Spanish and Mexicans arrived. It's one of the few springs easily viewed in modern San Francisco.

El Polin Spring and Tennessee Creek, which flows from it, have been restored to include marshy areas and reintroduced native plants. More of the water now flows along the surface, as former culverts have been removed. A small area of riparian marsh has been restored and more native plants put back around the spring. In the dry weeks of summer the area is a favorite among hummingbirds and other small, thirsty animals.

Many old lake beds lie dead beneath the streets and neighborhoods of the city, the fish and otters they once nourished long gone. The lakes we see in San Francisco now include some original natural bodies of water, but others are wholly artificial. Those that existed before colonization have been deliberately altered by people.

Lake Merced was a single body of water in 1840. A stream that flowed in from the southeast (now Daly City) fed the lake. A remnant of that creek now runs down a cement ditch on the edge of the Olympic Club golf course, along John Muir Drive, south of Lake Merced. A second stream carried lake water to the sea. It was a surface stream that entered the Pacific near the west end of today's Sloat Boulevard, according to very early maps. The stream's outlet would shift as the sand dunes shifted. In November 1851, the outlet stream was blocked from the ocean by drifting sand, isolating Lake Merced from the sea. Later that month, after heavy rains, the lake waters broke through the sandy barrier and again opened the temporary stream to the Pacific. Contemporary accounts claim the lake level dropped thirty feet. A 1902 map shows the outlet stream still leaving Merced at its northwest corner and flowing into the Pacific at the west end of today's Wawona Street. Later that outlet was blocked.

Pine Lake also existed. It was formed when blowing sand enclosed the west end of the valley that now holds Stern Grove. A 1902 map of the city shows that the lake once stretched five blocks, between Twenty-Eighth and Thirty-Third Avenues, south of Wawona.

The Chain of Lakes (North, South, and Middle Lakes) in today's Golden Gate Park were originally a series of small ponds. Elk Glen Lake, also in the park, is another natural body of water. The area covered by Golden Gate Park originally contained a total of fourteen small lakes. Any that weren't destroyed by park landscaping were significantly changed.

The Laguna Honda along today's Seventh Avenue is much changed, but it is an original lake as well. The narrow valley that holds the lake is believed to have once carried an ancient stream down from San Francisco's higher slopes when the ocean level was much lower than it has been in recent centuries. Laguna Honda once had a sister lake near Seventh Avenue and Lawton.

Another small lake existed in the valley where Cole Street now crosses Parnassus. After the Gold Rush, until the 1890s, the area was used for dairy farming. Laguna Seca, as it was known, was then filled in and covered with housing.

Glen Canyon. One of the few surface streams still to be seen in San Francisco runs down Glen Canyon. It constitutes the headwaters of Precita Creek, which joins Islais Creek, named from the Ohlone word for hollyleaf cherry. The spring-fed stream emerges on the lower eastern slope of Twin Peaks and flows for half a mile, nearly the length of 122-acre Glen Canyon Park. Today you can still stand amidst dense native willows in the upper portion of Glen Canyon. Here Ohlone women would have come for materials for basket weaving. The men may have pursued birds, rabbits, or deer through this very thicket. Today at the foot of this city park, the creek is diverted into a tunnel and doesn't reappear until it empties into the heart-less cement-encased Islais Channel.

In 1869 America's first dynamite factory, the Giant Powder Company, blew up in Glen Canyon. Also, in the late 1800s, the canyon, then known as Rock Gulch, supported a private zoo and amusement park. A plan to dam the canyon for a reservoir was never carried out. In 1878, the city was authorized to cover Precita Creek. Dairy cattle grazed the canyon in the early 1900s, and by then the creek's water was being used for the boilers that generated electricity for the city's new streetcars.

A 1920s map shows a second tributary to Islais Creek running down the path now followed by Cayuga Avenue. At that time this stream, named Island Creek, was still flowing as far east as Folsom Street, then apparently disappearing into underground sewers. Upstream on Island Creek, lay the small Lake Geneva. It was west of the current intersection of Geneva and Mission Streets. This creek crossed into San Francisco from Daly City, near the intersection of Guttenberg and Bellevue Streets.

In the late 1800s, Islais Creek was San Francisco's largest stream. Its water was used for drinking, being controlled by Clarke's Waterworks, a private company. A photo taken in 1904 shows that lower Islais Creek was still an open estuary then, where freshwater marsh met tidal saltwater marsh. It would have been a rich piece of bayshore habitat. The Islais Creek marsh extended as far inland as today's intersection of Highway 101 and Interstate 280, more than a mile from the current bay. It is also a mile downstream of where the once free-flowing creek is now forced into the underground tunnel that dumps it into the bay. That original marsh included the north side of Hunters Point. It is likely that Islais Creek was navigable by small boats as far west as today's San Bruno Avenue.

Two of several extensive salt marshes covered areas of the south-eastern section of what is now the city. An 1827 map by British Captain Frederick Beechey show two creeks in eastern San Francisco with multiple tributaries: Islais and Yosemite. South of Hunters Point a large marsh surrounded the channel of Yosemite Creek, which ran to the base of Bayview Hill on the north side. The marsh extended west to Third and Yosemite Streets. The southern headwaters of Yosemite Creek included an upland marsh and three springs that still exist on the north slope of McLaren Park. In this area lives an endangered insect, the San Francisco damselfly. This marsh, which is near the intersection of Oxford and Bacon Streets, is tiny. Both lakes that now exist in McLaren Park are artificial, but draw from springs and run-off from natural marshes there. The south slope of the ridge in McLaren Park also gives rise to springs. These fed Sunnydale Creek before it was put underground. That stream flowed into Visitacion Valley and into what was once Visitacion Bay, east of the present Cow Palace and south of Bayview Hill.

Another still-flowing stream is spring-fed Lobos Creek, its underground source apparently nearby Mountain Lake. Both are in the southwest corner of the Presidio. Even 150 years ago, there was no surface connection between the two. Lobos Creek runs a half mile before it empties into the Pacific at the west end of Baker Beach. The Ohlone came here to gather cattails, acorns, and stinging nettles.

If you want a hint of what precolonial creek valleys may have been like, look through the fence on the Lobos Dunes boardwalk, off the Presidio's Lincoln Boulevard. Here, twisted and hardy, live oaks stand as they have for millennia. They line free-flowing Lobos Creek and border a small patch of restored coastal dunes. The original dunes survived here until after World War II. This was the location of the last sighting of the blue Xerces butterfly before it went extinct in the 1950s.

In the 1860s Lobos Creek water was diverted into redwood flumes and carried eastward along the coast for over three miles; then the water was pumped to the top of Russian Hill. A private company engineered this feat to sell Lobos Creek water to a thirsty and fast-growing city. The water for Lobos Creek is seeping through the sandy soil from Mountain Lake which lies uphill.

Mountain Lake is unique in several ways. It is the only natural lake in the Presidio and in fact it is the only natural lake in the whole eighty-thousand acre Golden Gate National Recreation Area. It holds a singular spot in San Francisco's history. It is here that the De Anza expedition camped for two days in 1776. From here the Spanish troops scouted for the future locations of the presidio and mission to be built on the peninsula. When the street heading north toward the Golden Gate Bridge was widened, the western part of the lake was filled. But recent years have seen extensive restoration efforts, see Chapter 18 for more on Mountain Lake restoration.

East of Mountain Lake Park, at Euclid and Palm Avenues, there was once a pond that was a favorite place to hunt wintering ducks. Known as Kelly's Pond, it was filled in in the 1880s and now the houses of Jordan Park cover it.

In Cow Hollow, there was a small lake known as Washerwoman's Lagoon, roughly bounded by today's Lombard, Gough, Filbert, and Octavia Streets. During the Gold Rush, it became a center for vegetable production and clothes laundering. In the 1850s, although some locals were still sending dirty clothes to Hawaii or Canton, China, to be washed and sent back, much of the growing city's laundry was done here. By 1882 the lake was polluted and blamed for spreading cholera. As a result, it was filled in and buildings were put up.

The waters of San Francisco Bay originally reached today's Bay Street. North Beach was exactly that, a beach at the north end of the peninsula. Many nineteenth century Italian families settled inland from Bay Street because they could pull their fishing boats onto the sand and walk to their nearby homes.

Most of the early sailing ships anchored in the area where today's Embarcadero runs, north of Market Street. Telegraph and Russian Hill protected those ships from much of the wind coming through the Golden Gate. The eastern slope of Telegraph Hill dropped straight down to a narrow muddy strand along the cove. You can still see that steep cliff face if you look uphill from Battery Street north of Broadway. To those arriving on the ships, this cove and landing was the place named Yerba Buena. When the Gold Rush began, the distant mission settlement and presidio were not yet recognized as part of "Yerba Buena" by the newcomers. One it became part of the United States, the Americans quickly renamed the whole peninsula "San Francisco."

All that remains of Rincon Point is the rise supporting the western end of the Bay Bridge. Originally the point was a hill right at the high tide line and surrounded by water when the tide washed in. Most of Rincon Hill was used for bay fill, but before it was leveled, it formed an irregular peninsula, its highest point at First and Howard. North of Rincon Point, the high tides reached to the eastern side of what is today's Montgomery Street. South of Market, high tides reached west to First Street, once literally the first street you came to if you turned your back to the bay and headed inland.

To the east, south and west of Rincon Hill was an expanse of marsh and mudflats fronting the Bay, covering part of the areas we now know as South of Market and China Basin. This marshy area ran from Third Street to Seventh Street and extended north of today's Folsom Street. A botanist writing in the 1890s described a swamp near the present corner of Sixth and Harrison Streets. Most of it was filled in well before 1900. Near Second and Mission was Happy Valley Spring, a source of drinking water for early residents. Water from the Happy Valley Spring would have run down into the brackish marsh.

Mission Bay extended through the western portion of that marsh from Townsend (originally Town's End) south to the eastern slopes of Potrero Hill. Mission Creek emptied into Mission Bay, where Channel Street now runs. In 1874 the state legislature deemed Mission Creek no longer a navigable stream, which meant it could be partially filled. Its mouth now lies just outside the Giants baseball stadium and is known as McCovey Cove, honoring the great slugger. At Mission Creek's upper reaches, there was a shallow tidal basin near the area that's bounded today by Harrison and Shotwell, between Seventeenth Street and Twentieth Street. Proceeding west was Arroyo de los Dolores, for which the nearby mission was named. Down that arroyo flowed a stream that fed a sizeable lake. This lake (Laguna de Manantial, later called Lake McCoppin) ran from Fifteenth Street to Nineteenth Street, bounded on the east by Howard, on the west by Guerrero. A spring sent a rivulet down the arroyo from Twin Peaks, roughly along the path of Eighteenth Street, ending at the lake. By 1873, most of the lake was filled in, but the fill was soft. This weakness led to death and destruction during the 1906 earthquake. Buildings atop the lake fill collapsed as the earth vibrated and liquefied.

Further north, a smaller creek flowed roughly along Fourteenth Street, entering Mission Creek near today's Folsom Street. An early explorer mentioned a shallow lake in today's Hayes Valley. Without drilling beneath today's homes and streets, we can't confirm this lake's existence. Another stream headed downhill from Twin Peaks and ran southeast. Bayard Taylor wrote in 1849: "Three miles from San Francisco [Portsmouth Square] is the old mission of Dolores, which is watered by a perpetual stream fed from the tall peaks towards the ocean [west]."

North of Market there was a small saltwater lagoon (Laguna Salada) near the present corner of Jackson and Montgomery. In 1847 San Francisco's first bridge was built across that lagoon's narrow outlet. A spring-fed stream ran down the route of today's Sacramento Street. The stream fed a small freshwater lake immediately east of where Sacramento intersects Montgomery today. This area—around Portsmouth Square—had soft soil, inadequate support for the shoddy construction that characterized buildings and roads in the city during the early years. The natural conditions in general were extremely problematic. San Francisco's rugged contours and wind-driven sand dunes presented difficult obstacles for early inhabitants. Here's an eyewitness description from newspaper editor James Ayers, who first arrived in 1849:

> When one looks back and recalls the topographical features of San Francisco at that time, he is amazed at its selection as a site for a great city. It had, indeed, nothing to recommend it for that purpose except its magnificent harbor. There was absolutely no level ground.... Where it was not shut in by almost precipitous and rugged acclivities it was obstructed by formidable sand hills ... immense sand dunes covered what is now the fairest part of the city. At the intersection of Bush and Kearney streets was a sand hill that rose to a height of forty or fifty feet. On Market Street near Third, and reaching halfway to Fourth, was another great sand mountain.

Beyond the inconveniences, the ground beneath people's—and animals'— feet presented deadly challenges to daily living. In his memoirs, General

William T. Sherman recalled San Francisco before the Civil War: "I have seen mules stumble in the streets and drown in the liquid mud. Montgomery Street had been filled up with brush and clay, and I always dreaded to ride on horseback along it because the mud was so deep a horse's leg would become entangled in the brush below and the rider was likely to be thrown and drowned in the mud." Ship parts, cargo in boxes and discards were used in the efforts to build "safe" paths atop the seemingly bottomless muck. Today the little museum in the old Rincon Post Office on Mission Street displays examples of the timber, bottles, pots, tools, boat rigging, and other discards found buried in San Francisco's waterfront mire.

Here's what Gertrude Atherton had to say, looking back from the comforts of the mid-twentieth century:

> There was a time, not many years ago, when San Francisco halted far east of Van Ness Avenue, and with the exception of the Presidio and the settlement around the old Mission Dolores, there was nothing to be seen but miles of sand dunes, and the afternoon winds lifted their shifting surface and swept in through the streets of the city. Sometimes one could not see the opposite side of the street through the blinding dust and there were so many afflicted eyes that occulists came from other parts of the country and retired with comfortable fortunes.

Original streams, dunes, lakes, and marshes were altered as today's street grid came into existence. Most of the shallower portions of San Francisco Bay have now been filled. Captain Beechey's journal (from his 1826–1827 visits) describes the old San Francisco shoreline as being largely alluvial from Fort Point east and south all the way to Yosemite Creek. He remarked on the 167-foot-high sandstone cliff on the east face of Telegraph Hill, which some early visitors called "Sketch Hill." Beechey also recognized the presence of jasper and serpentine where San Francisco's rocky core was not covered by dunes. On Angel Island, Captain Beechey found clay slate on the southwestern portion, with alluvial material making up the north edge of the island.

Beechey also pointed out that earthquakes "are rather common." The San Andreas Fault—and its potent earthquakes—is the other irresistible force, besides human effort, that has shaped the terrain from ancient times to the present day. San Francisco remains vulnerable to constant alteration, both natural and artificial. Much of the city stands on sand. Couple that with buried streams and lakebeds, marshy margins with undependable landfill and the high value of any plot of land and you get construction that is only good until the next earthquake. You get a city where flux is unavoidable, where the unexpected should be expected.

CHAPTER 3

Green in Winter, Brown in Summer: Precolonial Flora

Native Americans were the ultimate keystone species, and their removal has completely altered ecosystems, not only in the Intermountain West but throughout North America.

—CHARLES E. KAY, "ABORIGINAL OVERKILL AND NATIVE BURNING," 1995

WHEN EUROPEAN EXPLORERS FIRST ARRIVED at San Francisco Bay in the eighteenth century, they found many unfamiliar plants. There were live oaks, madrones, buckeyes, bay laurels, toyons, willows, and wax myrtles, plus the native shrubs and smaller plants of sand dune and coastal scrub. There were several varieties of lupine, plus ceanothus, poison oak, and manzanita. The climate was harsh. In order to thrive, plants had to adapt to salty winds and fog, abrasive sand, shifting dunes, some days of intense sunshine, porous soil that lacks nitrogen, and droughty summers. One hardy plant was so abundant that the original village, which eventually became San Francisco, was named for it: yerba buena. Naturalists found 120 plant species in San Francisco new to science.

On the overland Portola Expedition in 1769, Father Juan Crespi kept a thorough journal. As they made their way up the coast between what is now Santa Cruz and Half Moon Bay, he wrote:

> We went in view of the shore, over high, big hills all covered with good soil and grass—though almost all the grasses had been burned—and all very bare of trees.... [T]here are many willows in the creek bed.... It is perfectly astonishing to see the quantity of brambles all through these places; they are a great hindrance to travel. There is no wood in the valley, but the mountains close by have good stand of savins [coast redwoods].

Later, on the same expedition, Father Crespi wrote this about the Santa Clara Valley: "At night the scouts returned from their exploration, bringing back no report of any harbors; what exploring they did was done with immense toil, they reported because of the many inlets, lakes, and mires they were faced with, and the country all rough and burnt besides."

Thus does Father Crespi describe the terrain after local Native Americans had burned off the dried grasses and shrubs, an annual land management process common in the arid west before Europeans and Americans took the land.

Among plants noted at Monterey by naturalists on the La Perouse expedition in the 1780s were sea wormwood, Mexican tea, southernwood, mugwort, starwort, Canadian goldenrod, yarrow, black nightshade, samphire, and water mint. Samphire is the name of a European member of the carrot family. Was this an American cousin, or an escapee from the mission garden? It is possible La Perouse and his men would have named many new California plants for science if the expedition had not been lost in the Pacific. Both ships of La Perouse's expedition broke up in a storm off Vanikoro Island in the Solomons. None of the crew was ever seen again by any European, though some may have survived on Vanikoro for some time. The tragic ending of this expedition kept any plants they found from being shared with scientists back in Europe, so we will never know what discoveries were lost, only to be rediscovered by later explorers.

Fortunately we do have many notes and journals and drawings from the California visit. They were sent back to France on a British ship before La Perouse and his ships left Hawaii heading toward their tragic end. It was a time when the French and British were not at war so co-operation at sea was routine that far from home.

The Ohlone's use of fire to control brush, forest, and grass created savanna habitat. The burning killed off brush, helping oak, buckeye and deep-rooted, perennial grasses to dominate the landscape. That would have also made it easier to hunt deer, ground squirrels and other dry land animals. The burned over areas in late summer and fall were often noted by early visitors before the missions tried to stop the practice in areas they controlled. The burning impressed at least one British visitor. Traveling by horseback south along the bayshore of the San Francisco Peninsula, Captain Vancouver in 1792 found the countryside welcoming:

> The plain on which we rode stretched from the base of these mountains [Coastal Range] to the shores of the port, and gradually improved as we proceeded. The holly-leaved oak [live oak], maple horse-chestnut [buckeye], and willow were increased from dwarf shrubs to trees of tolerable size.... [W]e entered a country I little expected to find in these regions. For about twenty miles it could only be compared to a park, which had originally been closely planted with the true old English oak. The underwood that had probably attended its early growth had the appearance of having been cleared away and had left the stately lords of the forest in complete possession of the soil, which was covered with luxuriant herbage.

Vancouver's party was traveling during the rainy season and he had no way of knowing that the Native Americans had long used fire to manage the oak woodlands, grasslands, and other habitats across California

New Plants Found. The first new San Francisco plant to gain scientific recognition was the yellow bush lupine, found by Archibald Menzies during Vancouver's visit. Menzies also collected a branch of the laurel that became the type specimen. He likely found that tree in the Presidio. In that same area, the silk tassel bush once thrived. It is now wild in San Francisco only at Glen Canyon. Menzies mentions a "poisonous plant," yedra, that was found in the Presidio. Yedra was the Spanish name for the abundant poison oak. Menzies also described what he called "a dwarf species of horse chestnut" near what is today Telegraph Hill. That's our California buckeye. When Vancouver anchored off Yerba Buena, Menzies said its name came "from the luxuriance of its vegetation."

Menzies made the scientific discovery of the Douglas fir. He likely encountered it outside of San Francisco. It was not until 1826 that the first Douglas firs were taken back to England by the explorer and plant collector David Douglas and thus got their common name. During his time in Northern California, Menzies noted ceanothus and two willow species. He also commented that the live oaks along the coast rarely reached fifteen feet in height. It is likely that any larger trees had already been felled by Mexican colonists.

Captain Vancouver and Menzies were enemies by the time the expedition ended. They had quarreled during the long and stressful voyage, and Menzies was threatened with court martial, a threat later withdrawn. Thus, sadly, Menzies' scientific notes were never published and forgotten in the archives as he went on to other naval assignments and then a medical career in England. Vancouver ignored Menzies' notes and died in England before he could even finish editing his own account of the expedition. Many of their natural history discoveries went unheralded. Later explorers had to rediscover the same new species in California. Vancouver did make some notes of interest, referring to narrow trails in the Presidio, "much discommoded with groveling bushes." He also commented on finding firewood for the ship, taking fuel from "small bushy holly-leaved oaks [coast live oaks], the only trees fit for our purpose."

The first Russian voyage around the world, begun in 1803, was commanded by Count Nikolai Rezanov. Rezanov's ships arrived on the coast of California in 1806. On board was George von Langsdorff, a renowned naturalist who was also Rezanov's physician. Langsdorff drew the Presidio as it looked from the Russian ship, the hills covered with brush or small trees all the way down to the beach.

In 1816 another Russian expedition entered San Francisco Bay. The naturalist on board, Adelbert von Chamisso, was the first to scientifically describe the California poppy, which he named *Eschscholzia californica* in honor of Johann Friedrich Eschscholtz, the ship's surgeon and also a botanist. It's likely that Chamisso found the poppy – eventually California's state flower – in the present-day Presidio. Chamisso also noted a single live oak downhill from the Mexican Presidio, and recognized the cinquefoil in bloom in October. He collected the first specimen of the wax myrtle from a wet area within the present-day Presidio. He found California hazel, which turned out to be a variety of a widespread species. Other plants Chamisso discovered in San Francisco include the California rose, California blackberry, alkali heath, and the aromatic yerba buena. More than one aromatic plant has been identified as yerba buena by writers, and even naturalists in the past. Missionaries apparently thought yerba buena was one of the plants in the *Satureja* genus, which are European savories. The species was eventually named *douglasii*, for David Douglas (1798–1834). The plant was considered a member of the genus Micromeria until molecular analysis caused it to be classified *Clinopodium douglasii*.

After the visit to California with Chamisso in 1816, Eschscholtz returned in 1826. In San Francisco, he collected several more plants new to botanists: the dune lupine, coffeeberry, twinberry, honeysuckle, and blue blossom ceanothus. It's likely he collected coffeeberry in the Presidio.

Britain's Captain Frederick Beechey visited the coast of California in 1826-1827. He noticed small red-barked trees in the Presidio, which we know as the Pacific madrone. In his reports of this part of his expedition, he also refers to honeysuckle. Beechey, like all early European visitors, was especially impressed by "yedra," poison oak. Europe has no similar plants. Here's what he wrote:

> [T]he most remarkable shrub in this country is the yedra, a poison plant affecting only particular constitutions of the human body, by producing tumours and violent inflammation upon any part with which it comes in contact; and indeed even the exhalation from it borne upon the wind is said to have an effect upon some people. It is a slender shrub,

preferring cool and shady places to others, and bears a trefoil crenated [scalloped] leaf.

The naturalist on the Beechey expedition was the intrepid and widely traveled Dr. Alexander Collie. In San Francisco, he found the first specimen of thimbleberry known to science. Like other early visitors, Collie noted the hills covered with blue blossoms in the spring. This was the flowering season of blue blossom ceanothus.

One of Beechey's officers was Lt. George Peard. During his visits to San Francisco in 1826-1827, Peard wrote in his journal about some of the plants he saw in what is now the Financial District in northeastern San Francisco: "Close to the beach ... the willow tree provided us with fuel and brooms. The lupin [lupine] springs up everywhere like a weed; and amongst the numbers of shrubs to be met with in the woods, I must not omit to mention the yedra [poison oak] ...a plant whose poisonous effects are said to be sometimes felt by persons passing near it.... The hedge strawberry grows luxuriously." Likely the last plant Peard mentioned was thimbleberry or salmonberry.

A Rich and Varied Flora. Other coastal scrub plants native to San Francisco include California buttercup, Douglas iris, broadleaf cattail, sticky monkey flower, California sagebrush, coyote brush, and seaside woolly sunflower. It's probable that beachburr and yellow sand verbena were native to the Presidio area. Western bracken and California polypody were two widely distributed ferns. The giant scouring rush and giant horsetail were found where the soil remained damp. Many of these plants are widely distributed and were first discovered in other parts of North or Central America.

Edwin Bryant was an early alcalde of Yerba Buena. In 1846, he described a horseback ride from Mission Dolores to Portsmouth Square. On that ride he would have crossed the future location of his namesake, Bryant Street: "Mounting our horses at sunrise, we traveled three miles over low ridges of sand, with sufficient soil, however, to produce a thick growth of costal live oak, and brambles of hawthorn, wild currant, and gooseberry bushes, rosebushes, briers, etc."

Bryant's botany was that of an amateur, but he accurately depicts the dense, low-growing coastal scrub that covered much of early San Francisco. The sand dunes of San Francisco were not barren. They supported growth of lupine, including Chamisso bush lupine with its purple flowers, monkey flower, poison oak, manzanita, ceanothus, coyote brush, coastal or beach sagewort – all dense shrubs that could tolerate wind and salty fog. Other plants found in the windblown dunes included: yellow bush lupine; dune tansy, with its chrome yellow flowers; and San Francisco wallflower. It was housing and commercial development of the sand dunes that permanently altered the natural flora. Apparently, feral cattle did not penetrate into what we now call the Richmond and Sunset Districts.

As late as 1871 James Bradley Taylor (1831–1902), writing of his visit to San Francisco with Ralph Waldo Emerson, described an April morning's excursion from the Occidental Hotel (destroyed in the 1906 earthquake). The hotel was on Montgomery Street near Bush. From there, Taylor writes:

> We passed through the Chinese quarter, and out over beautiful grassy hills, covered with blue and yellow lupine and a hundred delightful flowers…. Mr. Emerson was delighted as we drove along the beach of the great new ocean. We sat long on the platform of the Cliff House, and rested, and watched the sea lions that climbed and played on some rocks a short way out in the ocean, and the birds that settled by the hundreds on the same rocks.

San Francisco's eighteenth-century salt marshes were green with salt grass, spear oracle, pickleweed, and gum plant. The fleshy jaumea, with its complex yellow flowers, has returned as new salt marshes have slowly emerged along some of the current artificial San Francisco bayshore. One plant extirpated from San Francisco's minimal salt marshland is alkali heath.

Fort Mason offers a glimpse of what San Francisco's steeper bayshore probably looked like. Fort Mason, formerly known as Black Point, was named for the dark trunks of bay trees that once covered it. From the hilltop in the park, or from the foot of Van Ness Avenue, you can see the rocky slopes falling down to the boulder-strewn narrow beach. More accessible flatter areas of San Francisco's shoreline inside the Golden Gate have all been widely altered by development, pavement, and bay fill.

Running from Fort Point southeast to Hunters Point is a geologic fault zone. At the surface it presents an exposed or barely covered band of serpentine, found in a rock formation running the length of the Coastal Range in California. The centuries of seismic activity have exposed the serpentine along this fault line. Interestingly, the serpentine is an important component of the Franciscan geological formation, named for San Francisco.

When exposed or near the surface, serpentine has a strong effect on the survival of nearby vegetation. As it erodes with exposure to rain and air, serpentine produces a clayey soil high in magnesium and heavy metals — such as cobalt, chromium, and iron — and low in calcium. To survive on such soil, plants and animals must adapt, but that adaptation often becomes a delimiting characteristic in that they cannot live, or live well, anywhere else. Over two hundred California plant species, as well as untold numbers of insects, are found only on serpentine soils. There are several places in San Francisco where the effects of serpentine soil can be seen: the south end of the Golden Gate Bridge; below the Presidio's Inspiration Point, where serpentine was exposed by rock quarrying; Lone Mountain—the area around the Geary Boulevard tunnel—and on Potrero Hill. Early gardeners on Potrero Hill complained of the poor soil there compared to the nearby lowlands.

San Francisco's serpentine-tolerant plants include: bent grass, dwarf flax, a member of the purplespot gilia family, California aster, and short-leaf dwarf cudweed. Two Bay Area endemics grow only on serpentine soil: Presidio clarkia and Franciscan manzanita. That is one sub-species of Hooker's manzanita and is endangered; it survives nowadays as a cultivated plant and in extremely limited numbers in the Presidio, under control of the GGNRA. The original survivor had to be moved because of highway construction on the Golden Gate Bridge approach. A recent publication, *Presidio Plant List*, by Pete Halloran, lists 71 plants known to have been extirpated from that part of the GGNRA. Many of those grew on the serpentine soils there. Some adapted natives have survived. Sand dunes and serpentine soils are tough habitat, fending off many invasive weeds. In more accommodating habitat those weeds often come to dominate the plantscape, crowding out natives.

As the National Park Service's website explains, "Rare plants in the Presidio are found in either dune or serpentine communities because invasive non-native plants are not able to dominate these nutrient-poor areas." Indeed, the Presidio serves as an important "refuge" for rare plants: "Twelve plants found at the Presidio are designated as rare, threatened or endangered by the United States Fish & Wildlife Service and/or the California Native Plant Society. In addition, several other rare, threatened or endangered plant species have been re-introduced" in some of the Presidio's habitat restoration sites.

All of San Francisco's original lakes were lined with willows and tules. Broadleaf cattail grew wherever there was standing fresh water. Plants growing along spring-fed streams included common scouring rush, giant horsetail, water parsley, watercress, spearscale, spearmint, various clovers, water smartweed, salt grass, seaside plantain, numerous kinds of sedges and rushes. Moisture-loving trees like California hazel and native willows would have lined streams.

Native Oaks. There was some oak woodland in early San Francisco. As late as 1915 a photograph shows native live oak still covering much of Buena Vista Park. It is San Francisco's oldest city park, established in 1867. Later many of the Buena Vista oaks were cut down to make room for lawn and exotic plantings. Today there are oaks in the Presidio, Golden Gate Park and around Lake Merced. Oaks on the mesa along the northeast edge of Lake Merced are native. So are the regenerated oaks in the northeast corner of Golden Gate Park. Today's oaks in that area are second growth, as the original oaks were cut down during the rapid urban expansion after the Gold Rush. One other remnant of oak and manzanita scrub clings to the slope south of the churches lining Brotherhood Way, east of Lake Merced. The surface stream that once flowed along this valley was lined with arroyo willow.

On the slope east of Laguna Honda Reservoir, you can still see San Francisco's largest surviving remnant of coastal scrub. These 20 acres are owned by the San Francisco Water District and not open to the general public. The reservoir here was first built in 1863, enlarging an existing lake. The water from the underground aquifer here is still used to water parts of the San Francisco Botanical Garden at Strybing Arboretum, downhill in Golden Gate Park.

Some of San Francisco's windy hilltops were originally covered with native grasses: Twin Peaks, Bayview Hill, Buena Vista and McLaren Park's upper reaches. There would have been Johnny jump-ups and Pacific reedgrass. On some slopes from Land's End to Golden Gate Park's Strawberry Hill, native strawberries formed a dense ground cover. The geology of some of those hills reveals prehistoric tumult. Bedded chert, lifted up from ancient seabeds, can be found atop some of San Francisco's hills, for example, Twin Peaks and Billy Goat Hill (Castro and 30th). Chert is a sedimentary rock containing disintegrated shells of single-celled animals. Over eons these shells rained slowly down onto the sea floor. The resulting beds or layers hardened into rock over further eons.

The islands in the Bay were not continuously inhabited by Native Americans and thus the vegetation was not burned. Angel Island supported coastal live oak, toyon, laurel, madrone, and California buckeye. Alcatraz was named for pelicans, but also had grasses and small forbs that withstood the tearing salt winds. Yerba Buena Island was more sheltered, and both oak and toyon grew there before it became a home to feral goats.

Only scattered remnants of native plant communities can now be found within San Francisco's city limits. From Mt. Davidson to Crissy Field, from Candlestick Point to Yerba Buena Island to Lands End some small pockets of native flora have survived through neglect or else have been recently and painstakingly restored. Conservation of native plants came much later are more haltingly than efforts to save some larger mammals and birds.

CHAPTER 4

Before the Guns Arrived: Pre-Colonial Fauna

In the old California Indian tales, women married bears and bore their children. In Mexican California, the grizzlies were lasso'd by horsemen and set to fight bulls. When the Yankees came they raised a flag that bore a crude image of a bear and in the next sixty years or so hunted the real thing into extinction.

—REBECCA SOLNIT & MONA CARON, *A CALIFORNIA BESTIARY*

Are people more important than the grizzly bear? Only from the point of view of some people.

—EDWARD ABBEY

WE KNOW MUCH ABOUT THE larger animals that lived in San Francisco before colonization. For millennia, Native Americans lived in the San Francisco area, eating and harvesting local plants and animals. Two shell mound sites have been studied in San Francisco—one on the bluff north of Sutro Baths and another that was found during excavation for the current restored lagoon at Crissy Field. Bay Area archaeological sites have yielded bones of numerous mammals, including elk bones found at the Crissy site. Mammals hunted by local Native Americans were California sea lion, harbor seal, fur seal, sea otter, river otter, black bear, black-tailed deer, elk, and the lagomorphs. These included beavers, California ground squirrels, pocket gophers, and wood rats. Also killed by Native American hunters were raccoons, badgers, skunks, bobcats, grizzly bears, brush rabbits, harbor porpoises, common dolphins, and wolves. Bones of all these species have been found in ancient Bay Area kitchen middens and shell mounds. Smaller mammals—such as weasels, voles, shrews, bats, and moles—were not part of the Native Americans' diet, so we have found no telltale remains, and early explorers took little notice of these animals. Too bad. Based on current bat species' ranges, there were likely more than a dozen species of bat present.

Archaeological evidence and eyewitness accounts from the early nineteenth century show that a wide variety of plants and animals were eaten or harvested by Native Californians. Tribes in California were hunter-gatherers, using neither agriculture nor irrigation. The original Californians used bows and arrows, traps and tule nets to kill both water and land animals. In addition, early reports mention the large number of dogs around the native villages. Dogs were the only domestic animals in California before colonization. The landscape was managed using fire; unwanted plants were burned or dug up.

Archaeologist Jack M. Broughton conducted a seven-year-long study of bones in Native American middens around San Francisco Bay. Broughton wrote: "The Emeryville Shell Mound, located on the eastern shore of San Francisco Bay between the cities of Oakland and Berkeley, measured 100 X 300 meters in area and extended to a depth of more than 10 meters. It was the largest of what was originally a complex of about six mounds located on the alluvial flat of Emeryville." Broughton concluded that local native peoples extirpated some bird species. The larger the animal, the more likely it was to become prey for the Ohlone.

Broughton summarized: "Such large-bodied taxa as elk and sturgeon provided an ever-decreasing part of human diets across the occupational history of the site [at Emeryville] which spanned from about 2,600 to 700 years before present."

Broughton and his graduate students went through over 5,700 bird remains. They were collected and preserved at the University of

California, Berkeley, when the Emeryville Shell Mound was leveled for construction in the 1920s. Broughton's group found bones from 65 avian species, with larger birds the most common. Surprisingly, there were the bones of 15 raptor species including Bald Eagle. He found large geese species were among the first to decline, replaced over time by smaller geese and ducks in the natives' diet. Likewise, the hunters were forced further afield, collecting more and more cormorant eggs and adults from island colonies, then moving on to sea ducks after marsh birds were depleted. The first shorebirds hunted were Long-billed Curlews, Marbled Godwits, and Whimbrels. After they became scarce, hunters turned to the smaller sandpipers. Broughton estimates as many as 150,000 natives were living around the Bay before 1500. In 1579, perhaps the first Europeans to see Northern California, Sir Francis Drake and his expedition from Britain spent several summer weeks anchored in Drake's Bay off Point Reyes in Marin County. He found the Native Americans friendly, even worshipful. Drake's ships sailed up the coast from Chile, generally several miles offshore. Thus he missed the Golden Gate opening onto San Francisco Bay. Drake did anchor briefly near one of the Farallon Islands. There his men became perhaps the first visitors to gather seabird eggs on the Farallones and the first to kill the sea mammals they found there.

There are scant records of the time Drake spent in Marin. At that time natural science had little place in the politics and economy of northern Europe so this group of explorers did not take much note of nature. Drake did mention large deer herds. He also mentioned that food was plentiful, specifically "Muscles, Seales, and such like," and the large number of ground squirrels impressed him:

> We found the whole country to be a warren of a strange kinde of Conies, their bodies in bigness as be the Barbary Conies, their heades as the heades of ours, the feet of a Want [mole], and the taile of a Rat being of great length; under the chinne on either side a bagge, into the which she gathereth her mesate when she hath filled her belly abroad. The people

[Native Americans] eate their bodies, and make great account of their skinnes, for their Kings' coat was made of them.

We have no further written records of California for more than a century. Is is possible Drake's men left behind deadly microbes native to the Old World.

Epidemics Devastate Indians. Wildlife populations rebounded after 1500, as introduced diseases from Europe ravaged the Ohlone and their native neighbors. Menzies noted during his visit in 1792 that measles and dysentery were scourges among the Native Americans living around missions. Broughton proposes that the richness of birds and other animals found by the first European explorers in the eighteenth and early nineteenth centuries resulted from the diminishment of the native people, the alpha predators. Broughton contradicts the commonly held idea that ancient Native Americans were healthy, happy people living in harmony with the environment: "That clearly was not always the case. Depending on when and where you look back in time, native peoples were either living in harmony with nature or eating their way through a vast array of large-sized, attractive prey species."

Broughton suggests that by the mid-nineteenth century, imported European diseases had killed ninety percent of the Indians. Measles epidemics swept through the Indian population. Other killing diseases, against which the Native Americans had neither immunity nor medicine, were mumps, smallpox, syphilis, and influenza. All of these were first imported to California by Europeans or by other native tribes closer to areas previously settled by Europeans. There is some evidence that in the 1790s alone, various epidemics killed 60 percent of the coastal Indian population. One deadly epidemic would be followed by another.

Between 1806 and 1810, measles killed many Native Americans around San Francisco Bay. One estimate is that one-third of surviving Mission Indians died at that time, while Europeans rarely died from measles. Writing then at Mission Dolores in Yerba Buena, Father Martine de Landaeta said, "Measles have wreaked havoc upon the Indians of this province.... We missionaries here find ourselves with about 400 sick." In the first decade of the nineteenth century, Langsdorff noted, "A disease, hitherto unknown in New California, the measles, which had broke out this year and had for some weeks attacked great numbers of the Indians." Here's Broughton's further explanation:

> Recent analyses of archaeological fish and mammal materials from California and elsewhere in western North America document that those early historic-period faunal landscapes represent poor analogues for prehistoric environments, because they post-date a dramatic sixteenth- or seventeenth-century population-crash of native hunters. The superabundance of tame wildlife witnessed during the early historic period may only reflect population irruptions that followed the demise of their main predators [humans].

In addition to food, Native Americans made heavy use of animals for fur, feathers, shells, and bones. Bay Area tribes decorated baskets using feathers. Garments were often made from either feathers or fur. Deer skin garments were specially crafted by the hunters to allow them to get close to browsing herds and insure easier kills.

In 1806, Langsdorff noted Native Americans villages were carrying on their traditional culture as best they could. By then cattle had largely replaced elk or deer. The Indians near the missions were no longer allowed to set fires for land management. Langsdorff found them using fur and feathers for clothing, adornment, and to decorate baskets. He specifically mentions clothes made from sea otter fur, plus feathers taken from California Quail, Turkey Vulture, Northern Flicker, and Red-winged Blackbird. Two decades later, Beechey noted Indians dressed in garments of feathers, deer skins, or sea otter pelts He said the duck feather garments were quite warm. He also recorded the wearing of shell and feather ornaments by the men.

Even as colonization occurred, surviving Native Americans away from the missions continued to "manage" the landscape as they apparently had for centuries: by burning. Fire is an ancient tool for managing forest and grassland plants. Langsdorff noted the Native Americans not confined to the missions still set fire to the forests, and "burnt large tracts." Many native bunch grasses and trees, including the precious acorn-bearing oaks, actually benefitted from the fires, which removed much of the underbrush and plants that would compete for the precious soil moisture. Such controlled burning produced parklike habitat, good for oaks, deer, and rabbits. The naturalist and explorer Adelbert von Chamisso noted in 1816, while camped near Mission Dolores, "All night great fires burned on the land at the back of the harbor; the natives are in the habit of burning the grass, to further its growth."

For a century after the 1849 Gold Rush, Native Americans played a minor political and environmental role in the San Francisco region. First disease, then persecution and forced relocation of survivors, removed nearly all Native Americans from the San Francisco Bay Area. In 1850, T. Butler King wrote in his official report on California to the U.S. Secretary of State:

> It is quite impossible to form anything like an accurate estimate of the number of Indians in the Territory. Since the commencement of the [Mexican] war, and especially since the discovery of gold in the mountains, their numbers at the missions and in the valleys near the coast have very much diminished. In the fact the whole race seems to be rapidly disappearing. The remains of a vast number of villages in all the valleys of the Sierra Nevada, and among the foot-hills of that range of mountains, show that at no distant day there must have been a numerous population where there is not now an Indian to be seen.... It is said there are large numbers of them in the mountains and valleys about the head waters of the San Joaquin, along the western base of the Sierra, and in the northern part of the Territory, and that they are hostile.

Elk and Pronghorn. In the late eighteenth century, there were numerous European descriptions of the Pacific coast of California. One of the earliest accounts was written by Fray Crespi, who accompanied Portola to Northern California. He saw large herds of pronghorn in the Santa Clara Valley. He also noted large herds of deer. Father Francisco Palou was part of the expedition in 1776 that founded both Mission Dolores and the Presidio. In crossing the Santa Clara Valley, he noted a large elk herd:

> We descried in the distance a herd of large animals that looked like cattle, but we could not imagine where they belonged or from whence they had come. Some soldiers then went out to round them up, so that they should not stampede our tame cattle, but as the soldiers approached, they perceived that this was not a herd of cattle, but deer, or a species of deer, as large as the largest ox or bull, with horns similar in shape to those of the deer, but so large that they measured sixteen palms [11 feet] from tip to tip.

Also in the Santa Clara Valley, Palou tells of a pronghorn hunt:

> [T]here is another species of deer about the size of a three-year-old sheep. They are similar in appearance to the deer, except that they have short horns and also short legs like the sheep. They live in the plains where they go in herds of 100, 200, or more. They run altogether over the plains so fast they seem to fly.

Today we know the pronghorn is the fastest land animal in North America. They evolved their life-saving speed millennia ago, before the cheetah went extinct in North America. With the cheetah long gone from our prairies, there is no land creature in North America that can outrun the pronghorn.

La Perouse, visiting Northern California in the 1780s, estimated California Quail coveys numbered three hundred to four hundred birds. He listed several other animals seen by his crew: "sparrows, tit-mice, blue jays [scrub-jay], speckled wood peckers, sand-larks, tropic birds in the woods [orioles, tanagers], hares, rabbits, wolves, wildcats, bald-headed eagle [Bald Eagle], great and small falcons, goshawk [not likely], sparrow-hawk [accipiters], black vulture, great owl, raven, wild ducks." His list continues: "gray and white pelican with yellow tufts [mature Brown Pelican in breeding plumage], different species of gulls, cormorant, curlieus [curlews], ring-plovers [Killdeer, Semiplamated Plover], small sea-water hens [coots, alcids, and grebes], herons."

In one specific note, La Perouse says, "A bee-eater, which has been supposed to be peculiar to the old continent, was here [the Monterey area] killed and stuffed by the French ornithologists." Likely he is referring to a Western Kingbird—a species not related to the Old World bee-eaters— but they share bluish and yellow plumage and bold hunting behavior.

One of La Perouse's more interesting notes reflects the wealth of life in the sea before Yankee and British whalers began to have an effect in the Pacific. Off the Monterey coast, he writes, "One cannot express the number of whales by which we were surrounded, nor their familiarity." Likely these would have been hump-backed whales, as his visit did not coincide with the annual gray whale migrations.

Also visiting California in the 1780s, on the Vancouver Expedition, Dr. Menzies noted: big cats he termed lion and tiger. Most likely, he was referring to the cougar. He also mentions mountain cat. It is probable that he never personally saw a mountain lion and got conflicting descriptions from natives and assumed there were more than one species of big cat. He also wrote of pole cat [skunk], wolves, coyotes, foxes, fallow deer, small rat, mountain rat, ardillo which he describes as a species of *Scirus* or squirrel. A small rabbit which he mentions was very common near the Presidio. He said reindeer [elk] were plentiful inland. Offshore from San Francisco, Menzies shot a Black-footed Albatross, and noted that it must be a new species.

Here's how Menzies describes the area we know as Crissy Field along the northern San Francisco waterfront: "low track of Marshy Land along shore, with some Salt Water Lagoons that were supplied by the overflowings of high tides and oozings through the Sandy Beach; on these we saw abundance of Ducks and wild Geese." This was in November when wintering waterfowl, from colder climes to the north, converge on the San Francisco Bay Area.

During the 1806 visit by the Rezanov expedition, George von Langsdorff made notes on the animal life he noticed. He was Rezanov's personal physician. We can take Langsdorff, a German medical doctor, literally, as he wrote: "A strict adherence to truth ought not to be merely a matter of preference, it ought to be considered as a sacred duty by every traveler who undertakes to give the history of his adventures to the world."

> We often amused ourselves with shooting the crested partridges [California Quail] and rabbits, which abound upon the surrounding hills. One day we went out ... and conducted by some thirty or forty Indians, to catch hares and rabbits. This was done by a peculiar kind of snare. Inside of three hours, without firing a shot we had taken seventy-five.

Likely Langsdorff's "hares" were black-tailed jackrabbits, which can still be seen at Hunters Point. They would have thrived among the dunes. The rabbits would have been brush rabbit, now an uncommon resident of San Francisco's wilder corners. Yet as recently as 1959, William Berry, author of *Mammals of San Francisco Bay Region*, said, "Brush rabbits are readily observed in such protected areas as Golden Gate Park." Harold Gilliam, in his 1967 book on San Francisco, could still call the brush rabbit "common."

Other animals caught Langsdorff's attention and were described by him as: sea otters, sea dogs [harbor seals], American lions [cougars], American tigers [bobcats?], stags, roes [a European deer], wolves, bears, and polecats [skunks]. Of the last he writes, "The urine which this animal spurts from him to defend himself against his enemies exceeds in smell everything that can be conceived." Those polecats' progeny still commonly fill the foggy San Francisco neighborhoods with their strong-smelling repellent. It seems likely that Langsdorff had at least one personal experience with the skunk's mighty perfume, which we now know is specially secreted and not urine.

Langsdorff listed birds he saw in San Francisco's bay and marshes: herons, sandpipers, shorebirds, cormorants, gulls, grebes and loons, mergansers, ducks, and many geese in winter. Langsdorff's list continues: blackbirds, orioles, ovidus [no Latin meaning], Red-winged Blackbird, lark [possibly our Horned Lark], Western Meadowlark, Flicker, California Quail, wren, and many hummingbirds "in summer only."

It is likely that Anna's Hummingbirds were less common in winter then. They are now supplied with a great variety of winter-blooming exotic plants like albizia and eucalyptus, and can overwinter and sometimes even nest during San Francisco's mild winter. I once saw a female hummer incubating eggs during Christmas week in Sutro Heights Park.

Captain Rezanov's own journal mentions hunting deer as well as looking for bobcat, bear, and mountain lion. Around San Francisco he says: "I found most of the birds with which I had become familiar at Sitka [in Alaska]." His list includes cormorants, grebes/loons, White-winged Scoter, scoter sp., and Black Osytercatcher. There were also seals, sea lions and the precious sea otter. Almost unheeded, otters swam about the bay in numbers. Three decades later the sea otter was extirpated from the bay and has never returned as a breeding species. In 1816, Russian explorer Otto von Kotzebue commanded another Russian expedition. He described "flocks of wild geese, ducks and snipes, so tame that we might have killed great numbers with our sticks."

Lt. George Peard, on Captain Frederick Beechey's British expedition, listed animals he saw near San Francisco during winter visits in 1826 and 1827: elk, deer, wolf, coyote, fox, bobcat, mountain lion, jackrabbit, and cottontail. Both visits took place in November and December. Birds mentioned in Peard's journal are gray pelicans [Brown Pelicans], cranes, herons, geese, ducks, teal, wigeon, curlew, rail, waterhens [coot], plover, wagtail [likely Killdeer], kingfisher, woodpeckers, wrens, sparrows, hummingbirds, turkey buzzards [vultures], kites, hawks, jays, and "beautiful large horned owls."

Europe has no icterids, and this bird family was unfamiliar to men on the Beechey expedition. This family includes American blackbirds, meadowlarks, orioles, and cowbirds. Peard singles out "a sort of starling with red on the pinion joint," meaning a Red-winged Blackbird. Peard also noted, "The woods contain innumerable bevies of crested quail or California Partridge [California Quail]."

Captain Beechey's ship's surgeon and naturalist was Dr. Alexander Collie. On the Beechey expedition, Collie and others collected numerous specimens in or near San Francisco that were taken back to scientists in London: Great Horned Owl, Belted Kingfisher, Pine Siskin, a Least Bittern apparently found in the Presidio, American Avocet, Semipalmated Plover, Red-winged Blackbird, and Bufflehead. Collie said the avocet was abundant in San Francisco. While travelling to Monterey on horseback, Collie estimated some quail flocks on the San Francisco Peninsula contained four hundred birds. Captain Beechey himself kept notes on San Francisco fauna: "In the woods not immediately bordering the missions, the black bear has his habitation, and when food is scarce it is dangerous to pass through them alone in the dusk ... but when the acorns abound there is nothing to apprehend." True danger would have been attributable only to grizzly bears, which were still present in what became San Francisco. Not long after the Gold Rush neither black nor grizzly bear was ever reported in San Francisco again.

Here is Beechey's list of mammals: skunk, deer, elk, ground squirrel, gray squirrel, small rabbits, voles, sea otter, porpoises, whales, and harbor seals. The mountain lion he describes as "common," while wolves and foxes are "numerous." Raccoons were found only distant from the ocean. Coyotes were all around and dangerous to the free-ranging sheep. Likely the ground squirrel is the one now named for the captain himself, the California ground squirrel (*Spermophilus beecheyi*). Beechey repeated incorrect reports that the white bear [polar bear] sometimes came down from the north. The story was likely based on tales told by Russian visitors, who would have regularly seen polar bears in Alaska.

Beechey's lengthy list of San Francisco birds included the following: Great Horned Owl, Peregrine, Turkey Vulture, kestrel, Red-winged Blackbird, Anna's Hummingbird, Yellow-billed Magpie, California Scrub-Jay, California Quail, Band-tailed Pigeon, crows, plovers, snipes, and sandpipers "of several species." His list continues with Black Oystercatchers, herons, cormorants, Brown Pelicans, two species of rail, curlews, finches, sparrows, and buntings. Beechey described big flocks of Brown Pelicans landing on Alcatraz, their namesake island. He also wrote that many "shag" [cormorants] could be seen flying across the Bay.

The rich variety of ducks and geese impressed Beechey. He stated there were over twenty species in San Francisco, including Mallard and American

Wigeon. Even today it's possible to spot two dozen waterfowl species around the Bay in midwinter. Beechey was disappointed when his crew failed to capture a dark-bodied sea duck with a white head [male Surf Scoter].

By the time Beechey arrived in 1826–1827, Yerba Buena was no longer so remote. The Captain noted several American whaling ships in the bay when the *Blossom* sailed through the Golden Gate. Technically it was still illegal for non-Spanish ships to trade along the California coast, but local missions and settlements rarely enforced that law. As local commercial output was limited, settlers traded their tallow and cattle hides for ships' supplies from Europe and Boston. The ships' crews commonly purchased, or traded for, flour, beef, salt, and vegetables. In turn, locals received clothes, tools, special foods like cheese, and wine.

Dr. Paul-Emile Botta also reached San Francisco in 1827, aboard a French trading ship. He collected a number of natural history specimens in California, including the first Anna's Hummingbird described by science. It is likely that bird was killed in San Francisco. Back in Europe, the bird was named for Duchess Anna of Massena, wife of Botta's noble patron. The exact specimen was part of a large French bird collection purchased in 1846, containing twelve thousand preserved bird skins from across the globe. The entire collection and science's first Anna's Hummingbird now rest in the Philadelphia's Academy of Natural Sciences. Botta also found in San Francisco the abundant rodent still familiar in the city's park lawns, Botta's pocket gopher.

Botta sailed on a ship commanded by Captain Duhaut-Cilly, who wrote:

During our stay at Yerba Buena [San Francisco] we spent most of our considerable leisure time hunting.... The country abounds with hares [jackrabbits], rabbits, and tufted partridge [quail], and especially an astonishing variety of ducks and seabirds.

As for the collection I was making with Dr. Botta ... a multitude of beautiful shore birds; in the woods and on the hillsides, several fine species of hawks and other birds of prey; the thickets, magpies, blackbirds, sparrows, and several fruit-eating birds quite different from ours; and finally in the heath, a pretty species of hummingbird, perhaps the smallest that exists, with head and throat of glowing fire [male Anna's Hummingbird, far from the smallest].

The captain's "fruit-eating birds quite different" would have included this American endemics: Bullock's Orioles, Western Tanagers, Western Bluebirds, and Black-headed Grosbeaks. An educated Frenchman would have been familiar with waxwings and thrushes, which in Europe are nearly all earth-toned like our Hermit Thrush.

George Yount, an early settler in Northern California, observed in 1833 that "the wild geese, and every species of waterfowl, darkened the surface of every bay ... in flocks of millions. When disturbed, they arose to fly, the sound of their wings was like that of distant thunder."

Steve Richardson (1831–1924) grew up in San Francisco before the Gold Rush. His father built the first house in old Yerba Buena near the bay on what is today's Portsmouth Square. In his memoirs, Richardson recalled, "When I was 5 or 6 years old I often galloped as far as Mission Dolores [from Portsmouth Square, about 2.5 miles].... I often passed bears and wolves so close I could have thrown a lariat over them."

Salmon Runs. In 1841 Lt. Charles Wilkes commanded the United States' first-ever naval exploration expedition in the Pacific, formally named the U.S. Exploring Expedition. He noted Californians were not taking advantage of the abundant salmon runs: "The salmon-fishery, if attended to, would be a source of considerable profit." While they were still plentiful, the salmon impressed other observers. For example, Edwin Bryant had this to say about his visit in 1846:

> The Sacramento River, at this point [at Sutter's Fort], is a stream nearly half a mile in width. The tide rises and falls some two or three feet... It abounds in fish, the most valuable of which is the salmon. These salmon are the largest and the fattest I have ever seen. I have seen salmon taken from the Sacramento five feet in length. All its tributaries are equally rich in the finny tribe. American enterprise will soon develop the wealth contained in these streams.

Those huge salmon runs were doomed, but they were a temporary source of food and profit. Along the western slope of the Sierra, the heavy sluicing of hillsides by gold miners soon clogged up many rivers that had once hosted the annual salmon runs. Then came overfishing and eventual daming of spawning streams.

Captain William Dane Phelps was a sailor who first arrived in San Francisco in 1841. In his memoir Phelps relays a story he'd heard of a young Native American child carried off by a mountain lion. Phelps also tells of going ashore with some of his fellow sailors to hunt bear. He claimed they tracked a grizzly bear on horseback to Mission Creek from Portsmouth Square. The bear escaped by swimming across that creek.

Also in 1841, George Simpson of the Hudson's Bay Company was visiting Sonoma as a guest at General Mariano Vallejo's rancho. He found inland wildlife still abundant, just a few years before the Gold Rush changed California forever:

> The Californian is too lazy to hunt for amusement, and as to any necessity of the kind, his bullocks supply all his wants, excepting the red deer [black-tailed deer] is occasionally pursued on account of the peculiar hardness and whiteness of its tallow. Hence the number of wild animals is very considerable. Beaver and [river] otter have recently been caught within half a mile of the mission [Sonoma], and there are also the red deer, the wild goat [pronghorn], the bear, the panther [cougar], the wolf, the fox, the rabbit, etc.

Simpson joined earlier observers who found over-hunting already evident along the coast. Russian hunters at Bodega and Fort Ross, plus those on the Farallones, killed fur seals and sea otters for pelts. The Farallon Islands were inhabited by hunters with the Russian-American Company killing sea mammals, especially sea otters and fur seals. By the 1840s, seals and sea otters were nearly gone. It had taken only three decades of unbridled slaughter to decimate their numbers. In the 1840s, Russian California turned to farming for income. That failed and the Russians sold Fort Ross, abandoning commercial operations in California. After the Gold Rush, egg collectors pillaged the Farallones' seabird colonies to supply San Francisco restaurants.

New settler William Thomes describes his ship's arrival in the Bay, April 25, 1843:

> We saw right ahead of us Alcatraz Island, looking like variegated marble, with deposits of seabirds, and the air full of shrieking and quarreling gulls, while on the rocks were a hundred or more old sea lions, whose roars were enough to chill the blood of those who did not know that the animals were harmless, unless attacked.

> Off our larboard bow was a beautiful island, wooded and green, even to the water's edge. This was Angel Island, in those days as lovely a spot as the eye could rest on…. During my anchor watch [at night] I could hear the huge sea lions on the rocks, roaring and grumbling, and all over the town, what little there was, the barking of numerous dogs.

Thomes' shipmates traded plugs of tobacco for large smoked salmon at Yerba Buena. On a run to Sausalito for fresh water, Thomes was on a small boat that "ran close to Alcatraz Island, where the sea fowl had built thousands of nests, and the guano was over a foot thick in some places." Now Alcatraz is a sightseeing destination and part of the Golden Gate National Recreation Area. As prison guards no longer practice marksmanship on passing or perching birds, and the island is now a bird sanctuary. The seabird colony at Alcatraz has regenerated.

Thomas Farnham was another sailor who arrived in San Francisco before the Gold Rush. He jokingly described the Mexican Presidio this way: "Densely manned, also, are these piles of adobie and osseous ruins, not with rank and file of mailed warriors, but with dogs, vultures and jackals [coyotes]. This is Fort San Francisco, one of the strongest posts in the Californias." In Farnham's words, the bay was "surrounded by a country, partly wooded, and partly disposed in open glades and prairies of the richest kind, covered with flocks and herds of the Missions, and deer, and elk, and bears."

One of the last Russian trading ships to visit Yerba Buena before the Gold Rush was the *Naslednik Alexander* in 1845. On board was Alexander Markoff, an experienced traveler who published many accounts of his adventures. He gives us his version of the small village just before it became San Francisco:

> Over the whole immense bay the aromatic scent of nutritious grasses and flowers was being wafted. Around the shores, in picturesque array, the habitations of the Californians were scattered at long intervals, with green meadows and valleys between them, the horses, mules, cows and sheep grazing upon them. Far away in the sky the cry of wild geese could be heard.... Behind the village there were high green hills, with small brush upon them. Over them the wild zebra [burros?] roamed at will and the skillful Spaniard lassoed his steers.... The nearest ranch is not over half a mile distant from this village. This ranch is owned by a Spaniard and his family, a cheese-maker, who keeps a very large number of cows, from which he obtains milk enough to supply the village and also the vessels in port.... [On this ranch] is a garden in which there is an abundance of melons and squashes and even some apple and pear trees; beyond extend the pastures and fields planted with wheat, barley, maize, and pease.

Markoff hires a horse and heads south from Yerba Buena to visit the mission. He notes large herds of free-ranging cows and horses along the way. He notes many dogs: "There is such a multitude of dogs, that it is safe to calculate upon at least one for each inhabitant, if not two." Near the mission, Markoff finds an Ohlone woman,

> ...plucking the feathers of some quail. These small birds, of a brownish color, and high black top-knot consisting of only three feathers, have a white and palatable flesh, with a slightly sweet taste about it, and are very common in California, the inhabitants of which use them daily as food....Back of the [mission] village fields were visible in various directions, planted in wheat and barley, while on the right extended the

glassy surface of a small lake [Manantial], but behind that were groves of live oak.

Those trees would have been on the slopes of Twin Peaks.

Edward Kemble, one of California's first newspapermen, describes the natural scenery when he first arrived in 1846:

> The dense growth of dwarfed and wind-flattened shrubbery cover-
> ing these hills extended down within three hundred feet of the plaza
> [Portsmouth Square], or about the line of Dupont street [now Grant
> Street]. The brush was the cover of coyotes and rabbits, wildcats [bob-
> cat], and sometimes larger game, and was inhabited by innumerable
> quail, whose answering calls on that memorable first sunset walk, I can
> even now hear.

Kemble also recalled coyote howls carrying down the slopes of Russian Hill to the little town nestled around Portsmouth Square. Another report from the mid-1840s says the hills west of Rincon Point (Third and Folsom) were covered with shrubby oaks and abounded with game.

Then came the American takeover of California, the Gold Rush and rapid urbanization, transforming a small seaport into a bustling modern city. At the same time land plants and animals were hit by the full force of settlement and exploitation.

CHAPTER 5

Low on the Food Pyramid: Cold-blooded Animals

What was wrong with me, apart from colds and pleuritic flea-bites, was a lingering malaria; and that is now greatly overcome.

—ROBERT LOUIS STEVENSON, LETTER FROM HIS ROOM
AT 608 BUSH STREET, SAN FRANCISCO, 1880

No fish in the whole world has a more remarkable life history: a combination of life in both fresh and salt water, a notable migratory instinct, and final death at the age of four years. Occasionally, salmon develop and return to the fresh-water streams at an earlier age, but females return almost inevitably at four years of age.

—HAROLD BRYANT, *OUTDOOR HERITAGE*, 1929

SINCE EUROPEAN COLONIZATION BEGAN, SAN Francisco's few native reptiles and amphibians have been greatly reduced in numbers. Some insects are now extinct or endangered. The native fleas, however, persist in the face of poisons and other persecutions. The density of their victims has greatly increased. Indoor carpeting must seem like benevolence to any right-thinking flea.

The most singular example of "progress" destroying a species may be the Xerces blue butterfly. It was native to the sand dunes in western San Francisco. Development and the loss of lupine and other native flowering dune plants led to its extinction. It was last seen in the early 1940s. The California Academy of Sciences has a full collection of specimens, collected not far from the academy's headquarters in Golden Gate Park. There is now an invertebrate conservation group, the Xerces Society, named in memory of the extinct butterfly.

Another butterfly in precolonial San Francisco was the mission blue. This quarter-sized subspecies of butterfly is now on the federal endangered species list. It would also have been abundant in the dunes along Ocean Beach and extending inland to the highest hills. The blue's preferred plants are lupine and dune buckwheat, which once thrived on the restless sands. It lives its entire life only in lupine-dominated coastal scrub from San Mateo to Marin County. It is found nowhere else in the world. The only known remnant population in San Francisco is now on Twin Peaks, likely comprised of less than a thousand individuals. San Bruno Mountain and the Marin Headlands have populations that number in the thousands. Before urbanization most of western San Francisco would have been prime habitat for the mission blue.

The larvae of the mission blue feed on the leaves of three species of lupine. The adults derive nectar from members of the sunflower family that flourish among the lupine bushes. Since 2011 conservation groups have worked to restore and maintain lupine-rich habitat within the mission blue's native range. It takes people helping remove invasive weeds to maintain the lupine scrub that was once dominant on hills facing the Pacific Ocean's winds and salty fog. The mission blue is exemplary in its tiny natural range and its tenuous grip on survival which is entirely dependent on human assistance now that the Bay Area is urbanized. There are numerous species of native butterflies that still flourish in San Francisco. Some butterflies you may see on a summer day include common buckeye, green hairstreak, monarch, pipevine swallowtail, western pygmy blue and western tiger swallowtail.

There are dozens of native moth species around San Francisco. Some you may find inside or hovering around an outdoor light at night. Because so many are nocturnal there are myriad species that have only scientific binomials, not even getting a common name. Local moths include the large sphinx moth, polyphemus, girdler, various tiger moths and tussock moth. Moths are vegetarian and some species are closely associated with one family or genus of plants from ceanothus to apple trees.

In San Francisco, today, you rarely hear the Pacific chorus frog, although it's common in many suburban areas. Restoration efforts have brought our "singing" frog back to Mountain Lake. Several snake species still survive in San Francisco (not including the threatened San Francisco garter snake, which is now found only in San Mateo County). According to Chris Giomi of Tree Frog Treks, hikers can spot two garter snake species, a ring-necked, and even an occasional king snake. There are one toad, four lizards, and four salamander species left. The California slender salamander is found in back gardens across the city. It is highly sedentary, rarely moving more than a few feet during its entire lifetime. One study concluded that the salamanders now on Alcatraz and Yerba Buena Islands were introduced by human activity.

The four lizard species still found in San Francisco are western fence lizard, western skink, the northern and southern alligator lizards. The skink will often show a bluish tail on its sleek body. The more scaly fence lizard has blue half-moons on its otherwise pale belly.

The single native turtle species is the Pacific pond turtle, also called the Northern western pond turtle. The predominant turtle in the lakes of Golden Gate Park is the red-eared slider. The slider is a native of the eastern United States; a common pet species, it has been repeatedly released into the wild in San Francisco. There are also various species of feral soft-shelled turtles now living and breeding in Bay Area waters. The Pacific pond turtle is listed as a species of special concern by both the federal and California governments.

In San Francisco in 1841, Lieutenant Charles Wilkes and his U.S. Exploring Expedition collected a gopher snake over three feet long, and also collected a small arboreal salamander. This amphibian is purplish-brown with a few pale-yellow spots on its sides. It is still found in the city and on the Farallones.

The Wilkes Expedition also found the large, and more common, California newt. It is brown with a yellow belly and can be up to eight inches long. This species is slow-moving and brightly-colored but has toxic skin secretions containing tetrodotoxin. That's a neurotoxin in the sala- mander's the skin, muscles, and blood. Tetrodotoxin may kill many ani- mals, including people. Even skin contact may cause irritation or stronger reaction in people. As cute as he may appear, do not kiss this creature.

Early accounts note the presence of rattlesnakes in the unsettled parts of San Francisco. William Thomes came to San Francisco on a Yankee ship in 1843. He said rattlesnakes were a frequent danger in the little village around Portsmouth Square. Until extirpated by humans, rattlers would have appreciated the sudden importation of house mice and two species of rats added to the native rodents.

Native Fish. Bones from numerous fish have been found in Ohlone kitchen middens. The one fish we know lived in San Francisco's small streams is the three-spined stickleback. It has survived in Lobos Creek and that population is being used to re-populate the headwaters in Mountain Lake. Fish still caught in shallow salt water include smelt, sardines, and rockfish. The annual salmon run and the beachside smelt runs were major events among Native Americans. Streams in San Francisco and the Bay Area would have yielded salmon during the spawning run. Other fish that were present: steelhead, trout, sturgeon, lamprey eel. Merced and other lakes held whitefish, perch and suckerfish.

Of course, in the Bay and nearby ocean were Dungeness crab and numerous fish species. In 1786 La Perouse noted the presence of aba- lone, some with shells nine inches by four inches. He notes the beauti- ful mother-of-pearl lining the shell insides. He makes no mention of eating abalone, making me think this cultured Frenchman surely never tasted one.

Anthropologists believe Bay Area and other Northern Californian tribes had four main food sources: fish, shellfish, warm-blooded game, and acorns. Just the list of edible shellfish available to the coastal tribes is impressive: two abalone species, barnacles, two species of chiton, four species of clam, plus cockles, mussels, Olympic oysters and the yellow eggs of sea urchins. It is likely freshwater mussels will successfully repopulate Mountain Lake.

The Native American diet also included snails, but other earthy invertebrates just worked the land. Banana slugs were present in moist forests and heavy brush. They can still be found in the Presidio today. Earthworms are vital to the fertility of soil and thus to the richness of any habitat. Across California, many introduced species of earthworms are now widespread. In habitat that has been the least altered by humans, the native earthworm populations are doing best. However, our knowledge of California's earthworms is limited. One recent study apparently found some new species. They were always there, right beneath our feet.

It must be noted that not all wildlife suffered at the coming of colonization and the often dense population of towns and cities. As early as 1846, Edwin Bryant could complain, "I was not in a good humor, for the fleas, bugs, and other vermin, which infested our miserable lodgings, had caused me a sleepless night by goring my body until the blood oozed from the skin in countless places."

San Francisco is still well-populated with fleas. While working in modern office buildings, I more than once had to warn our staff that fumigators were coming in overnight to try to eradicate the fleas in the wall-to-wall carpeting. An early San Francisco resident complained that the tent city on Yerba Buena Cove seemed to be furnished only with fog, broken glass and fleas. Everything else, he found, was in short supply. He would not be surprised to return and find fog and fleas still thrive today. One recent paper on California's flea population revealed there are as many as 200 species and sub-species in the state. A flea for every purpose, I suspect.

One study estimates there are as many insect species in the Bay Area nowadays as in all of Great Britain, but the fact is, we don't really know what insects existed in San Francisco before colonization. The naturalists associated with the California Academy of Sciences, founded in 1853, set out to explore the natural world of the Bay Area, but the post-earthquake fire, in 1906, destroyed 60,000 specimens in the academy's insect collection.

One study looking at modern San Francisco city parks found fifteen species of ants, noting that a rich variety of ant species can coexist on even small parcels of open space. Soil composition and texture are highly influential on ant populations. Plants are less important than soil chemistry and consistency, yet urban forests with a high proportion of eucalyptus and other exotics have a negative impact on ant populations. Another study found no impact so far from invasive Argentine ants. This species is found along California's coast including the Bay Area. One statewide survey found three ant species to be dominant. The three are mutually exclusive in a given habitat: two of these species are harvester ants and the other is the southern fire ant. The invasive southern fire ant is still not present in San Francisco but is already established in the lowlands of the Central Valley and Southern California.

Urbanization, agriculture, and invasive species are most harmful to native insect species. The Argentine ant and the pathogens killing oaks and pines will have substantial impact on the insect fauna of the Bay Area in the near future. Already over half of the endangered arthropods on the federal list are found in the Bay Area. Among the endangered invertebrates still found in San Francisco according to the U.S. Fish and Wildlife Service: the white abalone, mission blue butterfly, and San Bruno elfin butterfly. Black abalone has also been named as a candidate species for listing as endangered. As the current increase in extinctions lowers the bio-diversity of the planet San Francisco will see it share of crises when one species after another faces oblivion. Even some of the smallest creatures around us may need people to intervene if they are to survive. For that to happen will require study and attention, public awareness and the political will to act.

CHAPTER 6

What Happened?

Both Spain and Mexico, always in dread lest some other power wrest from them this precious bit of earthly paradise on the Pacific, attempted to postpone the evil day by putting up a wall of exclusion against the entrance of foreign commerce, wither by land or by sea; but the hide and tallow trade brought ships in such numbers that the feeble efforts to keep them out broke down altogether, and the Golden Gate was finally swung wide to the world. As many as 135 of these ships [largely Yankee] arrived between 1841 and 1847.

—NELLIE VAN DER GRIFT SANCHEZ, *SPANISH ARCADIA*

Suppose, by some miracle of Hollywood or inheritance or good luck, I should acquire a respectable-sized working cattle outfit. What would I do with it? First I'd get rid of the stinking, filthy cattle. Every single animal. Shoot them all, and stock the place with real animals, real game, real protein: elk, buffalo, pronghorn antelope, bighorn sheep, moose.

—EDWARD ABBEY

PEOPLE HAVE ALTERED CALIFORNIA REPEATEDLY. People have enabled invading plants. Some proved hardier and more aggressive than the

native ones so they thrived and spread. New diseases and colonization disrupted the native human cultures and reduced their influence
on wildlife and habitat alike. Native American populations were repeatedly victim to epidemics for which they had no resistance. Eventually
the missions' herds of cattle began to supply the meat used by Native
Americans, even those trying to live in traditional villages. Beef replaced
elk, bear, and venison. Agriculture, hunting and eventually chemicals
took a major toll on wildlife. Urbanization, the statewide corralling of
water resources, highways, air travel—there is a long list of economic
activities that alter the environment and change survival requirements
for organisms of all types and sizes.

Rapid, drastic change hit California before the first Spanish arrived
in San Francisco. Both weeds and pathogens had quietly invaded the
West Coast. The oldest known adobe in the San Diego area contains
seeds from invasive European weeds. These aggressive plants may have
first hit North America in the east, thousands of miles from California,
and two centuries before the first mission was built. During the Gold
Rush, easterners often found themselves crossing North American
"native" grasslands full of the same weeds they'd seen back home.
Nearly all were unintended imports from ships connecting the Old
World to the New.

Soldiers, settlers, and Catholic missionaries first came to the San
Francisco area in 1776, while the eastern United States was just beginning
its revolt against Great Britain. The establishment of missions, a presidio
in San Francisco, the founding of the town of San José—all these steps
brought rapid and fundamental change. Before the Spanish colonization
of California, the Ohlone and neighboring tribes had dogs but no livestock. The missions and early ranchers immediately released cattle, horses,
sheep, and pigs into the countryside. Dogs and housecats also ran freely
about homes and missions.

Hunting with lasso and gun was common for mounted hunters once
horses became widely available after the 1770s. Not only were feral cattle and sheep hunted, but the native deer, elk, pronghorn, and bear, as
well. Carlos Hijar's memories of California before 1840 include a vivid

description of horsemen lassoing a black bear and hauling it back to a ranch for a bull-bear battle. The brutal fight was one of the Californios' favorite forms of outdoor recreation.

The mild climate encouraged rapid growth of the free-ranging live-stock herds, which multiplied faster than the human colonists. In 1791, Captain Alejandro Malespina's scientific expedition reached Monterey in California. Among other facts he gathered, Malespina estimated human and livestock populations and the quantities of farm produce. It was the only scientific endeavor sponsored by the Spanish government during California's colonial period.

Malespina cited 128 colonists at the San Francisco Presidio, including 56 women. There were 16 Indians there. At the mission, he counted only 2 colonists but 436 Indians. Cattle in both places numbered over 3,000, plus 1,700 sheep, 360 horses, and a few mules—all this a mere fifteen years after the Presidio and mission were founded. The mission had the only agriculture on the peninsula at that time, producing wheat, corn, barley, kidney beans, garbanzos, and lentils.

Vancouver's men benefited from the large cattle herds. The natural-ist on that expedition was Archibald Menzies. When Vancouver's party came ashore on November 15, 1792, the British were greeted by the local padre who, according to Menzies' journal, "ordered a Bullock to be caught from among the Herd that were feeding on the Pasture near the Shore." That free-range beef struck Menzies in a very positive way, after the crew found safe anchorage in Yerba Buena Cove: "The skirts of the Bay, and the hilly country behind was interspersed with brush-wood and clear spots of Pasturage on which a number of Black Cattle were seen feeding in Herds; these induced us to think favorably of the Country, which we should oth-erwise from general appearance be apt to pronounce naked dreary and barren."

All those cattle, reports Menzies, had come from a modest start. The Vancouver crew "were told that when these Northern [California] Missions were first settled about twenty Years ago [actually sixteen] there were but fifteen head of cattle to begin with and now the Country every-where swarmed with them."

In 1792 Vancouver reported the Santa Clara Mission was killing two dozen cattle per week. By 1806, Rezanov's expedition found that the mission at Santa Clara was slaughtering up to fifty cattle per week for food, hides, and tallow to trade. He then goes on to report secondhand that the Monterey Mission (now Carmel) had sent out horsemen to kill up to twenty thousand cattle because of the fear that they would destroy all the pasturage. Less than thirty years after Mission Dolores had been founded, free-range cattle were recognized as an environmental scourge.

In the Bay Area, as elsewhere in North America, commerce soon dictated how the land was used and what resources were plundered for profit. Historian James Hart, wrote of Yankee trading ships along California's coast even before it was part of the United States:

> From 1803 until the War of 1812 made it dangerous for American ships to be at sea, these New Englanders worked with Russia's hunters off the California shore, even snaking canoes into San Francisco Bay once in a while. When the war with England ended and after Mexican California was freed from Spain in 1821, Americans carried on business independently. By 1822 they had shifted to the more profitable trade in cowhides. The New England merchantmen collecting hides and selling Yankee goods soon so monopolized the region's economy that to Californians the terms Boston and the United States became synonymous.

The cattle business in the early nineteenth century was focused on tallow and cowhides. A nickname for exported cow hides was "California banknotes." Joshua Paddison, in *A World Transformed*, writes that California exported more than a million cowhides between 1822 and 1846. Much of that went via American ships to tanneries in Boston. There the leather was used for shoes, gloves, and other products. Often the tallow was sold to companies in Peru who turned it into soap and candles for use in the mining industry there. Arriving Yankee ships brought trading goods to Californians. Thus had cow skins replaced the earlier trade in otter and fur seal skins.

Many of the cattle were slaughtered and dressed out in the field, leaving plenty of meat and offal for scavengers. For some time, this was a boon for the wild alpha predator, the grizzly bear. Eventually the well-armed colonists in turn killed off the grizzlies. The last known grizzly bear to be shot in California was killed in Tulare County in 1922.

In 1826, Captain Beechey sent his naturalist/surgeon William Collie and a group of men on horseback from Yerba Buena to Monterey. As they rode horseback through what is now San Mateo and Santa Clara Counties, they noted many free ranging cattle, sheep, and horses. Sailors in the early nineteenth century tell of hunting cattle on Angel Island as well as on the mainland.

By 1830, it was estimated that fifty large ranchos in California supported two hundred thousand cattle, fifty thousand horses, and innumerable sheep. Those animals were nearly all free ranging. An 1831 estimate lists 5,610 cattle, 470 horses, and 40 mules belonging to the San Francisco Presidio. Mission Dolores at that time is credited with 4,200 cattle, 1,239 horses, 13 mules, and 3,000 sheep. It's possible these mission numbers are greatly reduced from the livestock counts in the previous decade, when the missions across California were at the height of their wealth and political power. That was before the Mexican government began giving land and livestock to private rancheros across the state at the expense of the missions.

Merchant Sir George Simpson visited in San Francisco in 1841–1842. He was checking on all of the major posts of the Hudson's Bay Company, for which he ran all North American operations. On December 29th, he arrived by sea, noting huge roaming herds of cattle and horses. No herdsmen could be seen. Simpson estimated that California at that time produced about sixty thousand head of cattle annually.

Simpson carefully eyed the regional economy during his stay. He estimated that General Mariano Vallejo, on his Sonoma and Solano County ranches, owned eight thousand head of cattle. Simpson also relates how the rich market for cows (hides and tallow) was already leading to changes in the free-range livestock populations. Sheep were being killed to give the cattle more pasturage. In dry periods of late summer, sheep will crop grasses to the ground, even pulling up the roots and devouring those.

That would have destroyed the chance of pasture regenerating when the fall and winter rains resumed. Good-bye, sheep.

Simpson found "horses almost as plentiful as bulrushes." He wrote of "hecatombs of beef," harkening to the large sacrifices of ancient Greece. Then he added, California is "where beef may be procured for little or nothing, where hemp grows spontaneously, where the pine offers an inexhaustible supply of resin, and where suitable timber for ship-building invites the axe." A devout capitalist, Simpson fumed, "California in a nut-shell.... Nature doing everything, and man doing nothing."

In the Bay Area that same year, 1841, Lt. Wilkes, commander of the United States Exploring Expedition, noted an early sign of environmental stress: "At the time of our visit, the country altogether presented rather a singular appearance. Instead of a lively green hue, it had generally a tint of a light straw-colour, showing an extreme want of moisture. The drought had continued for eleven months; the cattle were dying in the field." Yet he looked beyond that year's weather to estimate rich farming for the future in California:

> Wheat produces remarkably. According to the best authorities, eighty bushels have been gathered from one sown, and this with loss arising from treading out with horses [an inefficient thrashing method]. Indian corn, rye, barley and oats, are also very fruitful, particularly the last, which has been imported, and is now spread over the whole country around the Bay of San Francisco. Vegetables are extensively cultivated, and may be brought to perfection throughout the year.

By Wilkes's time the wild oats still prevalent in open areas of California were broadcast across the land, having escaped from cultivation, as did mustard, radish, fennel, broom, pampas grass, and many other cultivars.

In the late nineteenth century Yerba Buena Island was appropriately called "Goat Island" after its dominant residents. The first goats were released onto Yerba Buena in 1842 by two businessmen who thought the locals were sick of eating only beef. The goats would have meant death for any native shrubs on the island.

A shipload of Mormons arrived in the village of Yerba Buena in 1846. One of them, Mary Holland Sparks, wrote letters home. She described feral livestock at that time: "Wild horses and cattle are plentiful here. But if we are as smart as the Spaniards, we can catch them and tame them. Beef is very cheap here."

One account from 1848, during the Mexican-American War, tells of drunken American sailors on alert for a counterattack from Mexican soldiers. On a dark night near Portsmouth Square the sailors gamely fired on the expected attackers, driving off the "Mexican cavalry." By dawn's early light, more sober observers saw the attack had simply been a stampeding herd of wild horses.

Feral cows, horses, pigs, goats, and sheep competed with the native deer, elk, and smaller animals. Further inland, feral herds competed with pronghorn in dry grasslands. As the competition played out and deer survived—and now thrive, even in suburbs—pronghorn were pushed out of most areas where houses or ranches were developed. Elk barely survived in California. They have been reestablished in a tiny portion of their former range in coastal California. At one time, the only remaining elk in California were on a private ranch where they were protected from hunting. There is more on the elk saga in California in Chapter 9. There are no wild deer, elk, or pronghorn in San Francisco now.

Feral livestock changed the nature of the coastal scrub and inhibited growth of young trees. Along streams and around lakes the livestock would have been particularly hard on native willows. Without the protection of fencing, willows could never regrow along streams and ponds in areas used to pasture cattle or other livestock. Willows are critical protection and feeding habitat for many insects and riparian bird species. Small mammals like the mountain beaver (also known as ground bear or by its genus name, aplodontia) disappear where willows are grazed out. Feral pigs still roam California's coastal hills, competing with native animals for acorns, native plants, and invertebrates. While there are no wild pigs in San Francisco, they are still found and hunted in more rural parts of central California. Feral pigs are particularly prone to digging beneath oak trees in pursuit of acorns.

It wasn't just livestock that proliferated and spread across the land. Around towns, ranches, and farms, dogs abounded. Reverend Walter Colton (1797–1851) was a U.S. Navy chaplain. He served as alcalde of Monterey for three years in the 1840s, keeping a detailed journal of his time in California. Here's his description of the dog population in January, 1846:

> I never expected, when threading the streets of Constantinople, where dogs inherit the rights of citizenship, to encounter such multitudes of them in any other part of the world. But California is more than a match for the Ottoman capital. Here you will find in every village a thousand dogs who never had a master; every farm-house has some sixty or eighty; and every Indian drives his cart with thirty or forty on its tail. They had become so troublesome, that an order was given a few days since to thin their ranks. The marines, with their muskets, were to be the executioners.

There's reason to believe San Francisco was similar to the rest of coastal California in its dog population. Those dogs would not have been as effective hunters as cats, but would still have been very hard on ground-nesting birds, small mammals, and fawns.

There we have it: free-range livestock, dogs and cats galore, unrestricted hunting and fishing, slaughter of "vermin," tree-cutting, introduction of new species from across the globe, rapid urbanization. We must marvel at the wildlife and native plants that actually did survive or even thrive through all this change and assault.

CHAPTER 7

Tree Cutting: What Else Are Trees For?

In these times, the hewers of wood are an unsparing race. The first colonists looked upon a tree as an enemy, and to judge from appearances, one would think that something of the same spirit prevails among their descendants at the present hour. It is not surprising, perhaps, that a man whose chief object is to make money should turn his timber into bank-notes with all possible speed.

—SUSAN FENIMORE COOPER, *RURAL HOURS*, 1850

He who cuts down woods beyond a certain limit exterminates birds.

—HENRY DAVID THOREAU, *JOURNAL*, MAY 17, 1853

With the disappearance of the forest, all is changed.

—GEORGE PERKINS MARSH, 1864

ONE VISIBLE EFFECT OF SAN Francisco's growth was the removal of native shrubs and plants to make room for houses and streets. The demand for firewood, buildings and ships immediately claimed useful lumber, with the consequence that nearby hills were denuded. As early as 1849, San

Francisco was importing lumber. Entire prefabricated buildings were shipped from the Atlantic Coast. Some were even made of metal, until the 1906 earthquake showed how dangerous that was in a fire.

Before Spanish colonization of the San Francisco Bay Area, Native Americans managed the oak forests of coastal California. They used seasonal burning to keep down brush and woody perennials. Their fast-moving fires, set in the driest part of the year, did little damage to the mature oaks but killed-off the annual resurgence of brush. The resulting open woodlands were ideal for acorn gathering and deer hunting.

The Ohlone had many uses for native trees. Alder became arrow shafts and flutes. Alder bark was sometimes used for medicinal purposes. Laurel nuts were eaten and the wood was used for split-stick clapper musical instruments. When acorn crops failed, the Ohlone would resort to soaking the tannins from the nuts of California buckeyes and then grinding them up to eat. The buckeye nuts required more leaching than even the acidic acorns. Raw buckeye nuts could be thrown into a stream to poison and stun fish. Buckeye wood was good for making bows and drills for making fires. California hazelnuts provided edible nuts. The wood and slender limbs became weapons and fish weirs. The bark of the redwood was stripped and used to make walls of dwellings and storage sheds. The berries of elderberry trees were eaten raw or dried. The wood was used to make musical instruments. Hollyleaf cherry fruit was eaten and used as a flavoring. Ohlone also ate madrone berries. The madrone's wood, being extremely hard, may not have had other uses besides burning. Willows provided flexible material for weaving the baskets so crucial to activities of daily living, including carrying everything from acorns to babies, and for storing and transporting food, tools, and other items.

Seven species of oak provided acorns that were used as food by Native Americans in California. The oaks that dominated San Francisco would have been live oak. While acorn crops are unpredictable—some species of oak fail to bear nuts every year—once the tannins are leached out, acorn meal is a rich source of carbohydrates and would have provided useful nutrition, especially when added to meat or fish. Additionally, mold that was deliberately grown on acorn mush had antibiotic properties and was used to treat wounds and inflammation. Of course, oak wood was used in making a variety of tools as well as for firewood.

To the Ohlone coppicing must have seemed to have no end. Trees just kept regrowing. We now know that cutting off an oak at the base does not kill the tree. The oak root system is much larger than what appears above ground. If allowed those living roots will sprout new trunks. Often a grove of oaks may share only one or just a few interconnected root systems. Several nearby trunks may just be the above-ground part of a single tree with a single root network. That root system may, in fact, connect and share nutrients or water with neighboring root systems. The root systems can live for a thousand years in some oak species. Maximum longevity for coast live oak is usually capped at 250 years. A stand of oaks is not a group of individuals but more of an interconnected network. The grove may have only a few genetically differing individuals regardless of the number of trunks and limbs seen above ground.

From the earliest Mexican settlement, trees in San Francisco were used for construction and fuel. Colonial deforestation of San Francisco can be said to have begun with the first baking oven at Mission Dolores. Later, British, French, Russian, and American ships came and went, gathering wood at will. In 1792 Vancouver pulled into the bay, taking wood from a "small bushy holly" [live oak]. Trees nearest the shore and on islands in the bay would have been cut first. In 1816, Chamisso came ashore at the San Francisco Presidio: "On the naked plain that lies at the foot of the presidio, farther to the east, a solitary oak tree stands in the midst of a shorter growth of brush."

After 1822 there was no official attempt by newly independent Mexico to limit trade in California. That meant more ship traffic and more ships needing wood and water. Those that stopped in Yerba Buena would often go to Sausalito to find fresh water. In 1822, twenty trading ships landed in California. By 1826, that number had grown to forty-four. In his book, *Two Years Before the Mast,* Richard Dana describes his experiences aboard one of those ships, a Yankee trader. He tells about gathering wood for the ship in 1836, when it was anchored in San Francisco Bay near what is now Montgomery and Clay Streets: "A small island about two leagues from the anchorage called by us 'Wood Island' and [by] the Mexicans 'Isla de los Angeles' [Angel Island] was covered with trees to the water's edge; and to this two of our crew ... were sent each morning to cut wood ... in about a week they had enough to last us a year." The native trees nearly disappeared in the decades that followed. Today you cannot find a single islay bush—the hollyleaf cherry—anywhere near Islais Creek. The only known surviving native buckeye stands at Pennsylvania and Twenty-Second Streets, on Potrero Hill. Native coastal live oaks are found in scattered spots like the Presidio, Lake Merced's northeast corner, and northeastern Golden Gate Park.

In 1856, Henry Vere Huntley described a horseback ride from San Francisco westward to what is now Ocean Beach:

> At the Mission we left the road, and placing ourselves under the guidance of a gentleman named Wy----e, and whom we thought proper to elevate to the rank of a baronet, dashed in amongst the sand hills, and soon found ourselves without a road at all; but instead we charged across the country, and suddenly came upon a party of French charcoal-burners.

Just beyond the limits of settlement men were cutting down the shrubs and trees to make charcoal. Likely they would have found scattered live oak, buckeye, madrone, laurel and manzanita. Willow and alder grew along the creeks and lakes. Almost all those trees would have been useful in fireplace or kitchen stove. It is not fair to the early San Franciscans to think they were unusual or especially hard on forests. All during the eighteenth and nineteenth centuries much of western Europe was deforested for ship-building and other economic purposes. This culture came to North America with its European settlers. In 1821 Charles Fourier was already warning that business (the word "capitalism" had not been coined) was going to ravage the planet: "It is thus completely ridiculous to stop at making decrees [about forests] that enjoin civilization to be no longer itself, to change its devastating nature, to stifle its rapacious spirit ... One might as well decree that tigers should become docile and turn away from blood."

It wasn't until gardens were planted and Golden Gate Park was begun in 1870 that any major effort was made to plant trees in San Francisco. As already mentioned, most of the trees in the city's modern-day parks are not native. Yet in addition to the dozens of exotic species found in Golden Gate Park, it also has the live oak grove in its northeastern corner which is a recognized member of the Old-Growth Forest Network.

Along the California coast thousands of acres were planted in eucalyptus trees, beginning during the Gold Rush. After the first eucalyptus were brought in from Australia, the fast growing tree encouraged a speculative bubble. The early growth aided dreams of lumber fortunes to be made. That never materialized because young eucalyptus trees produce flawed lumber. The useful eucalyptus lumber in Australia came from trees at least 75 years old or more. No investor could wait that long for a return. The eucalyptus boom in California was a bust despite even state government encouragement.

There is a redwood grove in the botanical garden in Golden Gate Park. Planted there by men. A second redwood grove is found next to the Transamerica Pyramid in the Financial District. Both the building and its trees stand on landfill put in place after the Gold Rush. It seems highly unlikely there were any native redwoods in San Francisco in 1840.

Recent estimates are that over one hundred thousand trees grow along San Francisco's streets. Almost none of them are native. Most street trees have some level of legal protection within the city. Further thousands can be found on private land. Again, few of those are native. In Golden Gate Park the most forested area in the city contains over 170 species, mostly exotics. Today the most abundant trees in San Francisco include various eucalyptus species from Australia, Monterey cypress and pine, palm trees, albizia and many exotic street trees. The albizia and eucalyptus are particularly good at re-seeding themselves and expanding their territory. Where they grow in groves eucalyptus even produce chemical deterrents that reduce the competing plant cover. None of these plants would have been found in San Francisco in 1760.

CHAPTER 8

People Change Nature: The Introduced and the Invasive

It can be imagined what an agreeable surprise it must have been for all of us to see in the month of September for some leagues around Monterey the blossoming of such a luxuriant and copious general vegetation that the number of plants restored to life by this singular fertility was not less than 100.

—Dr. Thaddaeus Haenke, 1791

The invasive species that cause the greatest damage are those that alter ecosystem processes such as nutrient cycling, intensity and frequency of fire, hydrological cycles... These invaders change the rules of the game of survival and growth, placing many native species at a severe disadvantage.

—John Randall, et al. *Invasive Plants of California's Wildlands*

Dr. Thaddaeus Haenke was the first scientist with a Ph.D. to visit California. Even though he was familiar with tropical South America and Mexico, he was impressed by the botanical richness of coastal California. In fact, Haenke was among the first to begin the widespread propagation of California native plants in far-off places. He sent back to Spain the first redwood saplings believed to have been planted in Europe. He is credited with sending back those redwoods long growing near the Alhambra in Grenada. The Czech-born Haenke never returned to Europe, staying in Bolivia after the Malespina Expedition and dying there decades later.

From the first arrival of sailing ships and the first gardens at Mission Dolores to the present day, accidental or casual introductions of animal and plant species occurred in the San Francisco area. Many species that spread beyond human control are now considered invasive. Among the earliest arrivals were filaree, wild oats, wild carrot, and black mustard. As much as one-fourth of California's present plant life may belong to species introduced during the past 250 years. There are now well over a thousand known introduced plant species in the wild in California. Invasive animals brought to California vary from rats to fruit flies, from wild pigs to Wild Turkeys.

Introductions continue to this day. In August, 2017, another unintended event happened which may lead to an environmental disaster. Cooke Aquaculture, Inc. farms Atlantic salmon in the Pacific Ocean. Started in 1985 on New Brunswick, Cooke has grown to have operations on four continents: Asia, both Americas and Europe. At one of Cooke's operations a large net supposed to keep the Atlantic species from escaping into the open Pacific broke. Thousands of Atlantic salmon escaped into the sea between Cypress Island, Washington, and Vancouver Island, British Columbia. Only time will tell how many of the escapees were caught by eager fishermen or if some escaped and will breed in their new ocean home. There is only one salmon species on the West Coast that shares the Atlantic fish's genus, *Salmo*. That is the cutthroat, so it is that species which is most likely to be in danger of interbreeding with the newcomers if they survive.

Another example, the New Zealand mud snail was first found in the 1980s in Idaho and Montana. By 2000, it was first identified in California, east of the Sierra. The snail has now invaded several creeks that flow into San Francisco Bay. A second bay invader is the green crab which is discusses in Chapter 15. Yet a further example: originally noted in Japan, the spotted-wing vinegar fly had made its way to Hawaii by the 1980s.

First found in California in 2008, it has now has spread along much of the coast. Perhaps most threatening are a group of invasive Asian earthworms first identified on the East Coast and found in Oregon in 2016. The risk from these invaders is that they feed on the surface material in forests, quickly turning leaf litter and fallen plant matter into worm food and then feces. They drive out nondestructive worm species and clear the soil for erosion and desiccation, weakening forests trying to survive climate change and drought. These invasive worms also deplete the nutrients in the upper layer of soil making it much harder for seeds to germinate and survive. Ground cover disappears, rendering ground-nesting birds vulnerable to predators. The worms have been found in Josephine County, Oregon, which is just across the border from California. They can spread in compost, on earth-moving equipment, and in soil with potted plants. Where they become dominant, forest fires will likely become worse and some native species may die out.

Plant Inavders. One of the best known and perhaps one of the most hated invasive plants is yellow starthistle. It thrives in heat, in drought, along roads and highways and in empty lots. Its nasty spines and deep, drought-defying taproot make it a sturdy competitor in sunny places. Starthistle is believed to have come from its native Europe as a contaminant in alfalfa seed. It was first identified in Oakland in 1869, but its seeds have been found in adobe bricks in California dating from as early as 1824. Nowadays, starthistle can be found in almost every part of California except the high central Sierra.

The Spanish missionaries brought with them garden and farm plants from the Old World. Some naturalized. It's likely our feral fennel, radish, plum, and mustard date from the earliest mission gardens. The more successful transplants soon escaped from garden into the wild. Ships, covered wagons, trains, livestock and livestock feed, boots, and eventually airplanes brought unintended passengers into California: weeds, seeds, insects—tiny stowaways.

Many successful species were introduced intentionally. For example, various eucalyptus trees were imported from Australia, and large land snails from Japan. Scotch broom was first brought into the Sierra foothills in the 1850s. Native to most of Europe and North Africa, the shrub spread across many types of open habitat. Prodigious seed production along with drought tolerance encourages its survival. European beachgrass was planted in San Francisco in 1869 to help hold back the restless dunes along today's Ocean Beach. Now the plant is found all along the coast of Northern California where it over-shades most native dune plants.

The list of introduced plants now widespread in San Francisco is lengthy. It includes German ivy, nasturtium, New Zealand spinach, albizia, iceplant, hollyhock, Cape ivy, English ivy, periwinkle, Scotch and French broom, wild oats or cheatgrass, pampas grass (from Argentina), Bermuda buttercup (an oxalis with an exceedingly persistent root system augmented by tiny bulbs), and various species of eucalyptus. Other widespread introduced plants in San Francisco are poison hemlock, wild or sweet fennel, geraniums, wild radish, nasturtium, and Himalayan blackberry. The Himalayan blackberry, in particular, is apparently a favorite shelter for rats, as well as shelter and a food source for many birds. Blackberry is often the center of a bird-rich niche in the urban landscape. The Himalayan blackberry is a prominent invasive often targeted when native plants are being restored. Not even Monterey pine and cypress are native to San Francisco.

How pervasive are invasives? Here's information from the website for San Francisco's Recreation and Parks Department: McLaren Park covers 312 acres. One hundred sixty-five acres are designated as a Natural Area. Much of the ground cover in this park is now introduced species. Wild oat grassland alone covers nearly 80 acres in the park. On the bright side, McLaren Park offers the only relict of tall fescue prairie within the San Francisco Natural Areas System.

Tree Planting. Impounded water and irrigation enabled gardeners to plant exotics and tame sand dunes. In the late 1800s the U.S. Army planted forests of eucalyptus, palms, Monterey cypress, and Monterey pines across the hills of the Presidio. Between 1883 and 1892, the army planted 330,000 trees. None of these were native. Many of those trees still stand today. Others have died of old age or been felled. The goal of the original tree-planting was to curtail the wind and tame blowing sand dunes. The army also covered over several streams.

In the 1880s, Adolph Sutro planted eucalyptus forests on some of the higher hills in central San Francisco, such as Mount Sutro and Mount Davidson. He also planted trees at Land's End and Sutro Heights. Sutro had his own plant nursery and encouraged his real estate customers to plant Monterey pines and cypress, eucalyptus, and other exotic trees. The forest atop his namesake hill still has many of the eucalyptus planted by Sutro's workers. The undergrowth there is primarily English ivy. Sutro was not alone in planting urban forests. Quick-growing Monterey cypress, Monterey pine, and eucalyptus were planted in what is now Sigmund Stern Grove in the Sunset District. There are many eucalyptus trees throughout Golden Gate Park, at Fort Funston, the Presidio, McLaren Park, Candlestick Hill and along the edge of Lake Merced.

Though they are non-natives, both Monterey pine and Monterey cypress are well-adapted to the Bay Area's maritime climate. Both naturally grew in the coastal region to the south. The nearest native stand of Monterey pine is believed to be in coastal southern San Mateo County near Año Nuevo. Monterey cypress is now seen in coastal plantings around the temperate world. All these cypresses are descendants of two small relict populations originally confined to the mouth of the Carmel River in Monterey County. The many eucalyptus species, so dominant in the current San Francisco landscape are dangerous in fires. Several popular acacia species, also from Australia, have naturalized and can be seen in dense clusters up to twenty feet high. In the mild coastal climate of San Francisco, shrubs and trees from South Africa and South America have naturalized as well. Open spaces like Fort Funston and Fort Mason contain almost no native plants today.

In the earliest days of San Francisco, the land outside of the residential areas was often used for firewood and farming. Cow Hollow—along Union Street west of Van Ness Avenue—was named for dairy farms there in the late 1800s. Glen Canyon was a hunting ground for Ohlone people, then livestock grazing land for missionaries and later for Californio ranchers. In the late nineteenth century there were many small farms in the Mission District.

San Francisco's original grasslands and coastal scrub are almost gone. Most grassland fell before invasive plants, pavement, housing, and other heavy use. A large swath of coastal prairie in McLaren Park became Gleneagles Golf Course. Fortunately, a parcel of nearly natural habitat survives on the eastern slope of Mount Davidson, where trees were never planted. Among the native plants thriving among the short brush on that windswept hillside are huckleberry, golden yarrow, and Douglas iris. There are also grassland remnants on Bayview Hill, Mount St. Joseph, and Bernal Heights, each an elevated island surrounded by urban development. On Bayview Hill, which overlooks Islais Creek basin, some of the few islay shrubs left in San Francisco can be found, and perhaps its last breeding Wrentits.

Into the early 1900s the rolling dunes of the Sunset District were covered each spring with blooming lupine. Theodore Wores, a popular landscape artist in San Francisco in the early twentieth century, often painted Sunset District dunes when there was still blowing sand and blooming coastal scrub. A 1912 article in the *San Francisco Call* said: "Theodore Wores has discovered the lupines on the sand dunes near Ocean Beach." The *San Francisco Post* wrote in 1913, "Wores' idea is to preserve on canvas the wilderness of San Francisco as it was up to a year or two ago." Wores' paintings of the springtime dunes show hillocks of yellow and blue flowers from foreground to horizon, amidst patches of pale, bare sand.

Invasive plants dominate today's San Francisco. Once-common plants like California buckeye, scrub oak, silk tassel, laurel, and ceanothus survive in remnants only. Native ceanothus species and the California poppy, however, do have some presence in landscaping and gardens across the city. And the California section of the San Francisco Botanical Garden has an authentic representative planting of species that would have covered San Francisco's hills, dunes, creek sides, and serpentine balds.

Some introduced trees and shrubs seem to harbor and feed birds and insects, but it is a complicated situation. There is evidence, for example, that eucalyptus trees may be deadly to both wintering birds and monarch butterflies. Yet, ironically, eucalyptus have provided overwintering shelter for millions of monarchs in several coastal sites, according to the Xerces

Society. At the same time as the trees provide necessary shelter, their chemical make-up and their sticky leaves may prove deadly. The eucalyptus's natural herbicides prevent many other plants from growing beneath their canopy. You never see moss or lichen on a healthy eucalyptus tree trunk. The monarchs need native milkweed plants in order to reproduce in breeding areas. Like many migrant species of insects and birds, the monarch will also be vulnerable to climate change or habitat loss both on summer and winter territories. The population crisis of the monarch has led fans of the species to encourage planting of milkweed, once disparaged as a mere "weed."

Some introduced plants that grow fast and spread easily—like pampas grass and iceplant—form thick, dense monocultures that inhibit other plants' growth. They provide little useful shelter or food for animals, often nearly insect-free. Iceplants are members of the seafig family and include species like heartleaf iceplant and hottentot fig.

Do not forgive ignorance, please. In 1973 the U.S. Army Corps of Engineers looked for an easy way to control erosion as part of a flood-control project on Alameda Creek in Fremont. They brought in Atlantic cordgrass heedless of what that could lead to. The plant started to cross-breed with native Pacific cordgrass. And it spread rapidly, colonizing once open mudflats, destroying native plants, animals and bird nesting sites. At one time this voracious hybrid cordgrass had devoured over 800 acres of precious saltmarsh habitat around the bay. It was turning the mudflats of the bay into a sterile monoculture. The cordgrass not only covered over the mudflats so birds couldn't feed, its dense root system crowded out the invertebrates that lived in the mud plus it took over areas where no surface plants had grown before. In San Francisco it got established in the marshes around Candlestick Point. Now an eradication program is near completion, the cordgrass is nearly gone, according to officials at the San Francisco Bay National Wildlife Refuge Complex.

Snail and Hardy. Among the many introduced invertebrates to be found in San Francisco, one is perhaps the most notorious. It has various taxonomic binomials but is generally known as the brown or common garden snail. The snail was presumed to have been deliberately introduced to California in the mid-nineteenth century to be served and eaten as escargot, but it has become the diner, not dinner. Though it's occasionally eaten by some nonhuman mammals and birds, mainly, it thrives. A widespread pest, it is a voracious devourer of garden and native plants. It does well in many artificial environments, like ivy beds and artichoke fields. Originally a native of the Mediterranean area, it does especially well in the coastal and southern portions of California. It is marvelously successful in San Francisco's damp, mild climate, but less so where winter brings subfreezing weather.

Native Americans likely would have gathered and eaten some insect larva and red-legged frogs taken from marshes or lakes. Urban settlement multiplied the take of frogs. In the 1870s, native frogs were still being gathered from small lakes in Golden Gate Park for San Francisco's "French" restaurants. Later the much larger and more aggressive bullfrog was introduced from the eastern United States, imported by private businesses to supply restaurants. The nineteenth century had almost no environmental regulations of any kind so bringing in a new species was totally legal and unremarkable. No forethought was given to any possible consequences beyond the hope for profitability. In coastal parts of the Bay Area, the summers are still too cold for the bullfrog to breed. But in warm areas this large, aggressive predator soon wiped out smaller competitors. Today the bullfrog dominates in most of California, except for most arid regions of the southeast. The native California red-legged frog is threatened.

Another game species introduced from the east was the striped bass, which lives in sea water. Fishermen were pleased, as Harold Bryant wrote in 1929:

"The introduction of striped bass in 1879 has proved to be the most successful and important of any. Of fish collected in the Navesink River, New Jersey, 135 of various sizes from one and one-half inches to full-grown fish were placed in the Carquinez Straits near Martinez."

Here's the summary on the California Fish & Game website:

In a few years, striped bass were being caught in California in large numbers. By 1889, a decade after the first lot of eastern fish had been released, bass were being sold in San Francisco markets. In another 10 years, the commercial net catch alone was averaging well over a million pounds a year. In 1935, however, all commercial fishing for striped bass was stopped in the belief that this would enhance the sport fishery.

The striped bass remains a controversial species in California. Some of its detractors say it preys on smaller native fish species and may endanger their survival. There have been failed efforts in the California Legislature to outlaw the fish and have it eradicated. Meanwhile, the bass thrives.

Two other widespread species were released in California for hunting. Wild Turkey and wild pigs are now common in some oak chaparral habitat. Neither is likely to penetrate San Francisco's urban landscape.

There are numerous introduced arthropods now living in California. These include four species of fire ant, Japanese and two dozen other species of beetles, gypsy and cabbage moths, a dozen fruit fly species, and the honeybee mite. San Francisco's climate prevents the spread of some of these into the city, but almost no inhabited place on Earth with temperate or tropical climate has escaped conquest by the so-called American cockroach. Originally a native of Africa, it first came to the United States in colonial times—as early as 1625. Its scientific name, *Periplaneta americana*, was bestowed by Linnaeus, so we have him to blame for blaming this very successful scavenger on America. Unlike some cockroaches, this species is a good flier.

Another notorious pest that travels the world with humans is the common bedbug. It is believed to have originated in Middle Eastern caves shared by bats and humans. Ancient civilizations—Egyptian, Greek, Roman, and more—were well aware of this bug, and it is still widely found and suffered wherever humans bed down.

Eighteenth- and nineteenth-century sailing ships brought more than plants, people and trade. The ships imported rats, black and brown. In 1849 San Francisco suffered its first rat plague. One contemporary noted a house with a sign saying "Close the door, keep out the rats." The nocturnal rat would have been a champion egg and hatchling thief, especially hard on ground-nesting birds like California Quail, Snowy Plover, Killdeer, and Dark-eyed Junco. Rats also climb trees and will attack smaller nestlings if parent birds are not around. In turn, some rats would have been taken by native coyotes and rattlesnakes, but both those species were often persecuted by people. Coyotes have only returned to San Francisco in recent decades. The rattlesnake is likely gone as long as the city exists.

Our globalized economy with its constant trade and travel across skies and oceans is effective in spreading invasive species. A few hours inside an airplane is a far more efficient way to spread around the globe than months on a sailing ship. This is true for insect eggs, plant seeds, disease microbes, small animals, fungi or molds. The California Invasive Species Council now cites over 1,700 species of problematic organisms in the state. Many invaders like West Nile virus are microscopic but can make a big difference. There will no doubt be more introduced species, from microbes to the next species that follows the Eurasian Collared-Dove's wing-beats. That dove spread across North America in less than forty years after first arriving in Florida. It got to Florida on its own after being heedlessly introduced to the Bahamas from Europe which the collared-dove had previously over-run on its own. Before it reached Europe without any direct aid from people, the collared-dive was a native of South Asia. Like many invasives from cockroach to rat to feral pigeon, the collared-dove can take full advantage of the changes people make to the landscape, the plantscape and the overall environment. Once established a successful invader can be difficult to impossible to eliminate or even limit.

CHAPTER 9

Killing for Fun and Profit

[Common Murre] *Up to about 1880, "abundant" locally. At one time, "myri-ads" congregated on the chief breeding grounds, the Farallon Islands. Commercial egging, permanent occupancy of those islands by people, and petroleum on the ocean surface has, directly or indirectly, caused great reduction in numbers of the murres.*

—JOSEPH GRINNELL AND ALDEN MILLER, *DISTRIBUTION OF THE BIRDS OF CALIFORNIA*, 1944

THE UNCONTROLLED EXPLOITATION OF CALIFORNIA'S natural resources began with the first people, then accelerated with the Mexican and Russian colonies. As the colonial population grew, heedless profiteers found ever more efficient ways of killing wildlife and selling the products. The statistics we can cite are almost unbelievable: more Pacific sea otters were killed in a single year than now exist south of Alaska.

Flesh, wood, feathers, birds' eggs, and pelts were all profitable commodities in the nineteenth century. Completely unregulated "harvesting" enterprises quickly diminished California's wildlife and forests. The first heavily attacked species were the trees near shore, fur seals, and sea otters. The Spanish missions traded sea otter and other pelts. In 1786, La Perouse was at Monterey when the governor of California was ordered to collect sea otter pelts to be sent via Spanish ships for sale in Asia. The governor promised to collect 20,000 pelts per year. At the same time some animals were killed for sport (both bear species) or food (sea elephants, elk) and left little or no impact in the written record.

Russian fur trading was more organized and more lethal than Mexican. Russians first settled in Alaska and expanded southward. By the late 1700s, Russians and their Aleut crews hunted and butchered fur seals by the thousands for their plush, valuable fur. Otter and other sea mammals were taken as well. In Alaska, Russians caused the extinction of the Steller's sea cow. Fortunately, Georg Steller saw and described this ocean-going manatee in the early eighteenth century. No other naturalist ever got to see a live one. The Russian-American Company founded Fort Ross in Sonoma County in 1812 to help supply food for the fur company workers. The killing accelerated. During 1810–1811, an American trading vessel, the *Albatross*, loaded over 73,000 fur seal pelts provided by the Russian-led hunters on the Farallones. In California in 1810, 30,000 fur seal hides were collected during a five-month season. Two years later, the number reached 50,000. In 1812, General Vallejo said sea otters were so plentiful that oarsmen would kill them while rowing through kelp beds. In 1817, a permanent Russian hunting colony was established on the southeast Farallon Island. These hunters were mainly after fur seals and sea otters, but other mammals, like elephant seals, were killed for meat and blubber. That same year Camille de Roquefeuil estimated 8,000 sea otters were taken from the bay. Roquefeuil also noted "the great diminution of otters on the northwest coast." The Mexican government theoretically intended to control hunting on its territory, but didn't have the men or ships to do so. All this hunting was "illegally" done by Russians, outside the reach of the Presidio's paltry pair of cannons. The Spanish and then the Mexican government in California never maintained a permanent naval presence here so "Laws" went largely unheeded.

More and more, Russian hunters concentrated on the Pacific Ocean. In 1826–1827, Captain Beechey observed: "The sea-otter is not an infrequent visitor in the harbour of San Francisco, but very few of them are taken [because of scarcity], notwithstanding their fur is valuable ... these animals are becoming less numerous upon the coast; in 1786 it was stated that 50,000 of them might be collected annually, whereas at present [1827] the number is reduced to about 2,000." As late as 1830, the Russian trading operation was killing up to 10,000 sea otters annually. Those furs sold in China for about $60 each. Their economic value had grown exponentially in two decades. It was an otter fur boom. The highest fur seal kill was probably in the year 1834: 200,000. By 1840, fur seals and the smaller sea otters were both nearly exterminated, and Russian Fort Ross was sold to Jacob Sutter. To this day, sea otters are rarely found between San Francisco and Puget Sound. The fur seal has returned in modest numbers to the Farallones after decades of legal protection.

Another species that almost disappeared from California due to hunting was the elephant seal, also called the sea elephant. This large animal was killed for meat and blubber. There would have been several elephant seal colonies along the coast between San Mateo and San Francisco in precolonial days. By 1892, the only known surviving elephant seals were on Mexico's Guadalupe Island. After Mexico and the United States began protecting these huge mammals in the 1920s, the population slowly recovered. There are now over 150,000 elephant seals in the northern Pacific Ocean. The first breeding colony re-established near San Francisco was at Año Nuevo, south of Half Moon Bay. Elephant seals were noted on the beaches there in 1955, and not until twenty years later was the first modern-era pup born in California. There are also sea elephant colonies now at Point Reyes and on the Farallones.

Whalers Arrive. Sea-going hunters included whalers. Whaling was as widespread as it was celebrated in the nineteenth century. The first California record of a whaling operation devoted to killing the large animals was begun at Monterey in 1854 by Portuguese whalers. That summer season they killed two dozen whales. Each of the whalers earned $438 each that first season. When the price of whale oil fell to twenty-five cents per gallon, that company disbanded. Commercial whaling across the northern Pacific from California to Hawaii was relentless and intensive over the ensuing decades. With guns, harpoons, and factory ships, hunters were able to kill nearly every whale they found. We will never know how many whales were slaughtered but in 1873 a single shore station at Pigeon Point south of San Francisco recorded twelve whales brought ashore, another ten killed but lost at sea. We know from witnesses that over time whales became rarer and rarer near shore and had to be pursued further and further from land.

Writing in 1923 Edwin Starks describes one recent whaling season for a single ship:

> "Showing that ship whaling has not been entirely given up, I have before me the results of the whaling cruise last year (1921) of the *Carolyn Francis* along the coasts of Mexico, California, and Alaska. This boat with a crew of 42 men secured 158 whales, which yielded 145,000 gallons of oil. Of these there were 170 humpback, 32 gray, 2 finback, 1 sperm and 1 sulphur-bottom [blue] whale. Records were lost as to 15 whales."

The bones — ivory — from whale carcasses were of some value, but blubber was the chief prize in the nineteenth century. Rendered by factory ships or at shore stations; the oil was sent back to Boston and New York to be burnt in lamps. Populations of every hunted whale species dropped precipitously under the onslaught. Most whaling ceased with the international agreement that took effect in 1985-6. Since then only three nations still hunt whales: Iceland, Japan, Norway. California's coastal whale populations are still only a fraction of what they would have been in 1840. Humphrey the Humpback Whale entered the Bay in 1985 and again in 1990. His presence sparked wide media and public interest. That illustrates the rarity of a whale near the modern metropolis. Ohlone and early colonists could have seen numerous whales near shore or on the bay on any normal day.

In addition to the decimation of marine animals, hunting depleted many native terrestrial species. Any edible species was trapped or shot. Some nineteenth century gourmands considered Sandhill Crane a delicacy so the bird was hunted out of its former nesting ground in the Sierra. The Harlequin Duck was extirpated from its native rivers. At the time, California farms produced little meat beyond ranch cattle, and eggs came mostly from seabirds, not chickens. The rapidly increasing population demanded ever more protein.

Commercial hunting and egg-gathering went unregulated until the twentieth century. Large carnivores like bears and mountain lions were killed for sport as well as for restaurant menus. Some were shot simply for trophies.

Bayard Taylor (1825–1878) recorded a telling detail of life in Gold Rush San Francisco. He comments that choice grizzly bear steaks were sweet, solid, and preferable to the best pork. So long, Mr. Grizzly. Today the only grizzly bears in California are on the state flag and state seal.

In the 1850s, San Francisco's restaurant menus offered a wide range of wild game. John Henry Brown was San Francisco's first important hotelier. Here are his words on obtaining food for his dining room: "By every vessel that left for Oregon I would send for such articles as butter, onions, pickled tripe, hams, bacon, eggs or anything I could obtain in the way of provisions…. Another item of considerable expense to me, the hiring of two hunters and a whale boat to go off up the creeks after game; they would make two trips per week, and were usually very successful."

Oyster Business. Frank Marryat (1826–1855) gives this list from restaurant menus right after the Gold Rush began:

San Francisco bills of fare present at all seasons a great variety, and no one has a right to complain who has but to choose from bear, elk, deer, antelope [pronghorn], turtle, hares, partridges [grouse], quails, wild geese, brant [goose], numerous kinds of ducks, snipe, plover, curlew, cranes, salmon, trout, and other kinds of fish, and oysters…. It is not until you have been a long time without an oyster that you find how indispensable to your complete happiness this bivalve is.

Marryat goes on to describe how the lack of oysters in the bay led to one entrepreneur searching out a new source elsewhere.

The history of oyster harvesting and aquaculture is typical of human exploitation: deplete the local species, then import exotics that grow and sell faster. When the Gold Rush hit California, there was immediate profit to be found in harvesting the local native oyster from San Francisco Bay. The native species, known as the Olympic oyster, originally grew from Alaska along the coast to Baja California. Before the Gold Rush it was widely distributed around the San Francisco Bay. Heavy and unregulated harvesting, careless treatment of the bay and oyster beds and the Gold Rush era ethos of use it and abuse it quickly depleted the native oysters, leaving only sparse numbers of survivors.

Profit-hungry oyster suppliers then found an abundant population around Shoalwater Bay, Washington. From there larvae were brought down to San Francisco to mature. Even these oysters would not reproduce in California waters. Eventually, even this imported oyster population, so popular and profitable in Jack London's youth, succumbed to a combination of over-collecting and water pollution.

Attempts were also made to transplant larger Atlantic oysters, but the cold water on the Pacific coast prevented them from reproducing. Starting in 1875, eastern American oyster "seeds" were brought across the country on the newly opened transcontinental railroad. They were then grown in San Francisco, Tomales, and Morro Bays. The high point for commercial oyster production using the eastern oyster seeds was 1899, when an estimated 2.5 million pounds of oyster meat was collected from San Francisco Bay oyster beds. It was these transplanted eastern oysters that were pirated by the young Jack London and his associates. By 1908, bay pollution and silting had reduced production by 50 percent. The last eastern seed oysters were shipped to California in 1921, and the last of those oysters were harvested from San Francisco Bay in 1939.

In the 1950s, the oyster industry began recovering. Imported Pacific oysters from Japan were grown in Humboldt, Tomales, Drake's, and Morro Bays, and in Elkhorn Slough. Oyster production never resumed in San Francisco Bay. Today most commercial oyster larvae come from hatcheries along the Pacific coast and are two Asian species.

An article in an issue of *Scientific American* (2015) inaccurately claims the term "California Oyster" was a nineteenth century marketing invention. That article even went on to falsely conclude that there had never been native oysters in San Francisco Bay. Speaking with biologist Dr. Ted Grosholz I learned what modern science can tell us. Dr. Grosholz's laboratory is at University of California-Davis but much of his work is in Bodega and San Francisco Bays. There are surviving native bay oysters and recent reclamation projects have led to a population of up to two millions oysters living in their native waters. This population will fluctuate due to fresh water inflow and other climate conditions but the bay's natives seem well on their way to partial recovery. They live now in two protected locations: Eden Landing in Alameda County and San Rafael Shoreline in Marin County. This oyster restoration is being led by San Francisco Bay Living Shorelines Project. Dr. Grosholz went on to explain that DNA anaylsis shows that the Bodega and San Francisco Bay native oysters are just that; they have genetic distinction from the oysters that were once imported from Washington State. For decades their native ancestors clung to survival in small pockets of the Bay in spite of human activity and heavy pollution in the early twentieth century. The Olympic oyster in the bay thus survives in its native habitat and is protected, though its population is surely much reduced from what it would have been in 1840. This oyster prefers clear waters near the mouths of streams, and is sensitive to turbidity and low salinity. It cannot survive high or low temperatures when exposed. It is unlikely to be commercially harvested in California in the near future.

Today, Dungeness crabs are still a profitable delicacy, pulled from Pacific waters and served in many San Francisco restaurants. In the 1860s, newly arrived Charles Warren Stoddard wrote about crabbing in his new home: "We began our adventure at Meiggs Wharf [now Pier 43]. We didn't go out to the end of it, because there was nothing but crabs there, being hauled up at frequent intervals by industrious crabbers, whose nets fairly fringed the wharf. They lay on their backs by scores and hundreds, and waved numberless legs in the air— I mean the crabs, not the crabbers."

There is still an annual crabbing season in San Francisco Bay and nearby waters. The sport season opens November 1st and commercial crabbing begins two weeks later. The Northern California season ends on June 30th. In recent years, however, some crab seasons have been shortened or cancelled entirely due to toxic bloom, oil spills, or other environmental problems.

Elk Almost Exterminated. Early San Franciscan William Heath Davis recalled, "I often saw on Mare Island in the years from [1840 to 1843] as many as 2,000 or 3,000 elk. It was their habit to cross and re-cross by swimming between the island and the mainland, and I remember on one occasion sailing on the schooner *Isabel* through a band of not less than 1,000 which was crossing from the island to the main. It was a grand and exciting scene."

U.S. Army Lt. Joseph Warren Revere commanded the Sonoma military district in 1846, after the American conquest. Here's his elk hunting memory:

> We found, on rising the next morning, several of the neighboring rancheros, who had arrived, on their way to Punta de los Reyes, for the purposes of hunting elk, with which it abounds.... I resolved to remain and witness the sport.... I observed that the Spaniards had no arms; but they pointed to the riata [noose], the unfailing companion of all rancheros.... On our way, however, I observed one of the party dismount, near a small grove, and selecting a straight light pole, take from beneath his serape a crescent-shaped weapon, which he fixed to the top of the pole ... and it is used for hamstringing the elk.

Revere then goes on to describe the hunt and killing of six elk out of a herd he estimates at four hundred. It was not just sport, it was economically justified hunting:

> The tallow from the six elks filled two large hides, each weighting at least four hundred pounds. From the superior hardness, whiteness and delicacy of the elk's tallow, it is much requested among the rancheros for cooking purposes, and the hides are also worth something. The Punta Reyes is a favorite hunting-ground, the elk being attracted by the superior quality of the pasture—the land lying so near the sea, that the dews are heavy and constant, adding great luxuriance to the wild oats and other grains and grasses.

In 1846, Revere saw mixed herds of pronghorn and feral cattle as well as the abundant elk. Before long those wildlife herds were myth and memory. Just fifteen years later William Brewer listened to others' reminiscences during a visit to the San Ramon Valley in Alameda County: "Game was once very abundant—bear in the hills, and deer, antelope, and elk like cattle, in herds. Russell said he has known a party of thirty or forty to lasso twenty-eight elk on one Sunday. All are now exterminated, but we find their horns by the hundreds."

The precolonial elk population in California's grasslands and river bottoms has been estimated at half a million. Less than three decades after the Gold Rush began most tule elk were dead from hunting and habitat loss. Southern California cattleman Henry Miller rounded up twenty elk in 1874 and protected them on his ranch. By then few remained wild. Miller's elk herd increased, and in 1905 a few were transferred to Sequoia National Park. In 1914 and 1915 the California Academy of Sciences distributed 146 elk from Sequoia to nineteen other parks and reserves around the state. In 1932, the elk herd was given permanent protection at the Tule Elk State Reserve located in Kern County on state park property. Starting in the 1970s, elk were transplanted from there to other suitable habitat at Point Reyes, Grizzly Island in Solano County, and twenty other sites around California. Today California's elk population is about four thousand.

There were no fishing regulations in the nineteenth century just as there were almost no laws protecting mammals, birds, streams or forests. Harold Bryant points out in his 1929 summary of California's natural heritage that salmon were especially hurt by gold mining. Hydraulic mining washed away entire hillsides. The resulting gravel and sediment filled spawning streams. The salmon population plummeted. After mining dwindled, modern engineering began damming the same streams. Bryant concluded, "Originally one of the most abundant of fishes and the basis of the greatest canning industry in the state, [salmon] is becoming scarce.... The best, and the last great run of king salmon left in the state is to be found in the Klamath River." Sometime in this twenty-first century, we might see the last of the dams removed from the Klamath, thus restoring one of the crucial salmon spawning rivers in North America. Today the salmon fishing industry needs constant government protection and monitoring to survive. As we saw earlier, it can even face threats from its own supporters, like the unintended release of thousands of Atlantic salmon in

2017. Also, the fishing industry spawns clashes with other conservation efforts, including one slaughter of Double-crested Cormorants along the Columbia River. In the upper Klamath River Basin there is direct conflict between the water needs of the Klamath National Wildlife Refuge's need for waterfowl and Native Americans' rights to have ample river level for salmon fishing. Shallow water and warm water due to slow current are both detrimental to salmon. Many years there is simply not enough water in the Klamath River Watershed for all worthwhile uses, including agriculture.

Catch and Eat. Market hunting grew to become big business. Writing in the 1860s, J. G. Cooper noted Mourning Doves were shot for sale, even during the breeding season. At that time, live California Quail were often for sale, with some escaping back into the dunes of San Francisco. Cooper noted that in those days "market hunters rely chiefly on traps."

Animals were hunted in the interior, as well, and sold in San Francisco. Twenty years after the Gold Rush, Dr. John Strong Newberry wrote about the Sandhill Crane: "In the autumn and winter it is abundant on the prairies of California and is always for sale in the markets of San Francisco, where it is highly esteemed as an article of food." One scientist, whose observations illustrate the onslaught against native seabirds in California, was Dr. Adolphus Heermann. A surgeon and trained naturalist, Heermann spent 1849–1852 in Northern California. On the Farallon Islands, he watched egg gatherers raid Common Murre nests. The men scared away the adult murre, then raced to the nests before the Western Gulls could get the eggs. Heermann himself shot sea lions and seabirds on his visit, and collected a Tufted Puffin egg. In San Francisco, he shopped at meat markets for bird skins. In the markets, he recognized a new species, the Tricolored Blackbird.

Harlequin Ducks once nested on Sierra streams that drained the western slope. Hydraulic mining filled their streams with gravel, and the ducks were hunted. There's evidence the Green-winged Teal, Gadwall, Northern Shoveler, Northern Pintail, Wood Duck, Lesser Scaup, and Ruddy Duck were once common breeding ducks in central California. The Common Merganser bred on Bay Area streams in good numbers and on Alcatraz Island. Now only Cinnamon Teal, Wood Duck, Mallard, and Ruddy Duck can be considered common breeding ducks anywhere near San Francisco. The Canada Goose, an introduced species, is now present as well. It appreciates the lawns of playing fields and golf courses. According to Arnold Small, the geese have been breeding in the Bay Area since 1959. Since 2000, they've become common in San Francisco's Golden Gate Park.

In the late 1800s, San Francisco's egrets and herons suffered a fate common across the nation. To supply feathers for women's hats and clothing, hunters slaughtered the birds during breeding season, when their decorative plumes were at the peak.

Sport shooting for any purpose continued unregulated for decades. Unpopular animals like crow and coyote were supposed to be shot on sight. William Brewer's recollections include images of the indiscriminate and profligate wildlife slaughter. On a single trip to the Sierra in the 1860s, Brewer recorded:

> We camped at a fine meadow. The boys saw a bear, but he got away.... We got into the canyon of the South Fork of the Kings River ... the river swam with trout, I never saw them thicker. The boys went to fishing and soon caught about forty, while the soldiers caught about as many more.... We luxuriated on trout for the next two meals. The rattlesnake were thick—four were killed this day.... We killed a rattlesnake at ten thousand feet. I have never before seen them so high in the mountains. Dick also killed a grouse, a fine bird nearly as large as a big hen.

Most early records of Great Gray Owls in California come from shot birds that were stuffed for display in the local saloon or hotel. No living Great Gray Owl was reported in California between 1850 and 1910. It was only after widespread persecution by people ended that many species could return to their precolonial range and thrive. Some like bears, wolves, pronghorn, Great Gray Owl, Clapper Rail and Sandhill Crane never did.

Some animals have been targets of deliberate persecution. Native wolves, bears, coyotes, foxes, rattlesnakes, corvids, and hawks were hated by early settlers and shot on sight. It seems many people did not welcome predators they saw as competition to their own killing. We saw how Brewer's group killed five rattlesnakes in a couple of days. Any bear, whether black or grizzly, was fortunate to escape alive. Large birds were inviting targets for the marksman. Raptors, vultures, condors, large owls, and corvids were considered "varmints" and shot on sight. Adolphus Heermann regretted he was not able to collect a California Condor during his visit (1849–1852). He did shoot a Prairie Falcon he found on the Farallones.

Cooper wrote that Bald Eagles were a "very abundant species where not exterminated by the foolish ambition to 'kill an eagle' which inspires most gunners." Cooper goes on to say that Spanish inhabitants encouraged the eagle because of its skill at killing ground squirrels. He found some Californio ranchers raised young Bald Eagles that, when full grown, would hunt in the daytime and return to the house to roost at night.

For decades, Golden Gate Park employed a professional hunter to shoot all hawks and corvids. The attitude changed in the late twentieth century. As urban dwellers became less likely to own a rifle or shotgun it seems some Americans became more open to information that placed each species within the complex web of living creatures. After the hunter job was discontinued, the Red-shouldered Hawk repopulated its former range in the City and became a welcome rat hunter in city parks. It was only in the final third of the twentieth century that Great Blue Herons, Common Ravens, American Crows, Steller's Jays, and California Scrub-Jays were able to reestablish breeding populations in San Francisco. Some protected oak groves have regenerated. These are victories earned by native organisms. Add in the rebounding populations of elephant seals, fur seals, Bald Eagle, Brown Pelican, Peregrine and even California Condor and we have evidence of nature's resiliency and determination. However, none of these resurrections would have happened without direct and deliberate intervention by people who now so often can determine which species live and which will die.

CHAPTER 10

A Real Estate Boom: Gold Rush and Urban Growth

The hog that roots his own living, and so makes manure, would be ashamed of such company. If I could command the wealth of all the worlds by lifting my finger, I would not pay such a price for California. It is only three thousand miles nearer to hell.

—HENRY DAVID THOREAU ON THE GOLD RUSH

A rush and a scramble of needy adventurers, and, in the western country, a general jail delivery of all the rowdies of the rivers.

—RALPH WALDO EMERSON, 1848

Nature watches over all, and turns this malfeasance to good. California gets peopled and subdued, civilized in this immoral way, and on this fiction a real prosperity is rooted and grown.

—RALPH WALDO EMERSON, 1850

THE LARGE-SCALE ALTERATION OF SAN Francisco's landscape continued for decades. Marshes, streams, and lakes were filled in. This was done with no thought of earthquakes or flooding. Just as today major construction takes place in low lying areas that may well be flooded by rising sea levels. As soon as the Gold Rush began the hunger for land, speculation and profit exploded in San Francisco. One early arrival was writer Bayard Taylor. Here's what he found as the city expanded onto what had been the bottom of the bay:

> A better idea of San Francisco, in the beginning of September, 1849, cannot be given than by description of a single day. Supposing the visitor to have been long enough in the place to sleep on a hard plank and in spite of the attacks of innumerable fleas, he will be awakened at daylight by the noises of building ... carts and porters are busy along the beach.

The single most important impetus for the changes that came to the San Francisco Peninsula after 1848, was the explosive population growth in California, and San Francisco's emerging position as a port, banking headquarters, and commercial center. Thomas Cole, in his essay, "City Perched on a Frontier," tells it thus: "San Francisco claims to be unique, and it is. It is a boomtown, the very archetype of the tough, loony, and gloriously successful boomtown. And, unlike [other] boomtowns from Alaska to the Brazilian jungle, it lasted, thanks to grace and luck. Its history is dramatic and quirky, but above all it is sudden."

Indeed, there is plenty of contemporary evidence that many, at first, took San Francisco as a temporary place, both as residence and city. In 1855, the authors of *Annals of San Francisco* could already quote William Tecumseh Sherman: "Nobody feels a fixed interest here; all are ready to bolt as soon as a good chance offers. Everything is chance, everything is gambling." In the same paragraph, the *Annals* quotes Prentice Mulford as he describes an economy at its most rapacious: "Five years was the longest period anyone expected to stay. Five years, at most, was to be given to rifling California of her treasures, and then that country was to be thrown aside like a used-up newspaper."

Some who criticized the weather and muddy waterfront of San Francisco foresaw Benicia or other locations as the future's major metropolis. In 1850, General Persifor Smith was military governor and commander of the Pacific Division of the U.S. Army. He observed San Francisco was "no way fitted for military or commercial purposes; there is no harbor, a bad landing place, bad water, no supplies or provisions, an inclement climate, and is cut off from the rest of the country, except by a long circuit around the southern extremity of the bay."

General Smith moved his headquarters to Benicia, which he wanted to make California's capitol (and partially succeeded, as Benicia was the capital from 1853–1854). San Francisco's fog, fleas, sand, and wind seemed to militate for the area's great city being built elsewhere, not to mention that at first, San Francisco lacked any suitable natural source of fresh water. And yet, recurring fires, earthquakes, and sand storms all failed to stem little Yerba Buena's growth into a major city. Problems were ignored or overcome.

Easterner Fitz Hugh Ludlow visited California and Oregon in 1859 with the landscape painter Albert Bierstadt. Ludlow commented, "To a traveler paying his first visit, San Francisco has the interest of a new planet. It ignores the meteorological laws which govern the rest of the world."

In summer, 1849, writer Bayard Taylor departed San Francisco to see the Mokelumne River gold mining district east of Stockton. When he returned to San Francisco he was amazed:

I could scarcely realise the change that had taken place during my absence of three weeks. The town had not only greatly extended its limits, but seemed actually to have doubled its number of dwellings, since I left. High up on the hills, where I had seen only sand and chaparral, stood clusters of houses, streets which had been merely laid out were hemmed in with buildings and thronged with people; new warehouses have sprung up on the water side, and new piers were creeping out toward the shipping; the forest of masts had greatly thickened; and the noise, motion, and bustle of business and labor on all sides was incessant ... it was daily enlarged by from twenty to thirty houses.

Next the peripatetic Taylor traveled south to Monterey for the California Constitutional Convention, returning to San Francisco in November. At that time, Portsmouth Square was the hub from which the town extended. Taylor's credulity was tested again.

> The morning after I arrived, I went about the town to note the changes and improvements. I could scarcely believe my eyes. The northern point [Telegraph Hill] where the bay pours its waters into the Golden Gate, was covered with houses nearly to the summit–many of them large three-story warehouses. The central and highest hill [Nob Hill] on which the town is built was shorn of its chaparral and studded with tents and dwellings; while to the eastward the streets had passed over the last of the three hills [Rincon, now largely leveled] and were beginning to encroach on Happy Valley. The beautiful crescent of the harbor, stretching from the Rincon to Fort Montgomery, a distance of more than a mile, was lined with boats, tents and warehouses, and near the latter point several piers jutted into the water. Montgomery Street, fronting the bay [all the "land" east of Montgomery is now on bay fill], had undergone a marvelous change. All the open spaces were built up, the canvas houses replaced by ample three-story buildings, an exchange with lofty skylight fronted the water, and for space of half a mile the throng of men of all classes, characters, and nations, with carts and animals equaled Wall Street before three o'clock.

Joseph Perkins Beach came around the Horn to San Francisco in 1849. His journal describes what happened after his ship, the *Apollo* arrived in San Francisco. It entered the Bay and dropped anchor near Sausalito, where fifty ships were already anchored. That was September 18th. Eight sailors and a cook abandoned ship, presumably for the gold fields. By September 20th, all the *Apollo*'s passengers were gone and four more sailors had disappeared. Thus was Northern California peopled during the Gold Rush.

U.S. Representative Thomas Butler King's report on his visit to California in 1849 cited eighty thousand American immigrants to the state during that year, with another twenty thousand "foreigners." Most of those would have come through San Francisco, even if they were bound for the mining districts. That is a lot of population and commerce through a town that had numbered less than five hundred inhabitants in 1847, only two years earlier. Thousands of would-be miners and profiteers contributed to the population explosion. Accompanying the Gold Rush was the first real estate boom in San Francisco. It became one of the fastest-growing cities in history. Nothing was allowed to get in the way. Topography was reshaped for commercial purposes.

The first Swiss Consul to San Francisco was Théophile de Rutté, arriving at the end of 1849 during that Christmas season. He made these observations:

> At my feet stretched out this mushrooming city, grown out of the Mexican pueblo like a mighty oak out of an acorn…. The original crescent of Yerba Buena had disappeared and the sand of the surrounding hillsides had already filled it in to facilitate the growth of the city. The North Beach end now met Rincon Point with a line of giant wharves stretching out into the bay…. Toward the south, it was an entirely different picture. In the foreground swamps and green meadows rose to meet the gentle slopes of the San Bruno Mountains. In the middle of the plain stood the little village of the Mission.

Englishman Frank Marryat was in California from 1849 to 1851. In June, 1851, he came back to the city after nine months of hunting and mining inland. Here's what he saw upon return:

> On landing at San Francisco, I found so many changes on every side, that my knowledge of the locality was at fault; wharves extended on all sides into the sea, and the spot where I had last landed was scarcely recognizable, it was now far inland; the steam paddy [a steam-powered earth mover] had worked incessantly, and the front of the town still advanced into the bay.

Filling the Bay. The original Yerba Buena waterfront ran from the eastern face of Telegraph Hill, along the current Montgomery Street, and then curved around Rincon Hill, which stood on a peninsula. Much of the current South of Market area was either saltmarsh or was under water. Starting as early as 1847 (before the Gold Rush), and into the 1850s and 1860s, tidelands were sold off. Moving sand and earth, and then building, were so emblematic of San Francisco's economic life that in 1855 the authors of *Annals of San Francisco* seemed simply to echo the popular creed of Manifest Destiny in their description of the local scene:

> The old character of the [Yerba Buena] cove has been completely changed, and at present, instead of the former semicircle of beach there is almost a straight line of building extending across the middle of the cove from the Rincon to Clark's Point [Broadway just east of Battery today]. In many places of what is now the very centre of the business portion of the city lie large vessels, which in the disastrous years of shipping, 1848 and 1849, got stranded or were used as store-ships or lodging-houses on the beach ... these ships remained where they lay, fast imbedded in mud, while long streets, hollow beneath, and numerous solid houses arose on every side, effectually to hem them in forever.

> Perhaps not many years hence the whole shores at North beach and South Beach (Mission Bay) and the bay itself to a considerable distance from the present high-water mark, will be covered with streets and houses, quays and long piercing piers, just as now is the cove of Yerba Buena.

Sand hauling quickly became a major enterprise. From Happy Valley, south of Market Street, a sand hill was hauled away to fill in what became Battery Street. South Beach was filled in starting in 1849, using sand from a dune at Brannon and Second Streets. The Yerba Buena cove shoreline moved a thousand feet eastward into the bay. One sand hill at Market and Third had been 80 feet high, another at Grant and Market measured 89 feet. Both were leveled. Some lots were sold when they were still under 25 feet of water. The new owner would hire workers and a steam paddy to fill it above sea level. One sandy point that protruded into the bay along North Beach was Tonquin Point, west of Telegraph Hill. It no longer exists. It was leveled as its sand was hauled away to fill in what is now Fisherman's Wharf. An early seawall was built from rock dynamited from the east face of Telegraph Hill. Some of that rock was also used for fill or ship ballast. When the hill itself became prime real estate, rock was then shipped in from Brooks Island, off Richmond. An 1850 photograph of San Francisco by William McMurtrie shows goats browsing on Telegraph Hill. Soon they would be replaced by streets and homes. A lower hill south of Telegraph Hill, known as Clark's Point, once rose near where Broadway crosses Front Street. It was completely leveled by dynamite and steam paddies.

All along San Francisco's bay front, the early "making" of new lots was tremendous: 184 acres were filled in around the Palace of Fine Arts and the Marina. In Mission Bay, another 250 acres were built up and then built on. Filling began thereabouts with the Folsom plank road from Third Street to Eighth Street in 1852. Noting the rapid fill of the south of Market marshes, Henry Langley wrote in the 1870 *San Francisco Directory*, "Hills have been leveled and valleys filled up, so that the Southwest part of the city has lost its former lumpy aspect, and now presents the appearance of a level plain." Historian Hubert Bancroft estimated 450 acres of new land had been created in San Francisco in fourteen years during the mid-nineteenth century.

San Francisco's population growth was relentless. In the 1860s, many miners left for new, supposedly richer fields. The Civil War was raging two thousand miles away. Yet San Francisco grew. William Brewer wrote in 1862:

San Francisco is not only the metropolis of the state, but in reality the most prosperous portion, growing the fastest, and the growth being healthy…. Its growth has been rapid, it has grown as if by magic. Fifteen years ago two or three ranch houses and barren sand hills marked the spot; today it is a city of over 100,000 inhabitants, and growing fast. Since I arrived here three years ago building has been going on at an almost incredible rate. I now live in a fine, large boarding house, with stores under it.... The first day of last January the first street railroad car started.

This boom town growth was not an unusual occurrence in the United States in the mid-nineteenth century. Chicago, for example, grew from four thousand to nearly a hundred thousand people between 1840 and 1860. By 1860, New York teemed with over a million residents.

In 1874, surviving veterans of the 1849 Gold Rush reunited in San Francisco for an anniversary celebration. In the Grand Hotel, former senator William Gwin told them, proudly, what they had wrought:

> When we landed here, the permanent population of San Francisco did not exceed one thousand; now it is over two hundred thousand. The ground beneath us was a shapeless mound of sandy desert. Diagonally across from where we are sitting is a strip of ground covered with almost worthless buildings, that sold the other day, as an investment, for $300,000. The 100-vara [333-feet long] lot, of which that strip was a small portion, cost, at the date of our arrival, $16, just the fee for issuing the alcalde's title.

Rural land use was just as susceptible to financial imperatives as city building lots. Cattle continued to be an important economic and environmental factor. In 1850 Congressman Thomas Butler King, reported that before the Gold Rush a cow, sold for hide and tallow, brought two dollars, but by 1849 that cow brought twenty to thirty dollars, and all for meat. The tallow and hide trade was gone. King remarked that the price range on a horse had been five to ten dollars but had jumped to between sixty and a hundred fifty dollars. King predicted a continued migration to California, noting there would be a need for widespread agricultural irrigation and that the state would need to develop its own lumber industry to supply building needs. All that happened as he foresaw.

In 1860, William Brewer was newly arrived from the East Coast. He participated in the state's new geological survey. His notes on the San Francisco Peninsula, dated June 28, 1861, read:

The fields are all dry and yellow, the herbage on the waste lands eaten down to the very roots, the fields of grain ripe for the harvest....But how dry it looked! Hundreds of windmills pump water from the wells for cattle and for irrigating the lands, but the streams are dry, and sand and clouds of dust fill the dry air.

Brewer, like many easterners, was not yet familiar with the rainy and dry seasons in California's coastal climate.

Not all the radical changes to the face of San Francisco were brought about by ranching, real estate boom, and construction. In western San Francisco, Golden Gate Park was built and landscaped in the windy sand dunes and around the small inland lakes. Work began in the 1870s and took decades. John McLaren, superintendent of the Park from 1887 to1943, did more than any other single person to produce what we now know as Golden Gate Park. He preferred to be thought of as "the boss gardener who conquered the sand." He is said to have supervised the planting of two million trees. There is a more thorough look at Golden Gate Park's natural history in Chapter 14.

Sutro Heights went through a similar transition in the late nineteenth century. Adolph Sutro would lease parcels of his huge land holdings to small farmers as long as they paid him back by hauling their horse or cow manure to his garden spot above Lands End. In both Golden Gate Park and Sutro Heights, the dominant trees planted by gardeners were species not native to San Francisco—eucalyptus, Monterey pine, Monterey cypress. These thrived in the salt fog, sand, and wind.

In addition to intensive tree planting, the Army changed much of the face of the Presidio. The old bluff-top that once held the original Mexican Presidio was blasted away during the Civil War to make a flat area for the new Fort Point. Elsewhere streams were buried and marsh filled in. Water was pumped from Mountain Lake and a golf course was built nearby. The former marsh, now known as Crissy Field, was filled in just before the 1915 world's fair, to serve as an airfield. By 1900, North Beach was protected by a seawall and the new Fisherman's Wharf was created.

As recently as 1916, the Southern Pacific train tracks south of Potrero Hill ran right along the edge of the bay. East of those tracks Iowa, Minnesota, Tennessee, Third, and Illinois Streets all run over bay fill. Further south in India Basin, Heron's Head Park was reclaimed from bay fill land that was formerly meant to be an industrial pier. Where there is parkland, there were once tidal flats, and in fact a portion of that park is now salt marsh.

In 1925, Islais Creek "reclamation" began and over 280 acres were filled in east of the current Highway 101. In 1940, the U.S. Navy bought Hunters Point, and removed a 170-foot high hill to fill part of the bay there. As with many earlier bay fill projects, when dry land was not available the navy turned to dredged material from the bay itself.

In the 1950s the nation's first all-concrete baseball stadium was built at Candlestick Point. Now demolished, to be replaced by multiple-use development, the ball park was built across mainland and onto bay fill. Some of the 170 acres at Candlestick Point were filled in after the Pearl Harbor attacks in preparation for a U.S. Naval base to defend the coast during World War II, but the base was never built. The landfill remains to this day.

City Versus Pacific. Ocean Beach has a long history of people battling the sea. Inevitably the Pacific Ocean brushes aside anything humans try to erect in its way. The first development along Ocean Beach was a sand trail through the wild blown dunes. That evolved to become the Great Highway. At one time the western portion of San Francisco was dubbed "The Great Sand Waste." The first major construction in the outer lands was the original Cliff House, built in 1863. Over time, more people and more buildings came to the ocean shore. The first Beach Chalet was built along the Great Highway on the ocean side. In 1909 a seawall was built to protect the building's foundation. But erosion continued and a winter storm in 1914 caused severe erosion all along the coast and was the end of that seawall. That first Beach Chalet was also doomed. Over the next century, wind-blown sand and storm-driven erosion have recurred despite all engineering efforts to allay their effects. Now climate change is kicking in. Later in this book we will discuss what is proposed to prepare the western edge of San Francisco for the inevitable rising sea level.

By 1900, North Beach was protected by a seawall and the new Fisherman's Wharf was created. During the 1906 quake, severe settling resulted in catastrophe when a four-story wooden hotel at 718 Valencia, near Twenty-Second Street, collapsed. It was the Valencia Street Hotel, built on fill where a lake, Laguna de Manantial, had been. Many hotel residents were still asleep when the predawn quake struck. Trapped in the wreckage, they were then covered by rising water from nearby Mission Creek. Later the entire area burned before any rescue effort could be made. A historian recently estimated that two hundred people perished in that single structural disaster.

The 1989 quake severely damaged a number of more modern build-ings in the city's swank Marina District, causing fires and deaths there as well. That section of town stands on a filled-in marsh, subject to liquefac-tion. Bay fill was completed there in time for construction of the 1915 Panama-Pacific International Exposition, which celebrated the rebirth of San Francisco after the devastation in 1906. An Oakland freeway, also on fill, collapsed in the 1989 quake, killing more than forty people in their vehicles.

Across San Francisco, buildings and parking lots still sit on bay fill that was laid down quickly, haphazardly, and for a fast profit. Modern engineering might be able to solve the quake safety issues posed by these places—or maybe not. The 58-story Millennium Tower, at Mission and Fremont Streets, is a luxury condominium skyscraper completed in 2008. A year later, there were signs that it was sinking. Where it is located would have been offshore in 1845, so it sits on bay fill. One consultant said the building had sunk sixteen inches by mid-2016. It had also tilted two inches at the base. Millennium Tower residents began reporting misalignment of fixtures, structural parts of the condos, and parking areas. Lawsuits have been filed. The twenty condo owners in the luxury building may have paid as much as $75-million dollars each. Now a next-door neighbor is being pulled into the wrangles that will go on for years and involve tens of millions of dollars. Transbay Joint Powers Authority (TJPA) is building a public transit center next door which has included tunneling in the soft earth. It's being billed as the "Grand Central Station of the West."

Estimates indicate further leaning and sinking should be expected at Millennium Tower. Apparently, this high-rise has pilings that go down eighty feet but are not deep enough to reach bed rock. The number of smaller buildings in similar situations around the bayshore is in the thousands. How stable they will be in the next earthquake only the next generation of quake survivors will see.

CHAPTER 11

Birds and People:
Killing and Protecting

The winter months ... at this season the bay is crowded with hosts of birds. Ducks and scoters swim about off shore. Murres and cormorants, grebes and loons dive and sport to their hearts' content. It is the gulls, however, that attract the greatest attention of passengers on the ferry boats. They follow the boats back and forth, picking up food thrown overboard.

—CHARLES KEELER, *SAN FRANCISCO AND THEREABOUT*, 1906

The brushy parts of Golden Gate Park in San Francisco abound with quail, and from the benches one can watch the squads of plump hen-like little creatures as they move about with stately tread or stand talking sociably in low monosyllables. If they hear a footstep on the walk they start up and hurry across the path like hens before a wagon, top-knots dropped over their bills, necks craned forward, and legs stretched as they patter along in double-quick time.

—FLORENCE MERRIAM BAILEY. *HANDBOOK OF BIRDS OF THE WESTERN UNITED STATES*, 1902

NOTHING MORE CLEARLY SHOWS THE vast changes in the bird life of San Francisco than the near extirpation of the California Quail since 1980. People have severely affected bird populations, mainly by hunting and by altering habitat, but in other ways, as well. In some cases, the change was just that humans stopped persecuting a species and it returned or thrived anew. For the most part, however, the alterations are in our use of guns, poisons, pavement, construction, landscaping, gardening, irrigation, and undergrounding of streams. The gradual warming of California's climate is the broad background to habitat changes wrought by urbanization, agri-business, and widespread irrigation. All these activities continue to affect the natural world so that some species are favored over others. Some birds now found in San Francisco would not have been present before the Gold Rush. Others have vanished forever. There are on-going changes in the city, with one species appearing and spreading rapidly while another quietly vanishes.

Bird species whose populations were eliminated or diminished in San Francisco include Warbling Vireos, Yellow Warblers, Pacific-slope Flycatchers that favor streamside forests. Among the birds common in pre–Gold Rush San Francisco but now greatly reduced or gone altogether are American and Least Bittern, California Quail, Scrub-Jay, Spotted Towhee, Bewick's Wren and Wrentit. It's likely that Nuttall's Woodpecker, Acorn Woodpecker, Oak Titmouse, and California Thrasher were living in suitable habitat in San Francisco before the onslaught of agriculture and urbanization. Early accounts of San Francisco mention grizzly and black bear, cougar, elk, deer, jack rabbits, coyote, wolves and skunks. Only the coyote and skunk can be found here today. Introduced tree squirrels and opossum also thrive in the city.

In 1899 Charles Keeler found Pygmy Nuthatches only in mountains, not in the Presidio or Golden Gate Park, where now they can be seen regularly. The raven, said Keeler, was "found generally in places remote from civilization." Roosting by the dozens in Golden Gate Park, ravens are now prominent among beach walkers on Ocean Beach. In daytime, you may find dozens of them patrolling the sand for anything a careless person may have lost or left on the sand. One major reason for the raven's resurgence is that they are not popularly considered vermin today and are not shot on sight as they would have been a few decades ago. Not long ago the raven and most of its corvid cousins were commonly persecuted by people in the United States.

In 1930, the California Academy of Sciences published the *Handbook of Birds of Golden Gate Park*. It was written by Joseph Mailliard (1857–1945), curator emeritus in the Academy's Department of Ornithology (now Department of Ornithology and Mammalogy). His book was a comprehensive list of birds he had seen in the park. Those he listed, and those he excluded, show how much has changed in less than a century.

Mailliard listed no swallow species. Now three species commonly breed in the park: Barn, Violet-green, and Tree. Barn Swallows nest on buildings, while the Tree and Violet-green use trees planted by the gardeners in decades past. Likewise, the Pygmy Nuthatch does not appear in Mailliard's book. It is now at home and abundant in the mature introduced conifers. Common today, the House Finch was also missing from Mailliard's list. Mailliard found the Red-shouldered Hawk to be "very rare"; it is now common, and its piercing calls can be heard in any season. Mailliard noted two Red-shouldered Hawks had been shot in the park by the "park hunter." That's a telling revelation. For many decades, a hunter was employed to kill hawks and corvids in Golden Gate Park.

Golden Gate Park is now more forest than scrub or grassland, so it no longer shelters Kestrel, Horned Lark, and Spotted Towhee as the park did in Mailliard's day. Other birds Mailliard considered common that are now rare or irregular in Golden Gate Park are the Common Yellowthroat, Bewick's Wren, American Pipit in winter (the pipit still winters at Fort Funston), Swainson's Thrush, Yellow Warblers nesting (abundant in fall migration now), Lesser Goldfinch, and Pintails. Perhaps most tragically, California Quail, the California state bird, was then abundant and is no longer. In his 1870 book, J.G. Cooper said of the quail, "In San Francisco they are constantly to be found for sale alive, and many escape from cages, scattering about the city.... [A] few rods from the suburbs, flocks of quails are frequent among the dense undergrowth which covers the sand hills."

As recently as 1971, a bird checklist for the San Francisco Botanical Garden listed quail as a common breeding species. I can remember driving through Golden Gate Park in the 1970s and seeing coveys ramble down the sidewalks, and individual birds standing alert on park benches. Their population is severely diminished today, and their future in San Francisco is tenuous, beset as they are by natural and feral predators, as well as lack of habitat. A few quail linger in the San Francisco Botanical Garden and individuals are occasionally seen elsewhere in the city. As recently as the 1990s they were nesting in the Presidio. Apparently, they are now extirpated there.

When he wrote, J. G. Cooper said the California Thrasher was a common wintering bird in San Francisco. It is no longer seen within the city limits. The thrasher requires the sort of coastal or hillside scrub habitat and streamside thickets that mostly are gone from San Francisco.

Over a century ago, Charles Keeler pointed out other ways, active and passive, that unthinking people who were attracted by birds wreaked damage on them: "[I]n every town within our limits are found the two most persistent and destructive enemies which our bird neighbors know—the small boy with his gun and egg collection, and the woman with her bonnet adorned with a mutilated carcass." That latter observation refers to the widespread shooting of egrets, herons, and other birds in the late nineteenth and early twentieth century. Their feathers were plucked for adorning fashionable women's hats.

Some bird species have been winners as people altered the landscape. By 1870, Cooper already could see the rapid increase in Barn Swallows as settlements spread across the state. The Barn Swallow had originally been confined to nesting in caves and cliff crevices. It quickly adapted to people's wooden bridges, barns, porches, and other structures. The closely related Cliff Swallow underwent similar adaptation in America, though its presence in today's San Francisco is uncertain from year to year. A colonial nester, this bird needs a large, protected area to nest, not simply a small nook which would be fine for a couple Barn Swallows. In 1874, ornithologist Elliott Coues wrote, "In the case of Cliff Swallows, the change is of very recent date, and many records are preserved of the precise time when, in particular localities, the birds deserted cliffs to build under the eaves, or when adopting this habit, they appeared and bred in places where they were before unknown."

The Cliff Swallow will often share overpasses and bridges with the White-throated Swift. The swift can also be found at sports stadia. As late as 1944, Joseph Grinnell could still describe this swift as nesting in "faces of cliffs, bluffs, canyon walls; preference seems shown for those of granite rock, perhaps because this assures best claw-holds and firmest attachment for nests." Humans have erected huge artificial cliff faces and canyons in cities and along freeways that attract these birds. The largest concentration of White-throated Swifts I've seen was at a tangle of freeway overpasses along Interstate 5 near Stockton. These swifts can be seen near some tall buildings, city parks, and freeway interchanges along US 101. No granite is required today. During migration their cousin, the Vaux's Swift, gathers in thousands in large chimneys such as those found in the old San Rafael brickyard.

The native Black Phoebe also makes use of buildings and bridges, especially those with rain-shielding overhangs under which it may nest. The widely dispersed Rock Pigeon, which originally nested in cliffs in the Middle East, is successful at exploiting human structures. Long before there were bird watchers, this species likely moved into the first towns built by people. It is now uncommon to see Rock Pigeons nesting on cliffs, though they have returned to their "natural" habitat in Garden of the Gods in Colorado and in similar places. Most Rock Pigeons now prefer a nice four-story building with an overhanging roof, especially if a park or parking lot is nearby.

In the nineteenth century, the House Finch was commonly found around homes and ranches. They were so abundant around Californio ranches, that early Yankee immigrants called them "adobe finches." House Finches were often kept inside as caged pets. Yet in the late nineteenth century Spencer Fullerton Baird said, "California cultivators wage an unrelenting war upon this bird." The finch killing would primarily have been done by grain farmers, as wheat was a major product of California in the late nineteenth century.

Other birds favored for cages in those days were Black-headed Grosbeaks, mockingbirds, and Lazuli Buntings. It was Joseph Mailliard himself who spotted the first wild Northern Mockingbird recorded in San Francisco. That was in 1932. Now mockingbirds are common in most neighborhoods of the city and its suburbs.

Cooper noted the Hermit Thrush was breeding "among the stunted oaks covering the sand-hills of San Francisco." That species is now only a winter resident, migrating down from montane forests. And the Savannah Sparrow was once a common wintering bird in San Francisco before nearly all the dune grassland was covered over.

In the nineteenth century, Elliott Coues noted Burrowing Owls living in San Francisco, and indeed, the Smithsonian owns a specimen collected in the city. At that time, the owls were among the most widespread and commonly seen birds across lowland California. In the 1920s, William Leon Dawson found them ubiquitous in grasslands. Today the Burrowing Owl is scarce in urbanized and heavily cultivated parts of California, a victim of habitat loss and pesticides.

Other population shifts among birds seen in San Francisco have been well documented. The American Robin was a montane species in the 1860s. J. G. Cooper said it bred in the Sierra above three thousand feet and in the Santa Cruz Mountains. In 1874, Baird said the robin was largely a winter visitor along the coast of California and only occasionally bred in coastal mountains. As irrigated parks and lawns replaced sand dunes, San Francisco became robin-friendly, even in summer. By 1916, robins were breeding in San Francisco. As recently as 1954, a book on birds of the campus of Stanford University, to the south, said, "Here they are a winter bird and leave in the spring to nest in the mountains." Now, robins nest widely across the Bay Area wherever trees border lawns with earthworms. Recently the robin was the most abundant bird in a national bird count during winter. This species is one of the few that seems fit to survive changes that may come with global warming.

Cooper never saw a Hooded Oriole north of Los Angeles. In his day (ca. 1870) Cooper wrote, "the Hooded Oriole is essentially a Mexican species, though it also extends northward into Texas and the Rio Grande, and into southern California and Arizona." In 1874, Spencer Fullerton Baird also described the Hooded Oriole as a Mexican bird. Charles Keeler's 1899 book on California birds describes the Hooded Oriole as common south of Los Angeles. It was not known to nest north of there. Hooded Orioles now breed in San Francisco and at least a hundred miles northward because the species has followed the horticultural spread of fan palms. These trees provide suitable—perhaps preferred—nesting material for the oriole's finely woven hanging nests. By 1941, the Hooded Oriole was seen in Santa Cruz County, and it had reached San Francisco by 1966. Now the oriole regularly nests in Central and Northern California. That's a range extension northward of more than four hundred miles. Occasional sightings now are being reported in Oregon.

Cowbird Invasion. One pernicious newcomer to the Bay Area avifauna is the Brown-headed Cowbird. Cowbirds are successful nest parasites. A female cowbird can lay dozens of eggs in a single summer, each in a nest built by another species. When the cowbird egg hatches, the chick pushes out the smaller nestlings of the host species and thrives with its co-opted parents. American Robins evolved alongside cowbirds, so robins can and do recognize and destroy cowbird eggs. Most western bird species do not have that ability, and are easily duped. The cowbird's fledged offspring need forest patches and heavily grazed fields to feed in. Once followers of the large bison herds on the Great Plains, cowbirds quickly recognized the new source of plenty that arrived with settlers. The pioneers' livestock left uneaten grain and the inevitable manure. That in turn attracted insects that fed the cowbirds. Elliott Coues described some cowbird flocks in the 1870s: "Every wagon-train passing over the prairies in summer is attended by flocks of the birds; every camp and stock-corral, permanent or temporary, is besieged by the busy birds, eager to glean subsistence from the wasted forage." So, although originally confined to areas east of the Rockies, the cowbird has now overrun much of the North American continent.

One cowbird was spotted east of Los Angeles in 1889. Then in 1895, Charles Bendire, a military man who took advantage of his various postings to bird intensively, reported seeing a few cowbirds in the Great Basin.

By 1907, one was seen in Bakersfield; more were seen then in Fresno and Fremont in 1911 and 1912. In 1926, two eggs were found in a Common Yellowthroat's nest at Lake Merced in San Francisco. By 1931 the cowbird had spread to Sacramento, and by 1934, to Berkeley, Oakland, and Yosemite National Park. By 1941, it had reached Eureka, and Tahoe by 1957. In 1969 Laurence Binford saw a Wrentit feeding a juvenile cowbird at Lake Merced. I once had to watch two Common Yellowthroats feeding "their" baby cowbird at Lake Merced. The cowbird fledgling was about three times the size of each parent. Wrentits are long gone and yellow-throats are scarce in San Francisco, but cowbirds have flourished all along the Pacific Slope.

Cowbirds now parasitize over a hundred species across America. In San Francisco, some species, such as Yellow Warbler and Hutton's Vireo, have declined, at least in part because of the Brown-headed Cowbird. Recent research shows cowbirds often destroy victim species' nests to force repeated nesting. This increases the cowbird's chance to lay an egg in a new nest. Strong fliers, mature Brown-headed Cowbirds don't need to stay near fields or forests. Though they are land birds, they are one of the most common songbirds seen on Pacific pelagic trips, often flying many miles from shore. It is no surprise that they were able to extend their range to every part of the United States where people have removed native plants to create grasslands, then cut through forests or chaparral to build roads, farms, and irrigation ditches. All these changes please foraging and egg-laying cowbirds.

A number of other birds have immigrated to the San Francisco Bay Area over the past two hundred years. The House Sparrow, mentioned earlier, was introduced in the 1870s. Nobody knows how long the Rock Pigeon has been in San Francisco, as it most likely came as a shipboard stowaway or was brought along for food during the Gold Rush. The European Starling spread into California from the eastern United States where it had been introduced in the nineteenth century. Sightings were rare in the Bay Area until the 1950s, but starlings these days can be seen in throngs of hundreds or more. Fairly recent newcomers are the feral parrots that flourish in noisy flocks in San Francisco. Their arrival dates from the 1980s, and today they are widespread in the city. They seem to feel right at home in the non-native eucalyptus trees. So a Latin American parrot and an Australian tree now form a new ecological niche in urban San Francisco.

The Canada Goose is now ensconced in Golden Gate Park. This is a species that was not resident in the Bay Area in the nineteenth century. As late as 1927, Ralph Hoffmann in *Birds of the Pacific States* described the bird as breeding in northeastern California from Lake Tahoe northward. At that time some wintered in the Central Valley. In early Christmas Counts, the Canada Goose was only occasionally seen. In 1959, the species began appearing every year on the San Francisco Christmas Bird Count, a handful each time. Then the count was discontinued for two decades after 1962. Annual Christmas Bird Counts in San Francisco resumed in 1983, with Canada Geese found each time in numbers now into the hundreds. The resident Canada Goose population is thriving in many Bay Area suburban parks and golf courses.

More recent arrivals are Eurasian Collared-Doves. Originally native to the Indian subcontinent, the collared-dove is now found across most of the Middle East and Europe as well as North America. Collared-doves were released in the Bahamas in the 1970s. From there they spread west. First confirmed in Florida in 1986, the doves moved on across the North American continent. A local birder showed me some near New Orleans around 2000. They had just arrived there, and they continued to expand their range to the north and west. It is likely they first bred in San Francisco in 2005. That's an expansion from Florida to California in less than thirty years with no deliberate aid from people. The newest permanent breeding species to arrive in San Francisco is the Great-tailed Grackle, which followed the same route as the Hooded Oriole, Northern Mockingbird, and many previously self-introduced species. The grackle began in the southeastern California desert, spread west, and moved quickly up the coast. This large icterid is already established in southern Oregon, several hundred miles from its historic breeding range.

Corvids Killed. One group of birds has seen its fortunes alter significantly in the past century: the local corvids including the Common Raven,

American Crow, California Scrub-Jay, and Steller's Jay. In the mid-nine-teenth century, crows were noted everywhere. One account in 1859 said crows were abundant along the road from San Francisco to San Mateo. But that was not to last as the corvids gained a reputation of being bad for farmers and other birds. By 1900 they were treated as varmints. In her handbook published in 1902, Florence Bailey had this to say about ravens: "Suspicious, wary pirates they are, always on the defensive to evade attack, keeping well out of rifle range of man." She describes those ancestral ravens as living in remote canyon areas. Now their progeny populate city parks and beaches all around San Francisco Bay. Her entry on crows takes pains to explain that crows may eat some corn or baby chicks, but they also eat far more grubs and other harmful insects than they were credited with.

In early San Francisco Christmas Bird Counts (1916 to1919) corvid spe-cies were almost entirely absent. One crow was reported for those years. It was reported during the count week but not on the day of the count itself. This shows how unusual a crow was considered at that time. Nobody would have taken notice of a "count week" Western Gull or Junco. That single corvid shows how the birds had been persecuted by man, shot on sight as vermin. In his 1923 handbook on Pacific birds, Willard Eliot does not even list the raven, but writes regarding the crow: "Although on the blacklist [shoot on sight] in many states because of the damage it does to crops, a recent announcement from the Agricultural Department would indicate it does not do the amount of harm imputed to it."

In 1927, Joseph Grinnell found no crows nesting in San Francisco. As late as 1944, Grinnell and his associates found no ravens anywhere near California cities and suburbs. Jays were also scarce in those days. In wasn't until the 1970s that the corvids could re-establish themselves without being shot. In the late 1990s, I helped with a raven census in San Francisco. We found over forty nesting pairs plus dozens of unmated youngsters who roosted primarily in Golden Gate Park. The crows now tend to be mostly on the bay-side of town while the ravens dominate near the open ocean and along Ocean Beach. Scrub-Jays are widespread wher-ever there is brush hide in. Steller's Jays moved into the area in the 1990s.

They are still limited to artificial habitat with dense conifer stands, for example, in the Presidio and Golden Gate Park.

How many ways can we kill birds? Light pollution at night and high-rises at all times are dangerous for migrants. So are transmission towers and electrical lines. Our trash and carelessly strewn waste can kill. I've seen a kingbird hung in fishing line, Osprey caught by the leg in plastic string, diving birds with plastic around their necks, a pelican with a fish hook sticking through its beak. We people can't seem to stop setting traps for other species. Even windows in private homes can be deadly to birds using our garden feeders or simply passing by. Then there are fishing trawlers that attract and drown seabirds. There's toxic lead shot in carcasses, lakes, and streams. Oil spills kill shellfish, seabirds, and mammals. Roadkill can do in little finches and large Red-tailed Hawks and species in between. An exhaustive list of things we do, whether or not by design, that maim and kill wildlife would fill several volumes.

People modify our environment to improve life for ourselves—it's what we do—but what helps us may have unintended consequences for entire ecosystems. Predators at the top of nature's food chains are most vulnerable: whales, grizzlies, lions, wolverines, eagles. They get the most concentrated doses when a chemical accumulates in vital organs. Pesticides often drastically affect bird populations. One small bird or rodent may have a modest amount of a toxic chemical in its flesh, but if a predator eats several every week and the chemical attaches to its organs or fat cells, the poison eventually accumulates to a critical level. The result may be direct—death by poisoning—or it may be more complicated and more devastating to the species, as in the case of DDT.

DDT Scourge. The native Peregrine Falcon thrived in San Francisco until modern pesticides gained widespread use. Among larger predatory birds the DDT did not kill the adult birds outright, but made their egg-shells too thin for parent birds to sit on them without breaking them open. The birth rate for eagles, Ospreys, Peregrines, and Brown Pelicans fell to near zero. DDT does not break down quickly in nature, so its presence lingered as did its deleterious effects. DDT is water soluble so it was spread through run-off into lakes, reservoirs, streams, estuaries, and thence and into bays and oceans.

In the 1960s, Rachel Carson's bestseller, *Silent Spring*, incited action against DDT, and it was banned in 1972 over strong opposition from its manufacturers. Canada banned it as well, and Mexico ended DDT use in 2000. It is no longer made or legally used in Mexico and North America. DDT is still widely used in some tropical countries for malaria control.

One effect of the end of widespread DDT use in North America was that the Peregrine's population rebounded; it has returned to San Francisco and many other cities, often nesting on high-rises or bridges. The Brown Pelican was reprieved as well. Now the species is plentiful in the Bay Area, after its breeding season in the south. Every winter and early spring some nonbreeding pelicans can be found around San Francisco's shoreline. After breeding further south the majority of the pelican population moves back north for the better fishing in the colder waters of the northern Pacific.

The Osprey population was severely reduced by the effects of DDT and bounced back after the pesticide was banned. In the early days, Osprey would have been a very common sight over San Francisco, along the bay and ocean and over the larger lakes. In 1874, Coues could say that some California island colonies contained three hundred or more Osprey nests. Post-DDT, the Osprey population began to recover in the late twentieth century. By the 1980s Ospreys were once again seen daily over Lake Merced. Now we have contemporary records of the species once again breeding in San Francisco.

The beaches and rock cliffs along San Francisco's north and western edges are heavily used by both resident and migratory birds. Among the usual breeding species are Western Gull, Black Oystercatcher, Red-tailed Hawk (also found in forested parks), Brandt's Cormorant, and Pigeon Guillemot. Birders are used to seeing Red-tails hunt over fields and in open country. These birds will adapt to a windy, coastal habitat. I once saw a Red-tail swoop down behind a Western Gull perched on the Cliff House above the ocean and carry that gull off with two ravens in greedy pursuit. When the strong wind comes in off the Pacific, gulls often line up on top of the Cliff House, all facing west into the wind. The Red-tail had only to approach from behind, unnoticed. A pair of Red-tails annually breeds at Sutro Heights Park. Ravens often nest there as well. Red-shouldered Hawks often come to hunt at Ocean Beach along the grass-covered dunes above the tide line. Some days there may be two hundred ravens scattered along Ocean Beach. Gull and tern flocks sometimes number twice that in one gathering. Sanderlings, Willets, Marbled Godwits and Snowy Plover regularly winter along Ocean Beach. The Snowy Plover is a threatened species along the Pacific coast. Other birds to be seen on Ocean Beach include Heermann's Gulls and Elegant Terns. Both migrate north in summer from their southerly breeding grounds. In summer, Elegant and Caspian Terns fish up and down the shoreline. Unlike gulls, the terns are almost looking down at the water as they fly by. Gulls usually look straight ahead. In fall, a lucky observer can sometimes watch a marauding Parasitic Jaeger chasing gulls or terns out over the ocean. Other wintering species include Glaucous-winged, Thayer's (no longer a recognized separate species), California, Ring-billed, and Herring Gulls. Bonaparte's Gulls pass on migration as do Western and Least Sandpipers, Whimbrel, Long-billed Curlew, and some plovers. The "rockpipers" are found at Lands End—Black Turnstone and Surfbirds. Wandering Tattlers use that area on passage but winter further south. Near the ocean the omnipresent Western Gull is often the only species as abundant as the raven or Brewer's Blackbird.

Offshore in winter you can expect to see Surf Scoters and Western Grebes in rafts. There are also usually Red-throated Loons and Pacific Loons that particularly like the waters below the Fort Funston overlook platform. Murres and other alcids can sometimes be seen in any season. They may join a feeding frenzy with gulls, cormorants, pelicans, and others when a school of fish is found near the surface. During the winter in the Southern Hemisphere—our summer and fall—there may be a half million or so Sooty Shearwaters far offshore, swirling over the waves like large insects. They breed half a world away and have one of the longest annual migratory paths of any animal on earth. When they are off the California coast they depend on upwelling to provide their prey. They nest near New

Zealand, then spend off-season near San Francisco. Inside the Golden Gate there is often a wintering raft of grebes—Western and Clark's. Some winters they are joined by a Red-necked Grebe, a species that normally winters further north. Common Loon, Common Murre and cormorants may cruise offshore along Crissy Field. I have found Black Turnstone on the rocks as far east as the St. Francis Yacht Harbor. Inside the Bay I have seen Black Oystercatcher on the rocks as far south as Hunters Point. One time I was lunching at Pier 23 and a Parasitic Jaeger sped past chasing a gull. Caspian Terns are regularly summer visitors south of the Bay Bridge. There's a large colony of Double-crested Cormorant nesting on the bridge. They use specially-built accommodations.

San Francisco also has a Double-crested Cormorant colony at the northwest corner of Lake Merced. The Lake Merced cattails shelter numerous nesting Marsh Wrens, a species not now found in other parts of San Francisco. The only Bank Swallow colony is at the south end of Ocean Beach in the cliff face at Fort Funston.

Some "Big Year" contests among San Francisco's avid birders have shown that over 250 species live in or pass through San Francisco every year. The annual Christmas Bird Count regularly tops 160 species, though it includes Mt. San Bruno. Despite all that people have changed and all we have paved and covered with buildings, birds still find useful habitats spread across the city.

CHAPTER 12

Mammals: Survivors and Ghosts

A Russian traveler up the coast north of San Francisco wrote in 1824 of seeing elk 'as large as a horse, with branching antlers; these generally graze on hills, from whence they can see round them on all sides and appear much more cautious than the small ones [deer]' ...though most have not been hunted in generations they retain their alertness to any sound or smell.

—REBECCA SOLNIT AND MONA CARON, *A CALIFORNIA BESTIARY*

The grizzly is the boxer. A game old beast he is, too, and would knock down all the John L. Sullivans you could put in the Sierras faster than you could set them up. He is a kingly old fellow and disdains familiarity.

—JOAQUIN MILLER, *TRUE BEAR STORIES*, 1900

MOST LARGE LAND MAMMALS ARE gone from San Francisco, perhaps forever. No more wolf, tule elk, mountain lion, mule deer, bobcat, bear or badger. Mammals remaining in the city are coyotes, California ground squirrels and Botta's pocket gophers, tree squirrels, several bat species, skunks, and raccoons. Some of these animals were driven out but have returned. The opossums sometimes seen in residential neighborhoods were introduced from the eastern United States.

Coyotes can now be found in many American cities from Manhattan to Los Angeles.

The coyote returned to San Francisco around the start of this century, but its presence may be tenuous because of conflicts with urban humans. Its reputation does not encourage people's tolerance of this smart predator. The issue of coexistence with coyotes grew heated in 2007, when a woman said coyote attacked her off-leash dogs in Golden Gate Park. In 2013 one photographer got pictures of baby coyotes cavorting in the park. See Robin Wilkey listing in Bibliography. Some fans of these wild hunters are working to educate residents about how to get along with them. In late July, 2017, I saw this warning on the Park Service's Presidio website: "DANGER. Temporary Closure of the Park Trail and Section of the Bay Area Ridge Trail to Dogs. Effective immediately, the Park Trail between West Pacific and Crissy Field and the Bay Area Ridge Trail between Arguello and Rob Hill Campground will be closed temporarily to all dogs (on or off leash) due to reports of aggressive coyote behavior."

What measures will the Presidio rangers take? Is there a doomed coyote in the Presidio?

Not mentioned in historic accounts, the quick and secretive long-tailed weasel persists. Dependable naturalists have reported sightings of this sausage-shaped predator from the area around Lake Merced and the nearby San Francisco Zoo. This weasel which prefers more open habitat would have thrived in the pre-colonial San Francisco. Its short-tailed cousin is most often a denizen of dense conifer forests in the west.

Perhaps the most ubiquitous introduced predator in California is the red fox. The California Fish and Game website reports that the one subspecies native to California is the Sierra Nevada red fox. Its range is limited to the conifer forests and rugged alpine landscape, above 5,000 feet in the southern Cascade Range, and above 7,000 feet in the Sierra Nevada. The Sierra Nevada red fox is so uncommon that the California Fish and Game Commission declared it threatened in 1980.

Exotic red foxes of different sub-species are found elsewhere in California but are introduced, not native. Fish and Wildlife explains:

> The earliest known red fox introduction occurred in southern Sacramento Valley lowlands during the 1870s.... Early settlers imported and released eastern red foxes for fox hunting and fur trapping. These highly adaptable carnivores fit into an environment unprepared for their predatory skills and diverse appetites— and the first non-native red fox populations became established in California's lowlands.
>
> After World War I, red foxes were also imported for fur farming and by the 1940s, California had 125 fox farms. Some foxes escaped and others were released.... By the 1970s, non-native red fox populations were firmly established in the Sacramento Valley, expanding into the San Joaquin Valley, and appearing in other isolated regions of the state... Non-native red foxes were not observed at Monterey and San Francisco bay marshes until the 1980s but they have become well-established.

The introduced red foxes are trouble for many smaller animals, especially ground-nesting birds and reptiles. The little canid has no trouble getting his feet wet to raid nests of rails and other marsh nesters. They are a major threat to the scarce Clapper Rails in salt marshes.

There are four species of tree squirrels in California, two native and two from the eastern American woodlands. A University of California "pest control" website delineates the four species:

> Eastern fox squirrels (*Sciurus niger*) were introduced...and are well established in most major cities of California. Some people enjoy seeing them and introduced them into new territories. In some cities eastern fox squirrels have moved outward into agricultural land...where they have become a pest of commercial crops. Eastern gray squirrels (*S. carolinensis*) were originally introduced from the eastern United States into Golden Gate Park in San Francisco.

Native western gray squirrels (*Sciurus griseus*) are found throughout much of California, primarily in oak woodlands of the foothills and valleys and in pine/oak forests, where they feed on a variety of seeds, fungi, and other plant materials. They also have a tendency to strip bark in order to access and feed on the cambium layer, causing injury to trees. Native Douglas's squirrels (*Tamiasciurus douglasii*), sometimes called chickarees, are found in mostly conifer-forested regions of the north coastal area and along the Sierra Nevada.

Of the four tree squirrels, the eastern fox squirrel, sometimes called the red fox squirrel, is by far the most serious pest to homes and gardens in urban and suburban situations.

Along with tree squirrels, the raccoon has proven to be adept at urban living. In residential neighborhoods entire families can be seen trundling along the sidewalks after dark, checking every porch or garage or back garden for edibles. When we lived near Sutro Heights we had to finally close up our cat door because the raccoons used it as much as the cat, and then a skunk came inside as well. Just as well, we should all keep our housecats, a subsidized predator, inside where they cannot savage the birds.

Among the most successful mammals introduced in the San Francisco area are the Norwegian (or brown) rat and the common black rat, both of which thrive in human-made habitats, from houses to barns, to dumpsters. They have stowed away on ships for centuries, spreading themselves (and their own parasites) to most parts of the planet. Gold Rush era accounts of San Francisco often mention both rats and fleas (plenty of the latter, at least, were native).

Today the rats often live alongside their dainty cousin, the house mouse. Not just a household pest the house mouse is global, often kept as a pet and provides populations that are exploited in medical and biological labs around the world. Here is an animal that often unwillingly suffers and dies for the people around it. It is believed the species originated in northern India. It was found along the Mediterranean by 13,000 B.C. From there it went to sea and now is found on most coasts outside the polar regions and tropical Africa.

Recent estimates show that San Francisco is not sharing the rat population surge that is hitting eastern cities. This boom is apparently due to warmer winters. Yet the city's rat population is not disappearing either. The one native predator I have seen eating rats in San Francisco is the Red-shouldered Hawk.

Sea Mammals. Once abundant, the sea otter has been saved from extinction but is still not to be found regularly around San Francisco.. The North Pacific Fur Seal Treaty of 1911 was an international agreement to protect the sea otter and fur seal from hunters. In 1915, a small colony of 32 otters was discovered living off the mouth of Bixby Creek near Point Sur. Their survival was kept a secret until 1938. Though granted further protections in 1970, sea otters are still the unintended victims of fishing nets, and remain rare north of Santa Cruz and over much of their former range south of Santa Barbara. The sea otter is not regular around the Farallones and still rarely seen in San Francisco's nearshore waters. The species has been reintroduced to Washington State where it is on the endangered list. There is no known breeding population of sea otters north of the Golden Gate in California or along the Oregon Coast. In the early twenty-first century, diseases linked to pollution have plagued the sea otter population. The sea otter struggles against hazards like a "nasty toxin" called microcystin, produced by cyanobacteria. Cyanobacteria can form mats and have long been popularly known as "blue-green algae." This bacteria thrives on the nutrients in fertilizers and human sewage. That waste spurs super-blooms as the cyanobacteria uses photosynthesis to produce its own energy. These bacteria are capable of nitrogen-fixing as well as creating its neurotoxin. Even if a bloom is born in a farm pond, it ends up in the coastal seawater. No farmer dumping excessive fertilizer on his farm intends to kill sea otters, but he often does unintentionally and indirectly by encouraging cyanobacteria. It's doubtful the current population of sea otter in California today is any larger than it was when Beechey was worried about it being so small in the 1820s. The total population along the California coast is now fluctuating between 2,400 and 3,000.

Harbor seals can be seen both in the bay and along Ocean Beach. They will sometimes follow a person with a dog, apparently curious about the four-footed predator that walks on land.

Harbor seals eat small fish, mollusks and crustaceans including shrimp and crab. California sea lions eat dozens of fish species as well as mollusks including octopus and squid. Both are predators that depend on clean waters capable of sustaining populations of a variety of prey species. Both are in turn eaten by orcas, one of the Pacific's alpha predators.

Most widely known of San Francisco's wild mammals are the California sea lion, many of whom now laze away their resting hours on piers at Pier 39. They have largely abandoned Seal Rocks and other natural resting spots to become a tourist attraction and perhaps profit from free hand-outs. The first sea lions moved to Pier 39 in 1990 and were greeted as a nuisance to boat owners. Now they are one of the most viewed attractions in a city that continually draws tourists from around the world. The Pier 39 sea lions now have docents to explain their lives to shore-hugging bipeds and even their own dedicated webcam. The peak population at Pier 39 topped 1700 in 2009 and continues to fluctuate depending on season, food supply and weather. The sea lions' loud barking can be a magnet for visitors from land-locked locales.

Dolphins and porpoises, gray whales on migration and humpbacks can all be seen from shore occasionally. Usually they are seen outside the Golden Gate. Over time it is not unreasonable to imagine elephant seals and northern fur seals also reappearing closer to the city than the Farallones where they have re-established themselves with government protection. If elephant seals do return to Ocean Beach they will need to be fenced off from curious people and their dogs.

If an explorer from the 1820s could come back to see San Francisco today there are vast changes that would amaze or appall. Certainly after the noise and crowds were looked over, this time traveler would note the lack of quail, rabbits and ground squirrels. These would have been abundant before the Gold Rush. So would deer though they would have stayed away from any Ohlone or Mexican settlement to avoid the dogs and hunters. He might be curious to know where are the bears, the rattlesnakes, the dreaded yedra?

CHAPTER 13

San Francisco's Islands: Fragile and Despoiled

Drawing near the island we found ourselves in a new and strange wonderland. There was but a bare, jagged ridge of rock, cut out in places into great cones and pyramids. Yonder was one shaped like a titanic beehive and about it swarmed a vast throng of seabirds in lieu of bees.

—CHARLES KEELER, *A TRIP TO THE FARALLONS*, 1906

That mystical clear day when you can see forever, far beyond the Farallones, out to infinity and beyond. A biting wind down from the Yukon, stretching the sky so tight you can almost see through it. San Francisco with pink cheeks, chapped lips, fog on its breath, eyes straining across the next hill, sharply etched wonders to behold. On a day like this, everything is close enough to touch: Angel Island only a giant leap away, Alcatraz across the street from Buena Vista. The views are so fore-shortened that the city seems one-dimensional, flattened against a wall of space.

—HERB CAEN, *"SAN FRANCISCO CHRONICLE,"* NOVEMBER 25, 1979

SAN FRANCISCO'S MOST DISTANT AND oceanic islands are the Farallones. Until European explorers came to California, the Farallones were the remote preserve of sea mammals, birds, and flying invertebrates. The Native Americans feared the islands and stayed away. It's not clear their small boats could have withstood the thirty-mile trip out from the Golden Gate or the twenty miles down from Point Reyes. In any case, Sir Francis Drake's expedition crew may have been the first men to deliberately set foot on the islands. Before Drake, the 211 acres of the scattered rocky islands were densely populated with seabirds and oceanic mammals. When Drake's boat landed there in 1579, the crewmen hunted sea lions for meat and collected seabird eggs. That pattern of exploitation would last for four hundred years. Eventually extensive hunting, commercial egg gathering (egging) and the introduction of invasive species would depopulate the island of most native animals.

Until 1810, sailing ships occasionally visited the Farallones to take seals or sea lions for meat, or to gather eggs. That minor predation was supplanted in 1810 when the sealing ship *O'Kain* arrived on the scene from New England, along with four other sealing boats. They landed men on the islands, and over the next twenty-two months they slaughtered an estimated 150,000 fur seals. Those pelts were sold in China for $2.50 apiece. Over the next decades that price increased 20-fold. Supply, it seems, increased demand. One estimate of historic American income levels in the original thirteen states in 1800 is $68 per capita, so 27 fur seal pelts had almost the same value as an average person's income. Soon after the *O'Kain* sailed off with its fur cargo, Russian fur hunters arrived.

Groups of seal hunters from the Russian-American Company lived seasonally on the islands for more than two decades. Hunters ate any animal available to kill, but their main target was the northern fur seal, whose pelt was valuable in China. At the same time, seabird eggs and meat were collected and shipped north to the Russian post at Fort Ross. In 1828, 50,000 seabirds were killed on the Farallones for food. The Russians left in 1841, a few years before the most profitable exploitation of the islands' wildlife.

The first lighthouse opened in 1852, compounding the environmental damage to the Farallones. The lighthouse brought permanent residents and their trash. They arrived with their pets, their goats, and the inevitable stowaway mice. Worst of all, voracious Australian hares were freed on the 120-acre Southeast Island. Habitat and wildlife populations disintegrated further. Fur seals, Steller's sea lions, and elephant seals were extirpated. California sea lions and harbor seals declined to low numbers by the end of the nineteenth century. Seabird populations were destroyed or reduced to remnants. Even the nesting ravens on Southeast Farallon were shot. Still plaguing the southeast island are house mice, in the thousands.

The latest effort to return the Farallones to a more natural preserve is an attempt to remove all the house mice. The density on Southeast Farallon Island can reach 500 mice per acre during population peaks. These rodents not only damage the plants on the island, but will feed on seabird chicks. They are a rich food source for visiting Burrowing Owls. Without plentiful mice, it is doubtful the owls would overwinter on the barren islands, where there are no other rodents and few large insects. Worse yet, after the owls have decimated the mouse population, they feed on the young Ashy Storm-Petrels. There are only seventeen islands in the eastern Pacific where this scarce seabird is known to nest. These islands are all off Mexico and California and bathed by the California Current in the nearshore Pacific. Data indicate that half of all the planet's Ashy Storm-Petrel nest sites in a normal year are on the Farallones.

The mouse–owl–storm-petrel complex is a clear example of how we humans can upset a natural system with one small move whether deliberate or unintentional. It is doubtful that anybody really intended to bring house mice to the islands. At least nobody turned housecats or mongooses loose to eat the mice as happened in Hawaii where both predators are now a scourge.

A Mania for Eggs. The Gold Rush created a rich market for fresh eggs. California at that time had no poultry industry, so commercial egging operations targeted the Farallon Islands. In 1854, over half a million seabird eggs were gathered for sale to San Francisco restaurants and stores. Only the Western Gull eggs were avoided, as their thin shells would not survive the rough return voyage. Some eggers also avoided the Tufted Puffins because of their ferocious bite. Eggers gathered from easier targets, including the Common Murre, all cormorant species, and other birds whose nests are open and accessible.

In 1880, the eggers and the lighthouse keepers had a violent confrontation because the eggers thought a new foghorn would scare off the nesting birds. The U.S. Army evicted the resident eggers, but daytime egging forays continued. In 1896 only 100,000 eggs could be found for sale on the mainland; that was the end of commercial egging on the islands, but Farallon residents continued to gather seabird eggs until 1905.

On June 5, 1886, Harry Taylor of Alameda went to the Farallon Islands aboard the steamship *Madrono* carrying supplies to the lighthouse keepers out there. He wrote about how pleased he was with the large number of seabirds he saw at the height of the breeding season on the islands:

> I was filled with astonishment at the vast number of guillemots [mostly Common Murre], gulls, puffins and other birds, which being disturbed from their positions on the rocks by approach, flew into the air in massive flocks, and created a perfect din by their startled cries...I was told by the light-keeper that three of four species of hawks visit these islands every year to feed on the guillemots. I was shown an old raven's nest built of sticks in an inaccessible place where young had been raised the year before.

In his book copyrighted 1899, Charles Keeler gives us a catalog of pelagic birds at the turn of the twentieth century. He describes a walk on Ocean Beach after a violent winter storm, where he counted corpses: an albatross (likely Black-footed), Pacific Loon, Northern Fulmar, Brandt's Cormorant, Western Grebe, White-winged, Black and Surf Scoters, Rhinoceros Auklet.

Keeler visited the Farallones one July in the 1890s. At that time, Greek fishermen ran egging operations on the islands. They concentrated on murre eggs. These eggs had shells hard enough to could survive the jolting they got from the slamming of waves and the ship's rolling before the wind, on the journey to San Francisco for sale. Keeler saw eggers carelessly scare off the nesting adult Brandt's Cormorants, leaving the eggs open to predation by the ever-vigilant Western Gulls also nesting on the islands.

Other nesting birds he noted on the island were Cassin's Auklet, Tufted Puffin, Pigeon Guillemot, and Ashy Storm-Petrel.

Tenuous Shelter for Many Creatures. We now know that hoary bats and arboreal salamanders also live on the islands. Many migratory animals use the islands as they head south or north: various birds, dragonflies, bats, and even butterflies. All resident birds and predatory mammals suffer during El Niño years when upwelling diminishes and fewer fish can be found near the surface. Die-offs occur among alcids, cormorants, pelicans, sea lions, and larger fish. Also, warmer ocean waters can foster larger than normal poisonous cyaobacteria blooms. How much worse this will be made by climate change we do not yet know.

The Farallones have long offered diverse and plentiful fishing grounds. The sea life on the shelves and in the depths around the islands is rich. Dozens of species, from great white sharks to rockfish, thrive in the waters. Fishermen's favorites—rock and ling cod—are found around the Farallones. In El Niño years, some tropical fish like mahi mahi and albacore may show up around the islands.

Increasing Efforts to Protect and Preserve. By 1917, the spread of automobiles and other gas-powered vehicles increased the oceanic transport of petroleum. Spills, accidental and deliberate, produced an endless oil slick around the islands. Tankers emptied their ballast tanks before entering San Francisco Bay. Waste oil covered the Farallon shores, killing seabirds and mammals. Concerned lighthouse officials contacted the newly fledged Audubon Society, which went to work.

The co-founder of the Bay Area's first Audubon Chapter was wealthy coffee importer, Carlos B. Lastreto, a San Francisco native. In 1919, he and Dr. Barton Evermann, a prominent ichthyologist, formed a committee to stop the oil dumping. At this time, Evermann was Director of the California Academy of Sciences. The two men met with various oil company officials and won voluntary agreements to have waste oil pumped into tanks on shore and recycled. They also got support from scientific groups along the California coast and the California Fisheries Society. There was no federal agency with a strong will to control pollution at that time. That move to stop the oil dumping was a crucial early step in protecting the precious Farallones and the wildlife there. Government agencies offered little help because their territorial jurisdiction extended only three miles offshore from the mainland. Apparently, no attempt was made to enforce rules within three miles of the islands.

In the mid-twentieth century, nuclear waste and contaminated ships were sunk into the deep waters off the Farallones. Between 1946 and 1970 over forty-seven thousand drums of radioactive waste went into the Pacific Ocean there. In addition, many radioactive ships from the Bikini Atoll atomic tests were towed to the area and sunk. There is no clear answer on what effects this radiation has had or whether the drums are still sealed.

In August 1930, the Golden Gate Audubon Society conducted a field trip to the Farallones. Participants were disappointed: only four Common Murres could be found. They apparently did not know that by time any nesting birds would have gone into the ocean with any of that summer's fledglings. We have no data from this period on how many murres were still nesting there. The only land birds found were Rock Wrens and House Sparrows, though Western Gulls and Brandt's Cormorants were abundant. By 1959, the Common Murre population had dwindled to 6,000 breeding birds, partially due to overfishing and use of nets that caught birds, causing them to drown.

Climate change has worsened the effects of El Niño events on the Farallones, severely curtailing the upwelling of cold water. This makes the sea warmer. Then the near-shore Pacific becomes infused with toxic cyanobacteria which can kill fish and sea mammals. This warmer water also abets numerous infectious diseases that kill ocean life from plankton and starfish to sea otters, sea lions and Common Murres.

Despite recent effects of climate change, there have been positive milestones: Rhinoceros Auklets resumed breeding on the Farallones in 1972, elephant seals in 1973, the last feral rabbit was killed in 1975, the first baby northern fur seal was born there in 1996, and ten years later there were 80 pups. These things would likely not have happened had not the island been protected. Back in 1906 President Theodore Roosevelt had declared North and Middle Farallon a wildlife refuge. Starting in 1967 biologists and conservation workers took up residence in the dilapidated buildings of

Southeast Island. The workers were from the Point Reyes Bird Observatory (now Point Blue) under contract with the U.S. Fish and Wildlife Service. Then in 1969, South Farallon Island was added to the refuge. In 1972 the human-operated lighthouse was replaced by an automated system. Much of the Farallones were designated as wilderness in 1974. Still, the islands cannot be isolated from global changes. The need for care continues.

Marine Sanctuary. In 1981, a major advance in protecting the Farallones and their waters was made when the United States. designated the islands a national marine sanctuary. Here's the description from the sanctuary's website:

Designated in 1981, Gulf of the Farallones National Marine Sanctuary (GFNMS) spans 1,279 square miles (966 square nautical miles) just north and west of San Francisco Bay, and protects open ocean, nearshore tidal flats, rocky intertidal areas, estuarine wetlands, subtidal reefs, and coastal beaches within its boundaries. In addition, GFNMS has administrative jurisdiction over the northern portion of the Monterey Bay National Marine Sanctuary, from the San Mateo/Santa Cruz County line northward to the existing boundary between the two sanctuaries. GFNMS maintains an administrative office and public Visitor Center on Crissy Field in the Presidio of San Francisco.

The Sanctuary prohibits humans from attracting great white sharks, which fish in the waters off San Francisco. The sharks are especially likely to be present in fall, drawn by elephant seal and sea lions gathering to feed or rest on shore. The Sanctuary is taking steps to understand and protect the deep-sea coral and sponge habitat that lie well beneath the Pacific's surface. These are prime feeding and breeding areas for many ocean species. All islands but the southeast one, where researchers live, are now in the Farallons Wilderness Area.

Some years ago, in the spring, I spent an hour on South Farallon. I was there courtesy of a Point Reyes Bird Observatory supply boat. California sea lions and harbor seals were abundant in the water off a small cove, a few lined up on the narrow, rocky beach. High up in the cliff faces I could see the small nesting caves where Tufted Puffin came and went. Each returning bird carried a line of fish in its beak, and would land at what seemed like full flight speed. Each landing puffin would hit the lip of the rock then bounce inside. The steepest slopes of the island were colored black and white with upright Common Murre, their high-pitched whistles mixing with the sound of wind and waves. Some sea stacks held Pelagic and Brandt's Cormorant nests. Somewhere in the cracks of the rocks Pigeon Guillemot had hidden nests. On the island itself, the ground was divided and subdivided by screaming and territorial Western Gulls nesting among the rocks and stubby plants. Occasionally I'd spot burrow openings where Cassin's Auklets and the storm-petrels come and go by night to avoid predators. The bird sounds and density were a fraction of what was here through the long centuries before men intruded. The only signs now of people's presence are two wooden houses, wooden board-walks, an antenna, and a lighthouse, some scraggly trees—but these mea-gre remnants signify two centuries of human residence.

Currently the Farallon Islands have breeding populations of Steller's and California sea lions, Common Murre, Pigeon Guillemot, Western Gull, Cassin's Auklet, Tufted Puffin, Pelagic and Brandt's Cormorant, Leach's Storm-Petrel, and nearly half of the world's Ashy Storm-Petrels, about four thousand pairs. Thanks to governmental protections extended to the islands and their wildlife, four returning species have resumed breeding after an absence of over a century: northern fur seals, northern elephant seals, Rhinoceros Auklets, and Black Oystercatchers. All native wildlife on the islands is now protected. Currently the Farallones are home to the Pacific coast's largest colony of breeding seabirds south of Alaska.

Research over the past four decades by Point Blue has shown that Common Murres are now breeding earlier in the year, in response to cli-mate change and its effects on upwelling in the California current. The small Cassin's Auklet is dependent on krill for food. In some recent years now there has been little or no krill. Without abundant krill, the auk-lets' population crashes and there is little successful breeding. In 2005 and 2006, there was little of the usual nutrient-rich ocean upwelling; that killed off the krill, which in turn meant no Cassin's Auklet chicks fledged on the Farallones. Even the few auklets that laid eggs and hatched chicks could not feed them to maturity. If the failure to reproduce—triggered by climate change—becomes a frequently recurring pattern, it will be disastrous for a seabird whose lifespan may not exceed six years.

Seal Rocks and other offshore rocks along Lands End eastward to China Beach have nesting seabirds on them most summers: Brandt's Cormorant, Western Gull, Pigeon Guillemot (though they also use mainland cliffs), and Black Oystercatcher. All these nesting birds are highly dependent on the usual upwelling of cold, nutrient-rich water that feeds and sustains their prey. In 2007, there were some signs of nesting interest among a group of Common Murre on the largest of the Seal Rocks. If they return regularly to nest it will be the first time since the nineteenth century. California sea lions still use the Seal Rocks for loafing and sleeping, though now they prefer the wooden docks at Pier 39. Again, El Niño in a given year, and perhaps climate change over the long run, can severely affect all animals using the rocks as well as marine life, including fish, in nearby waters.

Islands in the Bay. San Francisco includes islands inside the Golden Gate. Most of these were isolated from the mainland when the sea level rose about nine thousand years ago. Angel Island is almost entirely within Marin County, with only 0.7 percent of the island officially within the boundaries of the City and County of San Francisco. Angel Island is only approachable by private boat, a long swim, or the ferry service from Tiburon in Marin County.

Alcatraz Island was named for the pelicans seen roosting there by early explorers. Here's how it looked in 1849 to Bayard Taylor as his ship sailed in through the Golden Gate: "We are in front of the entrance to San Francisco Bay. The mountains on the northern side are 3,000 feet in height, and come boldly down to the sea. As the view opens through the splendid strait, three or four miles in width, the island rock of Alcatraz appears, gleaming white in the distance." That white was from seabird guano, much contributed by Brown Pelicans.

The pesticide DDT, in wide use after World War II, decimated some bird populations, including Brown Pelican. The pelicans and other vulnerable species nearly died out in California. After DDT was banned in 1972, those populations rebounded, and now those birds are back in large numbers.

When Alcatraz was a federal penitentiary housing dangerous felons like Al Capone, the island was nearly devoid of wildlife. Bored prison guards practiced their marksmanship by shooting any bird that flew past. Alcatraz Prison was decommissioned in 1963. Ten years later, the island, including the crumbling prison ruins, was incorporated into the Golden Gate National Recreation Area. Protection of the island helped bring back breeding birds: Western and California Gulls, Brandt's and Pelagic Cormorants, Pigeon Guillemot, Black-crowned Night-Heron, and Black Oystercatcher, along with Black Phoebe, Anna's Hummingbird, and House Finch.

Yerba Buena Island has been heavily developed and is transected by the Bay Bridge. It is about 150 acres in area. At one time, it was called "Goat Island" for the animals that roamed its slopes. Two American Indian burial sites once found on the island have been destroyed through the building of roads, the bridge anchors, and modern structures. The U.S. military took control of the island in 1867. Twenty years later, tree planting began. Some of the eucalyptus trees planted then are apparently still standing. The fragrant mint, yerba buena, for which the island is named, has apparently been extirpated there. In 2000, botanist Michael Wood published a catalog of plants he found on the island. Some live oak woodland and coastal scrub survived decades of development and military ownership. Among the native plants that Wood found are dune gilia, Dutchman's pipe, yellow bush lupine, common montia, toyon trees, polypody fern, purple needle-grass, sticky monkeyflower, California buckeye, arroyo willow, and giant horsetail. Still he found more species of introduced plants than native.

Adjacent to the natural island is the wholly artificial Treasure Island, constructed in 1936–1937 as the site of a world's fair. It has the expected urban bird population and exotic plants. There is evidence that this former U.S. Navy base still contains toxic waste and radioactive material left behind. Clean up and radiation detection work led by the Navy continued into 2017.

In addition San Francisco has partial claim to Alameda Island. Most of the island is inside Alameda City and Alameda County. Yet the far northwest tip of Alameda Island is officially inside San Francisco. The land there is a marsh and rich in wildlife. Offshore are floats that are used by harbor seals. A breakwater is a popular roost for migrating Brown Pelicans. Golden Gate Audubon Society reports a high count of over eight thousand pelicans one evening. Most years the peak count hits two thousand. In addition the marsh is a nesting ground for a colony of Least Terns, an endangered species in California. Also it is home to a long-established colony of nesting Caspian Terns. Shorebirds found there include migrants like Willet and nesting American Avocets. At the present time there is no public access. That marsh and the rest of the land at Alameda Point were part of the decommissioned Alameda Naval Air Station. Much of that land is now being developed for business and industrial use through the City of Alameda. In addition the Veterans' Administration now controls 400 acres which are planned to house a treatment facility and columbarium. Altogether San Francisco's islands range from artificial and residential to pelagic wilderness. Each of San Francisco's islands will need close attention and intervention as sea level rises, the climate changes, and the inevitable appearance of new invasive species, new diseases, and new forms of pollution.

Golden Gate Park

Dreary sand dunes, blown about by the fog-laden wind fresh from the ocean, and barren hills, that seemed to give no promise of fertility, lay between San Francisco and the sea when in 1870 work was commenced on the Golden Gate Park. The seemingly impossible has been accomplished, and today the park is a great pleasure ground full of beauty and surprise at every turn. Broad avenues wind through the miles of shrubbery and trees, with footpaths branching in all directions. Spirited horses and carriages speed along the way. Crowds of people enjoy the outing on foot while many bicycles flash by.

—CHARLES KEELER, *SAN FRANCISCO AND THEREABOUT, 1902.*

It feels wild. It is shaggy and labyrinthine and confusing. There are places in it so hidden away and hard to find that few people have ever set foot in them. You can get lost in the place. After visiting it frequently for 30 years, I had barely scratched its surface. It wasn't until I began systematically exploring it that I really got to know it. And it took months. The paradox of Golden Gate Park is that its wildness is almost completely manmade.

-—GARY KAMIYA, *COOL GRAY CITY OF LOVE*

No OTHER AREA OF SAN Francisco could be more representative of the vast changes on this peninsula than the city's venerable, beloved, Golden Gate Park. The park itself incorporates some elements that have survived from pre-colonial times but it is largely an artifact. There has been much effort here by generations of people: irrigation, use of exotic plants, changing contours, hauling manure and compost to sand dunes so that there is nutrient-rich soil, road-building, construction of museums, a stadium, windmills, sidewalks, paths and bridges, playing fields and a golf course. This park is unique because it is self-contained and artificial. Few plants found in the park can be found in natural open space preserves beyond the city's boundaries. Golden Gate Park is now a rich and varied environment of plants and animals that could not find space or safety in private gardens or smaller parks. Today there are many dozen introduced tree species in Golden Gate Park. Much of today's park still derives from work begun with the vision and vitality of two men. William Hammond Hall (1846-1934) and then John McLaren (1846-1943) brought Golden Gate Park from the original windy sand dunes to a forested, heavily gardened recreation ground admired by resident and tourist alike. There are many fine, detailed histories of this park so here I hope only to illustrate how the park's development is a concentrated example of broad changes that were taking place simultaneously across San Francisco.

Comprising 1,017 acres, Golden Gate is far from being the largest urban park in the nation, but given the size of the city itself, the park seems grand indeed. San Franciscans clearly love this place. Its charm is in its combination of bucolic natural areas and finely manicured gardens, places to play, places to dream, places to connect and to learn, places to sleep illegally, places for music and other places for quiet. On a foggy August day, you can stop on a woodsy trail and feel the salty drops falling from tree leaves overhead that collect the moisture from the air. Some days of cold or windy weather you can walk a side trail and see nobody. Other days you can join a throng at some event on the Polo Field, the Great Meadow or at Kezar Stadium.

In 1870, when this land was set aside by the city government for a park, it was largely sand dunes. Before it was landscaped and planted, there were a few willow-bordered lakes on the site, some squatters in residence, and scattered oak groves in sheltered areas furthest from the windy beach. The most respected landscape expert at the time was Frederick Law Olmsted, designer of New York's Central Park. He warned San Francisco these lands outside the city limits were not suitable for a proper urban, forested park. Olmsted's conclusion about a park in the city was part cautionary, part damning: "There is not a full grown tree of beautiful proportions near San Francisco, nor have I seen any young trees that promise fairly, except, perhaps, of certain compact clump forms of evergreens, wholly wanting in grace and cheerfulness. It would not be wise nor safe to undertake to form a park upon any plan which assumed as a certainty that trees which would delight the eye can be made to grow near San Francisco."

If Olmsted's warning about the dune lands had been heeded, San Francisco's main urban park would be somewhere in Hayes Valley. It would be far from the Pacific and Ocean Beach, with only a tiny fraction of the beauty and variety found in Golden Gate Park's thousand acres.

When a young engineer, William Hammond Hall, was hired as the first park superintendent, he had little knowledge of plants or landscaping—but he knew where to look: not to the forested East Coast, but to the dune lands of western Europe.

First, Hall laid out the park's design including the panhandle that extends eastward from McLaren Lodge. At one time the panhandle was to extend all the way east to Van Ness Avenue. He laid out the two east-west roads that still snake the length of the park, avoiding square corners and straight lines.

The story of how Hall and his successors brought a forest to the dunes is one of many such taming-of-nature sagas of early San Francisco. He knew well the obstacles before him though he did not yet know how they were to be overcome. On his first detailed report to the park commissioners he explained the situation on the land: "The Golden Gate Park contains about 1,000 acres, of which 270 acres at the eastern end is good arable land covered in many places with trees and shrubbery; this portion may be converted into an attractive resort. The remaining 730 acres, stretching down to the ocean beach, is a waste of drifting sand. Forbidding as it appears at present...[we] will continue the work until the barren sand-hills are converted into verdant fields."

At that time Hall's optimism and determination would have seemed preposterous to an experienced realist such as Olmsted. In 1870, the park's plant nursery was established to support the greening of the dunes. At first, blooming plants were a low priority. Taming the wind and sand was the initial goal. Roses, azaleas, rhododendrons, and other ornamental flora came later. This nursery houses over 800 species of plants, some cultivated nowhere else. Now, with twelve greenhouses, the nursery continues to supply young plants for the city and its parks.

Trees, Then More Trees. Hall began work at the east end of the park and worked westward. Workers hauled in loads of horse manure, collected for free on the city's streets, and dug it in to enrich the sandy soil. Even though native trees were not prized by landscapers at that time, Hall saved native willows and oaks where possible. The oak grove on the ridge at the park's northeastern corner stands where oaks have grown through the ages.

Hall's men began the first tree plantings in 1871–1872. Most of the new trees were exotics, tolerant of sandy soil and salty winds. The trees also had to be drought tolerant to survive rainless summers. Hall favored evergreens, both conifer and broadleaf. Monterey pine and cypress became favorites for their fast growth, up to fourteen feet in height in two years. Eucalyptus might grow to eighteen feet with a four-inch diameter base in two years. Hall's crews created forest stands, interlaced with grassy glades. Hall wisely planted thick groves of trees so they could shelter one another from the sand and desiccating wind. As the trees grew, smaller ones were thinned out.

The future of Golden Gate Park as an urban forest was being set by Hall and his workers. On that very first list are many trees still in the park, or that have been succeeded by more of the same: eucalyptus, acacia (now a half dozen species can be found in the park), Monterey cypress, pines, both sequoia and coastal redwood, pittosporum. By 1875 sixty thousand trees had been planted—mostly eucalyptus, Monterey pine and cypress. Though the climate limited the choices the selected hardy species paid off.

As work crews finally approached the west end of the park they planted the dunes with European beachgrass to curtail sand movement before the inevitable strong winds off the Pacific. Later wind-resistant shrubs and cypress were added. Hall set the pattern for future park planning and planting. Even Olmsted was impressed and became a converted believer in Golden Gate Park. In 1876 he wrote to the San Francisco Park Commission and Hall: "I cannot too strongly suggest my admiration of the spirit and method which characterizes your undertaking, and I do not doubt it will be rewarded with results such as I have not hitherto thought it reasonable to expect under the circumstances. There is no like enterprise anywhere else."

The McLaren Age. Hall did not remain long at Golden Gate Park. He went on to become a key figure in forming California's state water policies that made the eventual agricultural and urban wealth of the state possible through a complex web of water systems. Hall was appointed California's first State Engineer in 1876 but he remained as consultant to Golden Gate Park until 1890. That is the year John McLaren became park superintendent. Upon accepting the job McLaren proclaimed, "There will be no 'keep off the grass' signs." McLaren remained in charge until his death in 1943. He was so revered by city officials that when he reached mandatory retirement age of 70 years, they amended the city charter to let him stay. He worked as park chief until he died, age 96.

McLaren had many strict standards. He would not hire anybody weak enough to wear a jacket for a job interview. He fired any worker caught smoking and he detested statues. When he could not prevent the city from erecting another statue in the park he would have bushes and trees planted around it to obscure its presence. Today the posthumous, smaller-than-life-size statue of McLaren himself is tucked into a tiny nook among his favored rhododendrons across from the Conservatory.

Because of San Francisco's unique standing among western U.S. cities, plants were frequently donated to the park, both by other states in the Union and by other nations. One example is an 1896 commemoration organized by McLaren. He wanted to celebrate the October 19th anniversary of the surrender of General Cornwallis at Yorktown. That happened in 1781, so the San Francisco event marked the 115th Anniversary. It was a great way to get donated plants. Each of the original thirteen states sent a native tree to be planted near the Pioneer Cabin just east of the Stow Lake boathouse. Among the trees that were donated were a white oak from the battlefield at Saratoga, New York; an elm from the Old North Bridge at Concord where the American Revolution began; a tulip tree from Virginia; and a red maple from North Carolina. Called the Arch of Colonial Trees, the grove is maintained to this day, although many of the original trees have been replaced over the decades since they were planted. It has been estimated that workers altogether planted two million trees in Golden Gate Park under McLaren's stern command.

Irrigation. Along with the need to amend the soil, the problem of getting water into the park was a challenge from the first. Sandy soil drains quickly, and in the months of drought, moisture in the form of fog drip is not enough to keep most plants alive. The lakes were too precious and small to be drained for the thirsty plantings. A reservoir was built atop Strawberry Hill. Some water from the lakes was used for irrigation but more water came from Spring Valley Water Company. The city paid for water to be piped in at a cost of forty cents for every thousand gallons. In 1902, work began on the first of two windmills at the west end of the park. It is known as the Dutch (or North) Windmill. Five years later, a banker, Samuel G. Murphy, donated the money to build the second windmill at the southwest corner of the park. It was completed in 1908, and still has the largest sails of any windmill on earth. The windmills drew up well water and pumped it along the surface for irrigation. Their work was short-lived, though. Electric pumps replaced the windmills in 1913, and after years of disuse, they suffered serious deterioration. Through the efforts of citizens of the city, money was raised for monumental restoration efforts. Now, the windmills stand as charming landmarks. The north windmill was restored by 1981, the Murphy Windmill by 2012.

Irrigation water, and the system that distributes it, is still the life source that keeps the Japanese Tea Garden, Botanical Garden, the golf course, the flower beds, playing fields, and lawns all in good health. The five-acre Japanese Tea Garden was the first public Japanese garden in the United

135

States. George Turner Marsh, a devotee of Asian art, sponsored the creation of the original garden as part of an exhibit for the 1894 Midwinter Exposition. After the exposition ended, the designer and gardener Makoto Hagiwara, proposed that the garden be maintained as an attraction. McLaren agreed, and over time, Hagiwara and his family, who lived on the site, expanded the garden to five acres. Makoto Hagiwara died in 1925, but his family remained caretakers of the garden until 1942, when they were removed to an internment camp. They were never allowed to return, and the garden deteriorated. Eventually, the tea garden was restored and the Hagiwara family name recognized and honored. Among the original features that remain are the Drum Bridge and the tea house. The pagoda and Zen garden were added later.

The fifty-five acre San Francisco Botanical Garden is largest such garden on the West Coast of the United States. Though it was originally begun by Park Superintendent John McLaren back in 1890, the extensive work did not begin until 1926, and it wasn't until 1940 that it was opened to the public. The work was paid for by donations from Helene Strybing. For decades her contributions were honored in the name: the garden was known as Strybing Arboretum. The San Francisco Botanical Garden Society, which supports the garden and maintains both a botanical library and a gift shop, changed the name of the garden to San Francisco Botanical Garden at Strybing Arboretum in 2004. There are several different plant communities to be explored in addition to native California habitats. There is a Mediterranean section, one with plants from Australia and New Zealand, Mesoamerican cloud forest and Southeast Asian cloud forest. The botanical garden is one of the richest birding spots in Golden Gate Park. In winter some of the exotic trees are regularly visited by Red-breasted Sapsuckers and you can see their parallel rows of round sap wells in the soft-barked trees.

Many of the animals now common in Golden Gate Park were introduced by people, from the fenced-in bison and feral turtles to the tree squirrels. The Canada Geese came of their own accord and adapted to a non-migratory livestyle, enjoying the lawns and lakes. Still Golden Gate Park is also home to native species uncommon in the residential parts of the city: Cooper's Hawks, Wilson's Warblers, Great Horned Owls, Violet-green Swallows, Hutton's Vireos, coyote, and Botta's pocket gophers.

Just as people created this environment from what nature had grown on the site, so the park will be changing and changed as long as there is a San Francisco by the sea. Epidemics may strike some plants, the climate will change and may even alter fog patterns, another earthquake is only a matter of time, unforeseen plant or animal invasions could occur. Thus the residents and lovers of San Francisco can expect to be tasked with the duty to protect, replant and alter the park as circumstances change.

In following chapters I will try to summarize many of the environmental challenges that can be foreseen from climate change to resource exploitation to restoration.

CHAPTER 15

_____

And Now...

Aside from the Farallones and Lands' End, Glen Canyon is the wildest and most unspoiled part of San Francisco. To hike through this deep notch surrounded by the highest hills in the city is to experience San Francisco's primordial landscape in its most dramatic form.... In 1889 the estate of the railroad tycoon Charles Crocker bought Glen Canyon from philanthropist and former mayor Adolph Sutro. In 1898, the Crocker estate, the largest landowner in the city, opened a pleasure garden and zoo in the canyon.

—GARY KAMIYA, COOL GRAY CITY OF LOVE

THERE IS NO WAY TO go back to what San Francisco was like in 1840, or even 1940. In some publicly owned open spaces, though, there are on-going small efforts to help some natural habitats to thrive or return. Recent studies of urban wildlife show that even small areas of habitat can have a positive effect on plant and animal populations. A native ant species would not need fifty acres to thrive, perhaps a fifth of an acre could suffice.

Restoration and stewardship efforts can be seen at Crissy Field, Crissy Lagoon, Lobos Dunes and Tennessee Hollow in the Presidio, at Land's End, Brooks Park in the Ingleside, Yosemite Creek, and on the mesa at the northeast side of Lake Merced. A portion of the twenty-five acres atop

Bernal Heights still holds a thriving native grassland. The eastern face of Mount Davidson still offers unique habitat with many native plants. And Bayview Hill, despite quarrying, abuse, and neglect, has a remnant array of native plants and birds.

Since the Golden Gate National Recreation Area took over the Presidio, significant restoration efforts have been made there. The Presidio is the largest contiguous area of public land in San Francisco, containing over 1,490 acres. Now, after substantial effort, it is an important preserve for native plants. About two hundred acres of the Presidio have been designated as native habitat, and the lagoon and marsh at Crissy Field have been reconstructed and restored. However, much of the Presidio contains buildings and paved roads. There is considerable privately rented housing and offices, and the world headquarters of Industrial Light & Magic occupies the former site of Letterman Hospital. Various palm and eucalyptus species are widespread and are now often used by the feral parrot population.

Crissy Field and the lagoon have a history that reflects two centuries of radical change in San Francisco. Two hundred years ago, the whole area was a shallow lagoon with a bordering salt marsh. After the 1906 quake, rubble and dirt were used as fill to create a site for the 1915 Panama-Pacific International Exposition. After that fair some of the area to the west became an air field for the Presidio, and the eastern portion became the Marina District, where private housing was built.

In 1997 major restoration of Crissy Lagoon was begun. The army had buried waste and old aircraft debris around the air field; all that had to be removed. The paved runways were ripped up. Tons of old asphalt, cement, and other debris from post-earthquake landfill were hauled away. A channel was constructed to open the new, small lagoon to the bay. The marsh and lagoon now cover 20 acres. Next to that area is a 29-acre grass meadow on bay fill. After the undergrounding of the highway approach to the Golden Gate Bridge, Crissy Field will have a surface connection to the uphill sections of the Presidio for the first time in decades.

When the Crissy Marsh was re-created, three native plants quickly volunteered: beach morning glory, spear scale, and eel grass. Twenty-three plant species were reintroduced in the marsh area, including Pacific swampfire, California cordgrass, fleshy jaumea, alkali heath, and California sea lavender. The cordgrass is a native species, collected from a marsh in southern Marin County. To protect against invasion by other species in this genus, the native cordgrass at Crissy Field is subjected to regular genetic testing. Six species of native plants are dominant now on the Crissy dunes: yellow sand verbena, pink sand verbena, silver beachburr, beach (or coastal) sagewort, beach suncup, and American dunegrass.

The phrase from the film *Field of Dreams* comes to mind: "if you build it, they will come." The restoration of the Crissy area has drawn Great Blue Heron, egrets, gulls, terns, grebes, diving ducks, Double-crested Cormorant, Belted Kingfisher, coots, resident and migrating shorebirds including Wilson's Snipe. Many bird species now use the area depending on the seasonal flux of bird populations.

Nineteen species of fish from twelve families were collected in Crissy marsh between June 2000 and July 2004. Numerically dominant species include arrow goby, three-spined stickleback, staghorn sculpin, cheekspot goby, and topsmelt. Two non-native fish species have also been collected: yellowfin goby and rainwater killifish. Like fish, macrocrustacean density and richness are highest in the summer months. Thirteen macrocrustacean taxa have been collected in beach seine surveys at Crissy marsh since 2000. The most abundant species are yellow shore crab and blacktail bay shrimp. Two non-native species have been collected: oriental shrimp and European green crabs (also called shore crabs).

The European green crab is an aggressive predator that eats clams, oysters, mussels, and other crabs its own size and smaller. The first Pacific sighting of this species was in Marin's American Estuary in 1989. They were probably introduced from the East Coast unnoticed. Since 1990 the European green crab has spread into the San Francisco Bay. Forty individual European green crabs were caught here in the summer of 2003. Two more were caught in the summer of 2004. The species has moved on, invading Oregon, Washington, and British Columbia.

The need for vigilance and action is constant, lest some of the more rugged invasive plants and animals take over. The channel must be artificially kept open to the bay; shifting sand regularly blocks it. Restoration and maintenance efforts, in other parts of the Presidio as well, must continue to be relentless, including genetic testing and plain old weeding. Crissy Lagoon cannot continue to exist without help from humans, and neither can Inspiration Point, Tennessee Hollow, Lobos Dunes, and other scattered areas.

Presidio Rare Plants. The Lobos Dunes project came about after a San Francisco city sewer line broke in 1994, eroding a section of hillside on the west bank of Lobos Creek. Over the decades, the dunes had been used as a parade ground and later a playground. The restoration project included putting in a pedestrian boardwalk and replanting the area with native shrubs, including silvery lupine, San Francisco lessingia, coast buckwheat, and dune gilia. The battle against invasive weeds here never stops.

On the north side, the dunes border a forest of Monterey cypress and pines that were planted long ago. Along the south edge of the dunes runs Lobos Creek, a rare length of surface stream in San Francisco. Lobos Creek is lined with native live oak and shrubs. At the eastern end of the dunes is a pocket-sized spring-fed marsh full of native willow. Invertebrates that take advantage of this small restored dune area include the Acmon blue butterfly and the bluet, a brightly colored damselfly. The creek flows less than a quarter mile before emptying into the ocean at Baker Beach. White-crowned Sparrows resumed nesting in the dunes in 2001. Anna's Hummingbirds can be found working the blossoms in season. It is a miniature example of what much of the western portion of San Francisco would have been like in 1840. Landscape painter Theodore Wores would feel welcome with his easel and brushes. Famous nature photographer Ansel Adams lived in a house that still overlooks Lobos Creek and Lobos Dunes. He once wrote:

> With a resolute whisper, Lobos creek flowed past our home on its mile-long journey to the ocean. It was bordered, at times covered, with watercress and alive with minnows, tadpoles, and a variety of larvae. In spring, flowers were rampant and fragrant. In heavy fog, the creek was eerie, rippling out of nowhere and vanishing into nothingness.

In the Presidio alone, a dozen rare plants survive and are carefully protected, including the San Francisco spineflower, a dune denizen. Dune gilia has bright blue-violet flowers and was first discovered for science in the Presidio. It can be found at Lobos Dunes and around Crissy Field. San Francisco lessingia, another plant first discovered in the Presidio, is named for a German aster expert, C. F. Lessing. Outside of the Presidio, this plant is now found only on San Bruno Mountain in nearby Daly City. On the serpentine slope of Inspiration Point, Presidio clarkia grows.

The Presidio website lists each of the rare plants and provides some habitat information. One of the most fascinating plant stories is that of Raven's manzanita. Peter Raven, who eventually became a renowned botanist, President Emeritus of the Missouri Botanical Garden, discovered this plant when he was a boy of fourteen. The single surviving plant was growing in the no-man's land between the old highway (US 101) and Crissy Field. Since then clones have been grown in other appropriate spots in the Presidio. Long ago, the plant had once lived on Mt. Davidson but has never been known outside San Francisco.

Some slopes proved too steep even for San Franciscans to develop so there is more chance that native plants can survive in those "unused" spaces. Mt. Davidson is covered with eucalyptus trees on its western slope, but a near-natural grassland covers part of the north and eastern slopes. Here you can still find Douglas iris, golden yarrow, mission bells (also called chocolate lily), snowberry, Pacific reedgrass, pink-flowered currant, blue elderberry, and yellow-eyed grass. Glen Canyon still has a portion of a free-flowing creek plus native willows, and crimson columbine. Two hundred years ago, this would have been a likely place to find Wrentit. The bird is only rarely seen now in San Francisco and may not annually breed here. These accidentally preserved open spaces provide remnants of the habitat that was San Francisco two hundred years ago. Altogether 1,100 acres of San Francisco Recreation and Parks land have been designated as Natural Areas, where restoration and protection of native plants is intended. This is in addition to what's being done in various units of the GGNRA.

Sometimes reversion to a wild state just happens. It only requires lack of interference from people. In the 1970s the Port of San Francisco was preparing to build a huge new shipping facility at Pier 98. The aborted project caused some bay fill to be put in place. After construction was abandoned, the natural action of waves and weather turned the fill into a saltwater marsh. Native plants and birds colonized the spot, still owned by the Port of San Francisco. Now these twenty-four acres are called Heron's Head Park which opened to the public in 1999. Over 170 bird species have been reported at this park including Harlequin Duck, all three scoter species, Caspian Tern and Red-necked Grebe. Even in a busy, crowded city nature can do a lot if given the chance.

Species May Adapt. The key to success in San Francisco for any bird or mammal is adaptability to the artificial habitat. In the intervening years since the padres, many native plants and animals have adapted to the changed conditions. San Francisco now has numerous raccoons, opossums, and striped skunks. Coyotes have returned to the city, though they still face prejudice and persecution. Hooded Orioles, Barn Swallows, Northern Mockingbirds, and Pygmy Nuthatches now breed where none existed two hundred years ago. Western Gulls, Brewer's Blackbirds, and ravens can find food in a parking lot or dumpster, or on the beach. During the 1860s, J. G. Cooper was noting the adaptability of species like Barn and Cliff Swallows. Both species began nesting on buildings and bridges. They were not the only birds who appreciated urban habitat. Of the doughty California Towhee Cooper wrote, "About towns, if unmolested, they become more familiar, entering gardens and making their homes about houses."

There is no going back to 1840. Or even to 1940. Each season, each decade brings changes, and some of those will persist far into the future. Humans have now become de facto managers of the natural world in cities across the globe. The best that can happen is a balance between the native and the introduced, between the long-time resident species and those that have been introduced or have moved in on their own. Whatever happens, this brief history is but a snapshot in time. Changes will continue, and in the future, climate change and its multiple effects may alter San Francisco's natural world as much as people already have in the past two centuries.

CHAPTER 16

Climate Change

One reason we make so little progress is that we keep waiting for our political leaders to lead.

—BILL McKIBBEN

Always remember the will to act is a renewable resource.

—AL GORE

CLIMATE CHANGE IS CREATING MORE short-term extreme weather events— higher winds, heavier rains and floods, more severe droughts and the accompanying fire hazards. Everything in the biosphere, from moss to mammals, must endure and adapt to new and changing environmental stresses. A 2016 study sponsored by the Farallons Institute found that climate change in the North Pacific will create unprecedented weather variation and put increased pressure on many species. Variations will include more intense storms, extreme temperatures, warmer surface waters, altered ocean currents and rising sea levels as polar ice melts. This, the study concludes, will affect not only plankton, krill, shellfish, fish, seabirds, and sea mammals, but also many organisms that never go near the water.

As I was finishing work on this book there was an unprecedented event in San Francisco. The high temperature on September 1, 2017, was recorded at 107 degrees Fahrenheit. That is four degrees higher than the previous all-time record for San Francisco, measured at the start of the twenty-first century. Nothing in the previous one hundred-and-fifty years matched those two hot days. San Francisco was sharing in a heat spell that was all along the Pacific Slope with inland temperatures topping 110 in some places. Will climate change make such days less of an anomaly and more routine? How will fog-loving plants like live oak, redwood and Monterey cypress respond?

Some plants and animals are altering their seasonal imperatives, nesting or blooming earlier than has ever been noted historically. Some migrant species—from butterflies and whales to birds and bats—may change their migration patterns. In fact, this is already happening. Some are moving north or upslope to more suitable habitat. This may cause direct competition with species already in that zone. Plants and animals confined to limited ranges or specific habitats are most likely to be in danger of extirpation. In Washington and Oregon state wildlife agencies recently began salmon-lifts. Netting the native fish and moving them out of their usual rivers when the current is too low and the water temperature too high. They jhave to be taken to colder waters to survive. The annual cycles of plants and animals may no longer match what's happened in past centuries. Some may adapt, many may not be able to.

Recent research indicates that at least 1,700 animal species in North America have already moved their ranges northward. This puts pressure on species that are possibly less adaptable, found only in northern areas or at higher altitudes. Those species now must compete with ones escaping from lower elevations or regions nearer the equator. There's substantial evidence that this rapid northward shift is leading to widespread species hybridization. In North America now there are "grolar" bears, a cross between polar and grizzly. There are hybrid coy-wolves (wolf/coyote crosses) and bobcat/lynx crosses as well. Hybrid whales, porpoises, sharks, seals, and butterflies have been documented. It's likely that plant distribution is changing on an even greater scale, as well, because there are so many more species involved.

Greenhouse Gases and the Sea. One of the several greenhouse gases that affect our atmosphere is carbon dioxide. Its effects can be seen from the atmosphere to the ocean floor. It signifies the complexities of the process we call climate change. We have long passed the point where earth's plants absorb enough carbon dioxide to balance the amount produced by human activities and natural processes. The warming Pacific is absorbing ever more carbon dioxide from the atmosphere.

Climate change has specific, drastic effects on the oceans. Two key things happen: (1) As the climate becomes warmer, so does the surface temperature of the ocean waters. Science tells us at least one prehistoric warming event raised ocean temperatures more than 15 degrees Fahrenheit. (2) As the amount of carbon dioxide in the atmosphere increases, the ocean absorbs more of this gas from the air. Carbon dioxide reacts with water to create carbonic acid (H_2CO_3) in the ocean. The direct effect is acidification—the lowering of pH—which affects everything from microorganisms to shellfish to sea mammals. For some organisms, acidification is lethal: if coral reefs dissolve, the coral dies; shellfish can't build shells. Acidic waters dissolve the calcium carbonate ($CaCO_3$) essential to sea shell formation.

Just how bad can this get? A scientific look back at a previous die-off caused by ocean acidification brings up terrifying images if you value any currently living creature. Volcanologist Seth Burgess studied the geological and biological changes that took place at the end of the Permian period about 250-255 million years ago. It wasn't simply the end of a geological age, it was the end of most living organisms. Fossil records show that 90% of all ocean organisms and 70% of those on land went extinct. Trees and coral reefs disappeared. Apparently fungus and bacteria thrived, their short live spans and rapid reproduction allowed much quicker adaptation to extreme conditions. Burgess and his fellow scientists followed a series of discoveries and likely connections to the resulting natural cataclysm of that time. Unusual volcanic activity in Siberia released huge amounts of carbon dioxide and methane into the atmosphere. That caused sudden warming and ocean acidification at the same time. It should be noted that now methane explosions are occurring in Siberia as the permafrost melts and stored methane is released. Burgess and his associates now believe the ocean water temperature rose ten degrees Centigrade at the end of the Permian. About today's situation Burgess told an interviewer he thinks comparisons between the Permian die-off and today's climate change are not ridiculous: "I think that the timescales over which the environment changes associated with mass extinctions are frighteningly similar to the timescales over which our current climate is changing. The causes might be different but the hallmarks are similar."

Research by Joshua Davis in Geneva shows a strikingly similar pattern in a smaller die-off in the Triassic. This one was about 201 million years ago and may have been triggered by volcanic events in the Central Atlantic Magmatic Province. That time, says Davis, greenhouse gases were baked out of the sediments, causing warming and ocean acidification. A new cycle of extinctions occurred then as well.

Warming water causes changes in oceanic upwelling and alters currents. That in turn changes nutrient levels that directly affect the types of small organisms that can survive near the surface. It is known that the normal upwelling of cold, nutrient-rich water off the northern California coast contributes greatly to the richness of sea life in the nearshore zone. When seasonal changes or El Nino stop the upwelling, die-offs occur because of warm surface temperatures and disruption of the food chain. Nutrient loss is hard on krill which is at the base of the food chain for numerous species. Further, warmer water encourages toxic cyanobacteria. Also, the warmer water allows more infectious pathogens to spread faster and last longer. We can expect this added environmental stress will be fatal to some species, at least in the ranges where they are now found. Some species will move north or south or further out to sea. Some are likely die off because they cannot adapt quickly enough during our neo-Permian extinctions.

Climate Change—Incompatible with Life? While acidification affects all the layers of ocean life, natural zones of low oxygen absorption are expanding across the surface. These regions affect all oceanic life from phytoplankton to whales. Oxygen levels throughout the ocean can be healthful or detrimental depending on tiny variations. Some years ago, the Monterey Bay Aquarium began trying to keep creatures from the deep alive in their aquarium so visitors could see these amazing, largely colorless benthic species, but they failed for some time. None of the animals survived. Experiments showed that it wasn't the reduced pressure at sea level, nor was it the flood of unaccustomed sunlight. Salinity did not seem to be critical either. Finally it was discovered that the high oxygen content of surface water is fatal to creatures that are used to a low-oxygen environment. Changes in oxygen or carbon dioxide content that would be negligible for a land animal are far more critical in oceanic habitats.

Climate change is already raising the level of seawater on the planet. Rising sea levels will alter coastlines, and San Francisco may find itself abandoning areas claimed from the Pacific and the bay more than 150 years ago. There is already controversy over buildings and development plans on land that was under Mission Bay before landfill changed the area. This even includes the baseball stadium where the Giants play.

Another source of environmental stress is salt water intrusion. It will affect plants and animals in areas adjacent to an ocean. Salt-tolerant species will come to dominate more locations. Cliff faces like those formed of ancient dunes at Fort Funston will erode. Low-lying areas like Sutro Baths, Ocean Beach, Heron's Head Park, Candlestick State Recreation Area, Fort Mason's old piers, and Crissy Field will be inundated unless seawalls are constructed to protect them. These open natural areas will be in competition for resources against places that produce revenue, like Fisherman's Wharf, Pier 39, the San Francisco Giants ballpark, Treasure Island, commercial concerns at Ocean Beach, and the Ferry Building, which are also susceptible to rising tide lines. If artificial means are used to keep back the bay or the ocean, how will those decisions get made? Will a commercial area be deemed more worthy than Golden Gate Park or Crissy Field? When decisions are made will expensive homes in the Marina compete with open space at nearby Crissy Field?

We do not know if climate change will increase or intensify El Niño events and other causes of ocean warming. But we have one definite example of an unexpected catastrophic event: "The Blob" of unusually warm water that sat in the North Pacific from late 2013 into 2016. That occurrence—and its severity—were historically unprecedented. In some areas of the Pacific, surface water temperatures rose seven degrees above average.

Oxygen levels in the nearshore Pacific dropped because the water was warmer and the traditional wind patterns disrupted. There was almost no upwelling of cold nutrient-rich water from the ocean floor. The heated surface water enabled a larger than usual bloom of a species of the planktonic diatom *Pseudo-nitzschia,* which produces a neurotoxin, domoic acid. The toxin-producing diatom was consumed by plankton, jellyfish, shellfish, and fish. In some coastal areas, the neurotoxin levels rose to thirty times greater than is considered a high level in average years. This toxin in turn ended up in the food eaten by larger predators: big fish and sea mammals. California sea lions and sea otters were found to be victims of the toxin. From plankton to whales, all life in the biosphere was affected.

The warm water, with its lack of nutrients, led to a dearth of sardines, anchovies, market squid, and other prey species; larger animals that depended on that prey starved. California sea lions, Common Murres, and Cassin's Auklets were among species that suffered starvation die-offs. Some species, including Western Gulls and Brandt's Cormorants, failed to reproduce. This happens among many oceanic species: when the food supply is insufficient the adult birds do not even try to reproduce that year. One bad year is not fatal to a species that lives ten years or more, but for smaller birds and some fish, a lost year or two could lead to extinction if the residual population has fallen enough already. Species normally found off San Francisco's coastline moved further north during the blob. Sardines, for example, had to go north to find waters where their eggs could survive. The warmth drew subtropical species north of their normal range, among them hammerhead sharks and ocean sunfish. It will be a sign of serious disruption if Hawaiian species begin showing up in San Francisco Bay.

Starfish Die-off. Widespread effects of the changes in the ocean have already been confirmed along the California coast. One phenomenon that made news, at least in coastal regions, was the dramatic die-off of starfish. The cause proved to be a viral epidemic, apparently enhanced by the warmer waters. Starting in 2013, scientists and divers noticed a wasting disease decimating the starfish populations in shallow waters. Over twenty species of Pacific Ocean starfish were affected. In some areas they were completely wiped out in two years, and some portions of the coast are still without starfish. The decimation had wide-reaching consequences. Starfish are important predators in the control of sea urchin populations.

Urchins have been described as ocean-going goats because they devour all the plants they can reach. With the starfish gone urchin populations exploded. Huge urchin concentrations ate every plant fiber to be found on the ocean floor. Algae and seaweeds vanished. In some cases, even the urchins themselves starved because they denuded their ocean grazing grounds. Some biologists are now working on urchin removal programs, but meanwhile, urchins continue to gobble up any kelp bud that appears on the ocean floor, then they move on.

Due to urchin grazing numerous kelp beds along the California coast have been destroyed or reduced to a fraction of their historic size and density. In 2017, one estimate said 90 percent of the kelp beds between San Francisco and the Oregon border had disappeared since 2008. Kelp forests have long provided critical food and shelter for many small fish and other organisms. Even animals as big as sea otters prefer kelp forests. The otters hunt in the kelp and tie themselves to long, flexible kelp stems while they eat or sleep off a recent meal, so that they don't just drift with current and tide.

The case of dying sea otters is another signature of ecological stress. Over three hundred dead otters in one study showed that about a third of them suffered from neurotoxin poisoning, but a majority died from a strep infection that has plagued the otters for years. Did warmer water and changes in prey availability lead to a higher mortality rate for otters? Did disrupted food supplies lead to malnourished otters thus made more susceptible to disease? Are the rampant diseases in starfish and otters portents of what climate change might mean for life in the Pacific? Will the heat blob return? Did it signal a situation that could become normal? There is much we do not yet understand about all that happened during the 2013–2016 hot-water event in the northern Pacific.

Climate change almost certainly means that a wide range of organisms will suffer more stress-linked maladies. In recent decades, diseases have hit live oaks, Monterey and ponderosa pines, sea otters, House Finches, corvids, starfish and other species. A virus has been identified as the cause of beak deformities in a number of American bird species. Vast areas of former ponderosa forest on the western slopes of the Sierra are now barren, the trees dead from drought and bark beetle infestation. A federal report estimates that California's national forests lost forty million trees between 2010 and 2016. Bark beetles, fungal infections, drought, and other blights killed off forests across several habitat zones. Trees that are not affected may come to dominate, and some of those may be introduced species, like eucalyptus and Russian olive. San Francisco will not be immune to such changes.

West Nile virus ran amok through California bird species in the early twenty-first century, killing off many corvids, especially the Yellow-billed Magpie. This bird is found only in California so there is no reservoir of the species beyond the reach of West Nile virus. West Nile still stalks much of California, and the state maintains a report scorecard online to track it. The virus is not native to America. Once established on the East Coast it swept across the continent in the first years of the twenty-first century. Control is elusive, as the vector for this disease is mosquitoes. As well as horses and hundreds of crows, West Nile virus annually kills humans, with seniors particularly vulnerable to it. Other major victims of West Nile are American Robins and California Scrub-Jays. Some abundant birds have a low susceptibility, for example, Turkey Vultures and starlings. Some individuals of a vulnerable species may show resistance and survive. May their progeny inherit the California earth. Other diseases that are transmitted by mosquitoes are expected to increase, including malaria, yellow fever, dengue fever, and Zika virus. Many of these have related strains that infect birds or mammals.

Our uncertain future. Disease is only one threat posed by climate change. A more subtle one is habitat disruption, which affects feeding, breeding, and migration. Millennia-old behavior patterns among animals may no longer further survival. Climate change will mean "adapt or die." Can monarch butterflies change the timing of their migration? Among plants, changes in climate conditions and water availability will produce threats and new habitat possibilities. Can Lake Merced's tules survive if that lake drops permanently to a lower level because of extended drought? Will rising sea levels turn that lake into an inlet or a brackish pool? What plants and animals will move into the niches abandoned by creatures that have to move or that die out? We can probably already be assured that Brewer's Blackbirds and dandelions will persevere. They can live in a broad range of habitats. Not so the Pygmy Nuthatch, which needs conifers, nor native lupines which prefer dunes.

Simply higher temperatures can make survival difficult for some species not adapted to high temperatures. In some mountain areas ptarmigan are already disappearing. They depend on snow in summer to regulate body heat. No summer glaciers and these birds overheat and die as they have no internal temperature regulation. We have very little information on how flexible some coastal species—both plants and animals—are when facing unusual heat for extended periods of time. Heat can always exacerbate dehydration among birds and mammals that cannot sweat. Most can only pant and will lose body moisture. Combine that heat with a drought and scarce water and it can be a survival crisis. Many species die after dehydration depletes more than 15 percent of an individual's body mass.

Evidence is already accumulating on the ways in which climate change is disrupting life cycles on land, particularly for organisms whose lives follow annual patterns. Some plants are responding to earlier springs by blooming earlier. In some areas the flowering has been moving earlier about two days per decade already. How does that affect migrant birds or insects that depend on that plant's flowers or seeds? There is evidence now that fertility of some species is negatively affected by warmer or dryer weather, longer summers, milder winters. There is one plant in high elevations of North America that is producing far fewer females. The dryer weather favors male survival because those plants require less water. Will the tobacco root plant eventually go unisex and then extinct? An opposite effect is being seen in at least three species of large sea turtles. Warmer waters tend to influence the species' eggs and produce more hatchling females and fewer males. When laid the eggs are gender neutral so environmental influence can be crucial. These are examples of multifarious changes in the natural world nobody would have foreseen in 1970. And there are likely many more changes that our observation and science have not yet detected and that we may miss altogether until it is too late.

San Francisco's climate is highly dependent on conditions in the Pacific. Will the increase or decrease of fog change the survival rate of introduced trees or native shrubs? "Rain" from heavy fog keeps many native and introduced plants from succumbing to drought. A Monterey cypress collects significant moisture from fog, then drops that water from its limbs and needles onto the plants and soil beneath it. Fog and wind patterns in San Francisco have long determined what plants thrive in what places. As those patterns change, so will the make-up of the plantscape.

We people will find ourselves faced with many life or death decisions as we choose which of our fellow creatures and plants on this planet we will protect and sustain. Which will be rewarded with conservation efforts and money? Which will die off, ignored because of indifference, ignorance, or lack of resources? Will people even spend the money to make the studies to be able to understand what is happening and why? The bitter global politics around climate change may make action by human agents slow or unrealistic. There seems to be no powerful entity immune to the profit-driven market system. Thus there is no entity to force ecological responsibility on hundreds of countries, thousands of corporations, and billions of people. In the end, we—having enabled climate change in its current severe form—will find ourselves doing biological triage on a massive as well as local scale. It is important to remember that direct action has so far saved—along with other endangered species—the Whooping Crane, California Condor, bison, tule elk, Raven's manzanita, mission blue and gray wolf.

A Throwaway Society:
Where All That Unwanted Stuff Goes

Now that time in San Francisco is gone, the sand dunes have swept over the Summer of Love, the Sutro Baths and Playland are demolished, and I returned that afternoon to see how the dunes and beach and ocean are making out in their loneliness. The Farallon Islands and the memory of the Coastanoan Indians had kept them company in my absence. The windmills are still stalwartly unmoved by the wind, the grayish bent trees shed their leaves in the salt-filled air. The beach was swept clean except for a few beer cans and prophylactics.

—HERBERT GOLD, *TRAVELS IN SAN FRANCISCO*

I covered the proposal to build a nuclear power plant at Bodega Head and others to build plants near the Bay and near Santa Cruz. It was at a time when nuclear was thought to be the energy source of the future, and even the Sierra Club was initially on record in support of nuclear energy to avoid the building of more dams.

—HAROLD GILLIAM IN *BAY NATURE*, INTERVIEW

IN ANY URBAN ENVIRONMENT, POLLUTION is constant. Cars give off gases and particulates. Tires wear down and tiny bits of rubber float across the earth. Small engines like mowers and air blowers put out unburned hydrocarbons. People flush their unused drugs or toxic chemicals into the sewer. Pesticides and detergents and paint residue are widely dispersed by heedless users. Every rainfall washes chemicals and trash from streets and gutters into storm sewers and then the bay. Boats, airplanes, buses, trucks, bicycle tires, Garden chemicals, cigarette butts, restaurant evacuation fans, trash and plastic debris—all these are sources of stuff that is bad for plants and animals—and people, in many cases.

At one time, the city park personnel went after the rat population in Golden Gate Park with poisons. As a result, all the Great Horned Owls were also poisoned and killed off. They are back as I write, but if a human disease or other problem connected to rats is detected, you can bet the poisoning will return and the owls once again may disappear. Around 2000, the National Park Service poisoned all the California ground squirrels that used to live near the Cliff House. The reason given was to stop erosion of the cliff face. That may have been the last ground squirrel population in the city outside of Candlestick Point. Chemical pesticides and herbicides are still widely used in gardens and parks. After four decades of widespread sales and use, there is a legal battle over the safety of the widely used herbicide, Roundup, a brand of the Monsanto Corporation. On its website Monsanto claims "When it comes to safety assessments, no other pesticide has been more extensively tested than glyphosate. In evaluations spanning four decades, the overwhelming conclusion of experts worldwide, including the EPA, has been that glyphosate can be used safely according to label instructions." Yet documents that have been hidden from public view are now coming to light due to a lawsuit against Monsanto, claiming Roundup's main ingredient, glyphosate, is carcinogenic. There are also claims that research into glyphosate's safety were stymied in the U.S. Now we know a branch of the World Health Organization says there is research linking glyphosate to non-Hodgkin's lymphoma, an incurable disease at this time.

Hazardous concoctions, in addition to harming unintended victims, always present the chance of spills, accidents, and otherwise unplanned pollution of water or soil. Some pollution is incidental but inevitable: oil from internal combustion vehicle exhaust pipes, air pollutants from internal combustion engines or spray cans, cigarette smoke and butts, toxic waste casually dumped on the ground. For decades, cancer-causing PCBs were used to keep electric transformers cool. The transformers were often located thirty feet up utility poles that could be hit by cars; collisions and wind could and did damage the transformers and release PCBs onto the ground.

Oil tankers are constantly sailing in and out of the Golden Gate, for example, although the risks of ship collisions and oil spills are well known. We have plenty of documented catastrophes. At 1:40 a.m. on January 18, 1971, a pair of Standard Oil tankers collided in the fog outside the Golden Gate Bridge. The *Arizona Standard* was headed into the Bay. The *Oregon Standard* was leaving the dock at the Richmond Chevron refinery. Stuck together after colliding, the ships drifted into San Francisco Bay. They finally anchored off Angel Island. Over 800 thousand gallons of the *Oregon Standard*'s cargo hit the bay. It was viscous, heavy, toxic bunker fuel. Then tides and waves spread it throughout the bay and along the coast from Point Reyes to Half Moon Bay. The death toll of birds and animals was great. Then in November 2007, the intoxicated captain of the *Cosco Busan* rammed his vessel into the Bay Bridge, spilling fifty-three thousand gallons of fuel into the water. The costs for repairs and cleanup ran upwards of seventy-three million dollars. There is every reason to expect spills to continue.

Our Plastic World. In 2010, the public had no idea that harmful micro-beads of plastic were being put into many consumer products and we were all guilty of spreading them across the planet. The San Francisco Estuary Institute and its partners are now studying the presence of microplastics and nano-plastics in San Francisco Bay. This research is being led by Dr. Rebecca Sutton. Her preliminary study found the bay was more contaminated by plastic than the Great Lakes or Chesapeake Bay. The plastic sources are myriad. Dr. Sutton compiled a fact list which lists the major microplastic components found in the bay and its sediments:

1) Foamed plastic particles from packaging, cigarette filters, and other items.
2) Microbeads that are pellets and fragments used in personal care products such as facial scrubs and toothpaste.
3) Fragments from the photodegradation of larger plastic items such as plastic bottles.
4) Nurdles, pre-production plastic pellets that are molded into larger plastic products.
5) Fibers derived from clothes and fabrics made with synthetic materials (polyester, acrylic) or fishing lines. Of all these preliminary studies show that microfibers make up a large majority of the plastic in treated wastewater released into the environment.

The two major sources of this plastic pollution are storm drains and sewage treatment outflow. Every storm flushes trash down the storm sewer system into streams and ultimately the bay. Wastewater treatment plants are not designed or equipped now to remove microplastic, so it passes through the system and into the "treated" water which is expelled ultimately to the ocean. Most stream born plastic is either fragments or fibers. In wastewater a large majority of the plastic bits are fibers. Many come from laundering synthetic fabrics used in clothes and linen. Nearly one-third of all plastic is used in one-time-only packaging in our throwaway economy. The move to eliminate plastic shopping bags from the economy is just a tiny first-step in trying to deal with plastic pollution. Plastic is cheap, durable and versatile which makes it both economically attractive and a common, lasting, global pollutant. It is also a highly profitable by-product of the fossil fuel industry which has considerable political clout in many nations including the United States.

It is known that plastic can absorb toxic chemicals already in the water. Some additives in plastic itself are also known to be toxic. Fish and smaller creatures eat or coincidentally take in microplastics. That can clog digestive tracts or gills. There is already evidence accumulating of some deleterious effects of plastic pollution on wildlife: disruption of reproduction, changes in hormone levels, triggering immune responses, messing with energy metabolism and disturbing liver function. Dr. Sutton is now launched on a long-term study of plastic in the bay that is aimed at finding out more about effects and finding ways to stem in-flow of microplastic.

The Ellen MacArthur Foundation is funding work to stop all this plastic pollution. In announcing their efforts, the Foundation wrote: "Most plastic packaging items are used only once before being discarded, often ending up polluting the environment. If nothing changes, there could be more plastic than fish in the ocean by 2050." Note that state and federal governments are not yet involved. Expect any effort to use public funds to curtail plastic pollution to unleash the lobbyists and spending of some very wealthy and powerful corporate interests who profit from heavy use of throwaway plastics.

Sometimes the perils are acute and instant disasters occur. In 2010, a failed Pacific Gas & Electric natural gas pipeline under San Bruno caused explosions and massive fires. Eight people died outright, and some thirty homes were utterly destroyed. That event remains a grim reminder that we have embedded beneath the cityscape a complex and ageing network of fossil fuel pipelines, each a potential hazard threatening death and pollution.

Science keeps uncovering perils and pollutants just as research continues to find new compounds that have appeal in the marketplace. We have only look back at what a "miracle" Teflon seemed to be when first sold to the public. It's only since the early 2000s that most of the public learned how dangerous chemicals used in non-stick coatings are. Microfiber clothing was hailed as a major advance by its promoters. Consider DDT, smoking tobacco, PCBs, synthetic opioids, electronics, neo-nicotinoids and most other profitable manufactured products. The chemical and materials makers and marketers use all their resources including lies to keep their product from being exposed as dangerous and ultimately banned. We now know that some oil company scientists were warning fifty years ago about the dangers of fossil-fuel powered climate change. From tobacco smoke to PCBs to Teflon it is often true that the manufacturer knows of health or environmental dangers before the public is informed. Deliberate silence can enhance profits. Quarterly profit statements and the resulting executive bonuses constantly took precedent for those companies. It's obviously easy to push off any concern for the planet's health and livability. It happens over and over. For decades, plastic bottles and the lining in metal cans have contained Bisphenol A (BPA), a compound that can leach into fluids. The first inkling that BPA might be dangerous dates back to the 1930s but the information was not widely known. The controversy over BPA's likely effects continues, with manufacturers curtailing the use of the chemical, various studies creating concerns about possible dangers, and the regulatory bodies making reassuring noises about tolerable levels. We continually wrap or bottle things in plastic without any idea what long-term effects the leaching of the chemicals in plastic may have on us or other organisms.

It seems we remove one environmental hazard while we nonchalantly broadcast another. Gone are DDT in pesticides, PCBs in power pole transformers, and lead additives in our gasoline. But our sewage is full of prescription drugs and hormones. Pharmaceutical companies constantly market new drugs. They may be tested on humans, but few pay attention to what such drugs do once released into the wild via trash cans or sewer systems. Wildlife—from bacteria to fish to crows—show signs of immunities to antibiotics developing in their genetic make-up. In England there is already concern that prescriptions compounds are hurting river otters there. Fish and other aquatic animals are especially prone to effects of our cast-off chemicals. Some medications even end up being absorbed by vegetables. There are no environmental standards for testing new prescription drugs, yet nearly all those medications end up in our sewers and ground water. Thus even we humans get to drink secondhand drugs. Like microplastics, they are not removed by standard water treatment plants.

San Francisco is moving toward removing plastic bags from commercial use, but plastic bags remain ubiquitous, littering the environment and winding up in local waters. Other non-biodegradable trash floats about our environment like confetti, or cigarette butts. Polystyrene foam—better known by its trademark name Styrofoam—is a good example. There are some ways to recycle it (you can check with EPS Industry Alliance for recycling tips), but in the past, tons of it have ended up dumped in the wild or in landfills.

Military Legacy. Long-lasting pollution is an endless issue. Heavy metals and radioactive material are especially likely in any area formerly controlled by the U. S. military. In the early days of America's use of nuclear power, there was very little systematic attempt to control where spent radioactive fuel or contaminated material was put. The most common approach was to bury it and forget about it. When Hunters Point and Treasure Island were military holdings, both were used as burial grounds for waste too inconvenient to ship elsewhere. Some radioactive waste in metal barrels was infamously dumped into the ocean around the Farallones.

But radiation lasts longer than human memory. Decades after the navy had left Treasure Island, a state health report, dated 2013, warned that radioactive shards buried there by the navy could endanger residents. The navy's leavings are still being studied to determine the danger to humans and other organisms on the island.

Hunters Point includes an eight hundred acre federal superfund site. Hunters Point is where the "Little Boy" atomic bomb was assembled during World War II. Later that bomb was dropped on Hiroshima. Clean up of radioactive soil and waste has been on-going there for several years. The U. S. Navy is still on the hook for clean-up costs. Past of the old base already contains modern, occupied housing outside the boundary of the superfund site. In the Summer of 2017 former workers in the clean up project came forward and charged that soil samples and testing had been fraudulent and that radiation was still in area supposedly cleaned up by a private contractor.

Another pernicious and chronic pollutant is lead. Lead paint is no longer made and lead additives have been taken out of gasoline, but lead contamination persists where these products were dumped or leached. Old lead-tainted paint still flakes off buildings. Any place where car or airplane batteries were worked on will have lead pollution, as did Crissy Field before it was cleaned up.

Another widespread source of lead poisoning is ammunition. The shooting range on the south shore of Lake Merced became controversial after decades when gunners fired lead into the lake while engaged in target practice. The skeet shooting range finally closed in 2015. Another source of lead at Lake Merced comes from weights used in fishing. Lead is especially hard on bottom-feeding fish, ducks, and the endangered California Condor, which eats deer carcasses that can be rich in bits of splattered lead from hunters' guns. In spite of outreach on this issue, and availability of lead-free ammunition, many hunters have not switched. Along with the condor, fish, ducks, and fish-eating birds still suffer fatal lead poisoning.

Issues at Lake Merced are typical of the controversies that still surround the open space in San Francisco. The public golf course at Lake Merced is also a source of manufactured stuff going into the water. Into the lake go golf balls, plastic bags, picnic detritus like styrofoam cups, carry-out food and drink containers, fishing line and equipment, oil from cars and lawnmowers and street run-off. The wrangles and conflicts are many as various recreational and commercial activities vie for dominance. This is a well-used lake that accommodates boating, fishing, a golf course, bird watching, hiking and jogging and more. It harbors breeding colonies of Great Blue Herons, Cliff Swallows (in the past), Double-crested Cormorants, Marsh Wrens, grebes and Canada Geese. There are a picnic ground, eucalyptus groves, areas of tule marsh, a paved trail heavily used by runners, and a small remnant of oak woodlands. In the late 1990s, the lake began losing water and that threatened almost all uses of the lake. A series of agreements were reached to divert more fresh water into the lake, now actually two lakes separated by an artificial sand dune, over which a road runs to the boat house and municipal golf course.

Golf courses bring their own environmental issues, and there are four courses inside San Francisco's city limits. Maintaining their perfect green turf requires heavy use of pesticides and herbicides. Golf course grass is a great consumer of water. And then there are those everlasting golf balls. Golfers hit them into the ocean and other water bodies—and the traditional ones take a thousand years to decompose. There are thousands in Loch Ness and perhaps as many in Lake Merced. In 1991 the MARPOLV

Treaty was signed and that effectively banned the practice of hitting old-fashioned, indestructible golf balls into the ocean. Apparently, there are modern golf balls that decompose more quickly. The Eco Golf Ball is made for use on cruise ships, where the pastime of hitting golf balls into the sea endures.

The medical industries, the chemical industry, packaging makers, the battery industry, clothing industry, cosmetic industry, the electronics industry, construction, agriculture, gardening—you can list almost every major source of profit and sales in modern American society and each will have its legion of chemicals, drugs, by-products, and waste that is part of everyday business. From bottle tops to battle ships, cellophane to cellphones, modern life is full of manufactured substances that were unheard of back in 1840. Many do not fit well into the natural world; in fact, they continue claiming victims long after they have been used, forgotten or discarded. It often takes time for the changes to happen. My great grandkids will read about how our generation still used lead bullets just as I recall my father plumbing our house with lead pipes in 1950. "Mad hatters" no longer use mercury. Ornithologists no longer use arsenic powder to preserve bird skins. Both John Cassin and John Townsend died from arsenic poisoning in the mid-nineteenth century after repeated handling of preserved bird skins. The lengthy list of chemicals that are no longer taken for granted runs from Freon to formaldehyde. Each pollution issue requires science, public concern, concerted action and usually political action.

Meanwhile, as corporations continue to find new products from new compounds to sell us, the impact of dense human populations on the environment is intense and often incomprehensible. We know not what we do, and what we don't know can kill us—as well as the animals and the plants around us. Business interests and the drive for profit often outgun public safety. It must fall to a responsible society and its governing bodies to try to reduce the damage done by the multiplying products of our modern culture. Finally, to survive, people will come to realize there is a finite carrying capacity on this small planet. That will led to confronting the underlying issue of population and how many people can survive over the coming centuries.

CHAPTER 18

Disturbance and Restoration

San Francisco has been pitched down on the sand-bunkers of a Bikaneer desert. About one-fourth of it is ground reclaimed from the sea—any old-timer will tell you all about that. The remainder is ragged, unthrifty sand-hills, pegged down by houses. From an English point of view there has not been the least attempt at grading those hills, indeed you might as well try to grade the hills of Sind. The cable-cars have for all practical purposes made San Francisco a dead level.

—RUDYARD KIPLING, 1889

SAN FRANCISCO HAS LONG UNDERGONE change from two sources: nature and people, sometimes in concert, sometimes in opposition, but always in flux. Humans act and the natural world feels the effects. From pavement to climate change to planting native lupine, people alter the environment in many ways. Also, San Francisco Peninsula's place at the edge of the planet's largest sea and atop one of earth's most active fault zones will mean inevitable future events which we cannot prevent. What follows those events becomes critical for all living things.

The geological reality of San Francisco is one of unpredictability coupled to certainty. There will be a disastrous earthquake. When that happens is beyond our ken for the time being. Writing months after the 1906 quake, Charles Keeler saw rebuilding as a way to make San Francisco a better place:

> As, in view of the tragic events which have converted miles of San Francisco into a dreary ruin, out of which through the heroic efforts of its citizens it is but now emerging, I read anew this account [his own book on San Francisco published first in 1902] of San Francisco, the throbbing life here chronicled seems strangely unreal. But this description of the dream city of our hearts may serve not so much as a reminder of what is forever gone, as an inspiration to the builders of the new San Francisco to hold fast to such traditions as are vital and good, and to incorporate them, glorified, let us hope, in the city of our imagination, already taking shape out of the chaos.

To know what creatures and plants live among us now will hopefully influence the inevitable rebuilding of San Francisco after the next quake. It can be hoped that along with architectural innovation, resource conservation and consideration of beauty, those future urban rebuilders will consider and value nature. Disregarding nature can be profitable in the short term, and it seems impossible for people to leave things alone. The small bits of open space in San Francisco are forever subject to social, economic, and political pressures. Many spaces are heavily used for recreation and entertainment. It would be hard to find more than a square yard of earth in the city that has not been directly changed by human activity a number of times in the past 240 years. These changes will recur; their eventual effects, though, cannot always be foreseen and often are not even considered.

It has taken more than two centuries of intense development and exploitation of the region's resources to make the San Francisco we see today. Here and throughout California, humans have greatly altered and abused the environment. Not simply paving grasslands and marshes; not simply mining, which trashes land and water; not simply releasing industrial and urban pollution into the air and water; not simply damming streams and using up centuries' worth of stored ground water; not simply dispersing pesticides and herbicides and dumping even more toxic debris. Many of these are part and parcel of the biggest disruption humans have caused in the environment: modern agriculture.

Though San Francisco no longer has farms and ranches, the products and by-products of modern agribusiness are in the bay, the air, the Pacific, and the food we all eat. Also, all Californians will pay in dollars and living conditions for some of the environmental damage done in the name of efficient agriculture. Allan Schoenherr's *Natural History of California* lists the many abuses perpetrated in the name of profitable agriculture: using groundwater in an unsustainable way, irrigation that concentrates selenium and other toxic elements, heavy use of pesticides, desertification, spread of invasive weeds, erosion, and over-grazing. His conclusion is sobering: "A day of reckoning is near, when California will be faced with the reality that its agricultural practices could lead to its own destruction."

Of course, not all human activity is detrimental or irreversible. Landfill and sewage engineering are far more sustainable now than they were a few decades ago. Recycling of resources has increased greatly yet some industries are built on throwaway or "disposable" products from drinking cups to diapers. The list of banned chemicals in the U.S. is justifiably long and getting longer. At the same time, corporations continually develop new chemicals and rush them into use before we understand their effects. The state and nation's politics are never free of corporations pushing to avoid regulation of new chemicals or products that can prove to be profitable. The story of Teflon is an example of this. The conflict between public health and profit seems unending.

Wildlife survival in the San Francisco area now necessarily depends on humans. It matters greatly what we humans do—directly or mindlessly—to habitat, ground water, air, oceans, soil, and trees. As climate change puts more and more stress on existing organisms and natural communities, human intervention or indifference will leave some species to go extinct and save others from time's erasure.

One significant example of how important human social and political behavior can be: use of DDT as a pesticide. First synthesized in

1939, it was ubiquitous in home and farm use by the 1960s. As a result of DDT leached into run-off and theninto rivers and the ocean. Thus DDT got into fish and ducks that ate them. Four alpha predators were pressed toward extinction along the California coast: the Brown Pelican, Osprey, Peregrine and Bald Eagle. DDT in the fish and other prey they ate concentrated in the adult birds and caused egg shells to thin and weaken. It was almost impossible for a DDT-laced bird to successfully hatch an egg. When I first birded in California in the late 1960s, I never saw a Brown Pelican and had no hope of ever seeing an Osprey or Bald Eagle.

Starting in 1962, with the alarm call in Rachel Carson's *Silent Spring,* some conservation groups began agitating for more study and eventually for a ban. The DDT makers quickly launched a publicity campaign to protect their profitable product, even hiring shills to go on TV and drink the stuff to prove it was harmless. Yet, over loud screams from the petro-chemical industry, the United States in 1972 banned DDT use in the United States. That federal law was signed by President Richard Nixon, a Republican. Now DDT's avian victims are well on the road to population recovery. It is common to see long skeins of Brown Pelicans off Land's End anytime from June through December. Some pelicans now stay year-round along San Francisco's coastline, although their breeding territory is further south. Osprey are regular breeders in Marin and now have colonized San Francisco and Alameda. The Bald Eagle is re-established in the Bay Area and may someday be a common sight over Lake Merced. Yet there is still DDT in river sediments and it shows up in ocean animals, as well. It is no longer made in the U.S. but is made elsewhere. DDT is still a mainstay in Asia and Africa, where it's widely used to kill malaria-carrying mosquitoes. Studies on DDT's effects continue because the link between this chemical and cancer is strong.

In the early twentieth century, a U.S. ban on killing birds for feathers was enacted. Yet even as recently as the 1960s, egrets and herons were still uncommon around San Francisco. Whole nesting colonies had been killed by market hunters seeking valuable plumes of the adult birds. Now you can expect to see Great Blue Herons nesting in Golden Gate Park and at

Lake Merced. Black-crowned Night-Herons nest on Alcatraz. Snowy and Great Egrets regularly visit the city to feed.

On Inspiration Point and along Tennessee Creek in the Presidio, native plants have been restored to areas that have been covered with introduced plants for over a century. Native plants and animals quickly began to colonize Crissy Lagoon and Marsh when it was "rebuilt." The long-term plan for restoration of more naturalized habitat from El Polin Spring downhill through Tennessee Hollow and into Crissy Lagoon calls for uncovering the main stream as well as its eastern tributary, Mason Creek. Much of that work has already been done. Eventually a visitor will be able to walk from El Polin Spring and stay next to the running stream all the way to its mouth in the Crissy Lagoon. This has not been possible since the late nineteenth century, when the army put much of the water through culverts and pipes.

In the southwest corner of the Presidio a lot of work has been done on restoring Mountain Lake. Goldfish, pet turtles, a sturgeon and an alligator have all been removed. Native wildlife and plants have been brought in, including the Pacific chorus frog, three-spine stickleback and the now-scarce native freshwater mussel. The stickleback has survived all these decades in Lobos Creek and fish from there have been brought to the lake. The mussels are filter feeders and will actually help maintain water quality in the lake despite the urban run-off.

Yosemite Slough, the intertidal channel between Candlestick Point and the Hunters Point Shipyard is polluted with lead and PCBs (Polychlorinated biphenyl). Clean up will take years. The plan, if money is available, includes restoring tidal marsh vegetation and dealing with 41,000 cubic yards of contaminated soil. Plans include construction of an interpretive facility and interpretive trails, an extension of the Bay Trail. Eventually, it is hoped, there will be restrooms, parking, and picnic areas on the north side of the slough.

Human efforts to restore some facets of natural landscapes nearly always center on construction or demolition, replanting or replacing – or some variations on these. But natural processes can take place without human intervention. Feral cats abound in some city parks and many pet cats are left to roam outdoors. The wild coyote has returned to the Bay Area and is a predator a city cat must avoid. Rock Pigeons may crowd rooftops and street corners, but Peregrines now nest on buildings and take many a pigeon right out of the sky. The starling is abundant, but American Crows, Common Ravens, and jays have returned after decades of human persecution. Local Cooper's Hawks will dine on starling as readily as the native finches, Nature will seek balance if given a chance; predator-prey relationships are part of the balance and will resume when human interference ceases.

The story of the fur seal in the Farallones is a dramatic case in point. The California Academy of Sciences website describes the saga:

The Farallon Islands, …west of San Francisco, once boomed with a colony of up to 200,000 northern fur seals. But between 1807 and 1840, American, British, and Russian sealers, who hunted the marine mammals for their prized satin-soft fur, extirpated them from the islands.

Examining bones excavated from Russian middens on the islands, the [research] team has identified the telltale jaws and teeth of fur seal pups less than three months old. Since these seals need at least that much time for their teeth to develop before leaving their birthplaces, the bones could have come only from pups born on the islands.

For decades after the hunting stopped, the fur seal was simply missing from the San Francisco area. Slowly, things changed, as the California Academy of Sciences website explains: "Over 150 years after sealers drove the Farallon Islands' colony of northern fur seals to extinction, the animals are beginning to reclaim their old haven." In 1974 the first documented live northern fur seal since 1840 returned to the Farallones. The first recorded fur seal pup's birth wasn't until 1992. Now the breeding colony numbers in the hundreds.

So it will continue. Decisions we humans make or fail to make will determine the winners and losers in San Francisco's outdoor habitats. Some organisms will find our urban environment suitable and thrive, others will struggle or even disappear, as they have over thousands of years since the first humans arrived on this continent and the North American megafauna disappeared. Beyond our direct actions—like hunting a species to extinction—indirect human influence is at least as powerful. We cannot accurately predict the effects of climate change, but change will come. Many effects will be uncomfortable or even catastrophic to humans and all other creatures trying to survive in the environment we all share. We must be aware of what is within our control and what may not be. No company, no person, no government agency can any longer plead innocence about how interconnected and interdependent every living thing on this planet is to the whole. Willful ignorance or heedless greed will only make the survival of people and other organisms more difficult on this spinning rock, with its finite resources and its trillions of living things. Over a century ago, John Muir explained to his fellow beings how the world works, often unseen: "When we try to pick out anything by itself, we find it hitched to everything else in the universe."

We are not alone on this planet; we couldn't survive if we were. We must be alert to what we can do to help other creatures survive. Knowledge and understanding of our surroundings is crucial. We can know and care what organisms are present now and which can make it through an uncertain future. People can and often are saving and aiding nature, even in crowded cities. Being aware and acting responsibly are crucial if future generations are to see a Brown Pelican soar past with wind under its wings, or watch a Botta's pocket gopher peeking out of his round burrow entrance, or follow bees coming and going from the yellow flower clusters on a healthy lupine bush.

ACKNOWLEDGEMENTS

THIS SMALL WORK HAS BEEN years in the making. I published a short, faulty version back in 2001. During four years living in London I was able to take advantage of the British Library and its complete collection of accounts of early Pacific exploration. I owe much to the fine British tradition of preservation of documents, buildings and art. The thrill of holding in my hands the huge folio containing Captain George Vancouver's notes and maps of the Pacific coast is one that would stick with any bibliophile.

The Bancroft Library at the University of California in Berkeley had many of the books and documents that launched my research.

Tree Frog Treks shared information with me on the reptiles and amphibians of San Francisco. They were helpful to a birder who can just about discern garter from gopher snake. Two professional biologists helped me understand two very crucial environmental issues, taking the time to explain to an inquiring journalist they had never heard of. Dr. Rebecca Sutton of the San Francisco Estuary Institute gave me a short course on her research into nano-plastic pollution in the Bay. Dr. Ted Grosholz of U.C. Davis gave me insight into the green crab invasion in the Bay Area. He also prevented me from being misled about the reality of native oysters in the Bay.

Two smart and honestly critical friends read a manuscript version of this book and made suggestions and corrections that helped me make improvements. Both know a great deal about the Bay Area and its natural world. Thank you, Tom DeVries and Robin McCall. Tom is a veteran journalist who's never met a topic he hasn't reported on. Robin is a lawyer for the California State Coastal Commission after her own career in TV news. Next my beloved and intrepid editor/wife, Kate, went over the manuscript with her sharp eye and questioning mind. Any mistakes that have survived all that are solely on my ledger.

The research itself led me back to some sources I have long neglected. Going back over old Herb Caen columns was a trip down memory lane. I lived in San Francisco's orbit most of the time from 1967 through 2007, four decades. During those decades Caen was for many of us the personification of San Francisco. Left Coast, glib and snide, tolerant and judgemental, cool and hot, urban with a twist of romance for the open countryside. His six-per-week chronicles in "The Chronicle" defined what was San Francisco for those of us who lived thereabouts. Fog in summer, rain in winter, aplomb in all seasons. Not Los Angeles. From Left Coast Bohemians to beats to hippies to techies…through much that cannot be forgotten: People's Temple, cults and crazies, Zebra and Zodiac murders, Milk and Moscone assassinations, 1989 quake…three-dot journalism at its strongest. Now with real estate prices to rival Manhattan and central London, San Francisco will surely time and again be felled by quake and tsunami, ever to be rebuilt as long as the human race endures. Nature has made this place irresistible to us mammals who are visually driven and love the scent of salt air reminding us of the salt marshes from which our first footed ancestors slithered.

This book would have been impossible without the bravery and knowledge of the many explorers who traveled from various nations to explore the California coast starting with Sir Francis Drake. By the late 18th Century many of the men who came were educated and recorded what they saw and understood about the land and the living plants and animals found there. Those many expeditions made San Francisco one of the few well-documented locations along entire Pacific coast of North America. By the time the Gold Rush hit in the mid-19th Century there was a pretty good record of what had been there before.

The photo on the front cover was taken at Seal Rocks by Dr, Thomas Kuhn, a long-time friend and neighbor when we lived in San Francisco. The back cover photo is by my friend, Peter Thiemann.

ANNOTATED
BIBLIOGRAPHY

Alcatraz Wildlife: http://www.us-parks.com/alcatraz-island/alcatraz-wildlife. html

Amarelo, Monica. *"Tiny Concentrations of Teflon Chemical Harmful to Public Health."* Environmental Working Group. August 20, 2015. http://www.ewg.org/ release/tiny-concentrations-teflon-chemical-harmful-public-health#. WX5S_Ijys2w

Arcuni, Peter. "The wasting of the stars: A look into the largest ocean epidemic in recorded history." *Peninsula Press.* Stanford University, CA. July 18, 2017. http://peninsulapress.com/2017/07/18/sea-stars/

Asher, Claire. "Climate change is disrupting the birds and the bees." BBC. London. August 7, 2017. Sea turtles and an American alpine plant are having their sex lives upset. http://www.bbc.com/future/ story/20170808-climate-change-is-disrupting-the-birds-and-the-bees

Atherton, Gertrude. *My San Francisco.* Bobbs-Merrill. Indianapolis. 1946. She sub-titled this book "A Wayward Biography."

Bagley, Katherina. "Mix Up" *"Audubon Magazine."* New York. Nov-Dec., 2013.

Bailey, Florence Merriam. *Handbook of the Birds of the Western United States.* Houghton Mifflin. Boston. 1917.

Bakker, Elna. *An Island Called California.* University of California. Berkeley. 1984.

Baldwin, Bruce G., Douglas H. Goldman, David J Keil, Robert Patterson, Thomas J. Rosatti, Dieter H. Wilken (Editors). *The Jepson Manual: Vascular Plants of California.* University of California. Berkeley. 2012.

Barker, Malcolm (ed). *More San Francisco Memoirs.* 1852-1899. Londonborn Publications. San Francisco. 1996.

Barker, Malcolm (ed). *San Francisco Memoirs.* 1835-1851. Londonborn Publications. San Francisco. 1994.

Beach, Joseph Perkins. *The Log of "Apollo." Voyage from New York to San Francisco, 1849. Journal of Joseph Perkins Beach.* Book Club of California San Francisco. 1986.

Bed bugs, how they conquered the world. Bedbugs.org. *http://www.bedbugs.org/ the-history-of-bed-bugs/*

Beechey, Captain Frederick. W. *An Account of a Visit to California 1826-27.* Reprinted from a Narrative of a Voyage to the Pacific and Bering's Strait. Book Club of California [Grabhorn Press]. San Francisco. 1941.

Beechey, Capt. Frederick. W. et al. *Beechey—Narrative of the Voyages.* Huish. London. 1836. Captain Beechey and his ship, *The Blossom* visited San Francisco in 1826-7.

Beechey, Captain Frederick W. et al. *The Zoology of Captain Beechey's Voyage* [1825-1828]. Four volumes. Compiled from the collections and notes made by Captain F.W. Beechey, the officers and the naturalist of the expedition. Henry Bohn. Covent Garden, London. 1839.

Bega, Sheree. "Preparing Ourselves for Climate Change" *Independent Online.* Parktown, South Africa. Nov. 13, 2013. The article warns that mosquito born disease like malaria and yellow and dengue fever may increase with the temperatures.

Bloom, Jonathan. "Luxury skyscraper Millennium Tower sinking in down-town San Francisco." KGO-TV. August 1, 2016. San Francisco. http://

abc7news.com/realestate/luxury-skyscraper-millennium-tower-sinking-in-downtown-sf/1452701/

Blumenfeld, Jared. "SF supervisors need to approve natural-areas program." *San Francisco Chronicle*. San Francisco. Feb. 27, 2017. About the effort to save the Mission blue butterfly. http://www.sfchronicle.com/opinion/openforum/article/SF-supervisors-need-to-approve-natural-areas-10963575.php

Bossard, Carla C., et al. (ed). *Invasive Plants of California's Wildlands*. University of California. Berkeley. 2000.

Boulton, April M., Kendi F. Davies, Philip S. Ward. "Species Richness, Abundance, and Composition of Ground-Dwelling Ants in Northern California Grasslands: Role of Plants, Soil and Grazing. *"Environmental Entomology."* 34(1):96D104 (2005).

Brennan, Summer. "Shell Game: There Is No Such Thing as California "Native" Oysters" *Scientific American*. New York. October 2, 2015. https://www.scientificamerican.com/article/shell-game-there-is-no-such-thing-as-california-native-oysters-excerpt/
I am assured by oyster experts that this article is misleading. There are native oysters living yet in California waters, and now protected by law.

Brewer, William H. Up and Down California 1860-1864. *The journal of William H. Brewer*. Francis Farquhar (ed). University of California. Berkeley. 1966. Brewer was hired to help with the first systematic geological survey of the state. It was a good place to be during the Civil War.

Browne, J. Ross. *J. Ross Browne His Letters, Journals & Writings*. University of New Mexico. Albuquerque. 1969.

Broughton, Jack M. "Pre-Columbian Human Impact on California Vertebrates: Evidence From Old Bones and Implications for Wilderness Policy" *Wilderness and Political Ecology: Aboriginal Influences and the Original State of Nature.* Kay & Simmons (ed). University of Utah Press. Salt Lake City. 2002.

Broughton, Jack M. *Prehistoric Human Impacts on California Birds: Evidence from the Emeryville Shellmound Avifauna.* Ornithological Monographs No. 56. American Ornithologists' Union. Washington DC. 2004.

Broughton, Jack M. and F. E. Bayham. "Showing Off, Foraging Models, and the Ascendance of Hunting in the California Middle Archaic" *American Antiquity.* 68:783-789. 2003.

Brown, Aleta. "Robbing a Golden Rookery." *California Wild.* Winter, 1999. California Academy of Sciences. San Francisco. This magazine is now defunct. This article is about the collection of murre eggs on the Farallones and the campaign by ornithologist Leverett Loomis to get it stopped

Bryant, Harold Child. *Outdoor Heritage. California, Vol. IX.* John McCarty (ed). Powell Publishing. Los Angeles. 1929.

Caen, Herb. *Guide to San Francisco.* Doubleday. Garden City, NY. 1958.

Caen, Herb. *San Francisco, 1976-1991.* Chronicle Books. San Francisco. 1992.

California Native Plant Society. https://www.cnps.org

Carr, Ada. "29 Million Trees Have Died in California From Bark Beetles, Drought" Weather.com. June 11, 2016. https://weather.com/science/environment/news/california-sudden-oak-death-epidemic-killing-trees-bark-beetles-drought.

Chang, Chih-Han. Johns Hopkins University. Baltimore. Website include information on invasive earthworms; soil, the final frontier. http://chihhanchang.weebly.com

Chevigny, Hector. *Lost Empire. The Life and Adventures of Nikolai Petrovich Rezanov.* Macmillan. New York. 1937.

Chu, Jennifer. "Siberian Traps likely culprit for end-Permian extinction." Massachussetts Institute of Technology News Office. Cambridge, MA. September 16, 2015. http://news.mit.edu/2015/siberian-traps-end-permian-extinction-0916.

Chung, Jayhee. "The life history of the invasive European green crab (Carcinus maenus) in San Francisco Bay." Spring, 2011. http://nature.berkeley.edu/classes/es196/projects/2011final/ChungJ_2011.pdf

Clarke, Kevin M., Brian Fisher, Gretchen LeBuhn. "The Influences of Urban Park Characteristics on Ant Comunities." Reasearchgate.net. July 29, 2008. www.researchgate.net/publication/233611069.

Clary, Raymond. *The Making of Golden Gate Park. The Early Years: 1865-1906.* California Living. San Francisco. 1980.

Cone, Marla. "Should DDT Be Used to Combat Malaria?" *Scientific American.* May 4, 2009. https://www.scientificamerican.com/article/ddt-use-to-combat-malaria/

Connor, Edward F., John Hafernik, Jacqueline Levy, Vicki Lee Moore, Jancy K. Rickman. "Insect Conservation In an Urban Biodiversity Hotspot: the San Francisco Bay Area." *Journal of Insect Conservation.* 6:247-259. Kluwer Academic Publishers. Amsterdam. 2003.

Conte, Fred S. "California Oyster Culture." *California Aquaculture.* University of California Davis. 1996. http://aqua.ucdavis.edu/DatabaseRoot/pdf/ASAQ-A07.PDF

Cooper, James Graham. *Ornithology, Volume I, Land Birds.* (edited by Spencer Fullerton Baird from Cooper's manuscript and notes) California Legislature publication. Cambridge, Mass. 1870. Cooper could not make a living at natural history and he never go to finish his second volume. He lived most of the time in the Bay Area.

Coues, Elliott. *Birds of the Northwest. A Hand-book of the Ornithology of the Region Drained by the Missouri River and Its Tributaries.* Dept. of the Interior, Government Printing Office. Washington. 1874. A compendium of every bird sighting by government biologists up to that time for a large area of the west.

Cutter, Donald C. *Malaspina in the Californias.* John Howell Books. San Francisco. 1960. This fine press book includes many reproduced illustrations including earliest known colored renderings of California Quail and Thrasher.

Cutter, Donald C. "A Redwood Collection by Tadeas Haenke." Conifers.org. http://www.conifers.org/topics/Haenke.php

Dell'Amore, Christine. "New Diseases, Toxins Harming Marine Life." *National Geographic.* Washington D.C. April 14, 2013. http://news.nationalgeographic.com/news/2012/04/130412-diseases-health-animals-science-environment-oceans/

Deppe, Ferdinand. *Ferdinand Deppe's Travels in California in 1837.* Gustave Arlt (trans). Glen Dawson. Los Angeles. 1953.

Dunham, Will. "South America's prehistoric people spread like 'invasive species'" Reuters, April 6, 2016. There is no reason to think the human effects on North America were any less catastrophic for wildlife.

"Earthworm Invaders" Smithsonian Environmental Research Center. Edgewater, MD. http://ecosystems.serc.si.edu/earthworm-invaders/

Eldredge, Zoeth Skinner. *The Beginnings of San Francisco.* Two volumes. Self-published. San Francisco. 1912. From the Expedition of Anza, 1774, to the City Charter of April 15, 1850. Contains copies of many maps of San Francisco as well as much of California.

Ellen MacArthur Foundation. On plastic pollution in the ocean: https://www.ellenmacarthurfoundation.org/news/ellen-macarthur-foundation-and-the-prince-of-waless-international-sustainability-unit-launch-2-million-innova-tion-prize-to-keep-plastics-out-the-ocean

Ellis, Michael. *"The History of the Farallon Islands."* Footloose Forays. Published online.

Esbig, Lawrence. "The Bigger the Predator, the Safer the Kelp." *The Daily Nexus*. University of California. Santa Barbara. Feb. 16, 2017. http://dailynexus.com/2017-02-16/the-bigger-the-predator-the-safer-the-kelp/

Farallon History on US Fish and Wildlife Service website: http://www.fws.gov/refuge/farallon/about/history.html

Farallon Restoration: http://www.restorethefarallones.org/learn/

Feldhamer, George A., Bruce C. Thompson, Joseph A. Chapman (editors). *Wild Mammals of North America: Biology, Management, and Conservation.* Johns Hopkins University Press. Baltimore. 1993.

Friedman, Roberta. *"Breeding a Success. Brown Pelicans Come Back to Their Offshore Rookeries." "Pacific Discovery."* California Academy of Sciences. San Francisco. Summer, 1990.

Gaar, Greg and Ryder Miller. *San Francisco A Natural History.* Arcadia Publishing. Charleston, SC. 2006. Contains many historic pictures of San Francisco as open space disappeared, farms were turned into housing.

Gilliam, Harold, Interviewed. "Never Give UP." *Bay Nature*. Berkeley. Jan-Mar, 2011.

Gilliam, Harold. *The Natural World of San Francisco.* Photos by Michael Bry. Doubleday. New York. 1967. Survey from weather and geology to wildlife and flora. A classic and a detailed snapshot of San Francisco at a moment in time.

Glen Canyon Park Natural Areas. San Francisco Recreation and Parks Department. San Fracisco. http://sfrecpark.org/destination/glen-park/glen-park-natural-areas/

Golden Gate Park: "Arch of Colonial Trees." San Francisco Recreation and Park Dept. San Francisco. http://sfrecpark.org/parks-open-spaces/golden-gate-park-guide/arch-of-colonial-trees/

Gorres, Josef. "Crazy Snake Worm." [Asian jumping worm]. Plant and Soil Science, University of Vermont. http://blog.uvm.edu/jgorres/amynthas/

Grinnell, Joseph and Margaret W. Wythe. *Directory to the Bird-life of the San Francisco Bay Region.* Cooper Ornithological Club. Berkeley. 1927.

Grinnell, Joseph and Alden Miller. *The Distribution of the Birds of California.* Artemisia Press. Lee Vining, CA. 1986. Reprint of original published in 1944 by Cooper Ornithological Club. Gives comprehensive picture of bird life at pint in time: Ravens almost extinct, Condors still flying free, Starlings almost unheard of.

Grinnell, Joseph, Harold Bryant and Tracy Storer. *The Game Birds of California.* Illustrated by Louis Agassiz Fuertes. University of California. Berkeley. 1912. Includes information on ducks, geese, swans, cranes, rails, all shorebirds, grouse, quail and doves known in the state at that time. Can you imagine hunting Black Oystercatchers? Clearly there has been some positive social evolution in the past century.

Guillou, Charles F. B. *Oregon and California Drawings. 1841 and 1847.* Book Club of California. San Francisco. 1961.

Gutierrez, Ramon and Richard Orsi (ed). *Contested Eden. California before the Gold Rush*. University of California. Berkeley. 1998. Anthology of history essays. Two most pertinent to this book are: "A World of Balance and Plenty" by M. Kat Anderson, et al. "Serpent in the Garden: Environmental Change in Colonial California" by William Preston.

Guy, Allison. "Some Kelp Forests Show Surprising Resistance to Climate Change – But It's Not All Good News." *Oceana blog*. Washington D.C. Dec. 20, 2016. http://oceana.org/blog/some-kelp-forests-show-surprising-resistance-climate-change-%E2%80%93-it%E2%80%99s-not-all-good-news

Haenke, Thaddeus. Biographical summary: https://www.unigoettingen.de/en/187059.html

Hakim, Danny. "Monsanto Weed Killer Roundup Faces New Doubts on Safety in Unsealed Documents." *New York Times*. New York. March 14, 2017.

Hansen, Gladys and Emmet Condon. *Denial of Disaster. The Untold Story and Photographs of the San Francisco Earthquake and Fire of 1906*. Cameron. San Francisco. 1989. Ms Hansen produced evidence that the quake and fire death toll far exceeded "official" counts.

Heizer, Robert E. and Albert Elsasser. *The Natural World of the California Indians*. University of California. Berkeley. 1980.

Hijar, Carlos, et al. *Three Memoirs of Mexican California*. Thomas Savage (recorder in 1877). Vivian Fisher (trans). Friends of Bancroft Library. Berkeley. 1988.

Hoffman, Ralph. *Birds of the Pacific States*. Houghton Mifflin. Boston. 1927.

Halloran, Pete. "Presidio Plant List." Golden Gate National Parks Association. San Francisco. 2002. Available at Golden Gate National Parks Association (GGNPA), Building 201, Fort Mason, San Francisco, CA 94123

Howell, John Thomas, Peter Raven and Peter Rubtzoff. *A Flora of San Francisco, California.* University of San Francisco. San Francisco. 1958.

Hunters Point radiation. "Further Hunters Point Shipyard land transfers halted while Tetra Tech's radiation cleanup fraud investigated." *San Francisco Bay View.* San Francisco. Sept. 17, 2016. http://sfbayview.com/2016/09/further-hunters-point-shipyard-land-transfers-halted-while-tetra-techs-radiation-cleanup-fraud-investigated/

Invasive plants. California Invasive Plant Council. Berkeley. Has list of all invasive species and description of possible restoration tactics. http://www.cal-ipc.org/ip/management/ipcw/pages/detailreport.cfm@usernumber=25&surveynumber=182.php

Issel, William and Robert Cherny. *San Francisco 1865-1932. Politics, Power, and Urban Development.* University of California. Berkeley. 1986.

Jameson, E. W. and Hans Peeters. *California Mammals.* Revised Edition. University of California. Berkeley. 2004.

Jehl, Jospeh and Ned Johnson. *A Century of Avifaunal Change in Western North America.* Cooper Ornithological Society. 1994.

Johnson. Paul C. *Pictorial History of California.* Douobleday, Garden City, NY, 1970.

Jurek, Ronald M. "California Shorebird Study." Paper presented at meeting of California-Nevada Chapter of the American Fisheries Society and Western Section of the Wildlife Society, Feb. 2, 1974. Monterey, CA.

Keeler, Charles. *Bird Notes Afield.* Paul Elder Publisher. San Francisco. 1906

Keeler, Charles. *San Francisco and Thereabout.* A.M. Robertson. San Francisco. 1906. Published just before the big earthquake, includes photos of pre-quake city.

King, Thomas Butler. *California: The Wonder of the Age.* W. Cowans. NY. 1850. A fact-finding report for fellow members of the U.S. Congress. King (1800-1864) was elected to the U.S. House of Representatives from Georgia. King Street in San Francisco was named for him.

King, Thomas Butler. *Report of Hon. T. Butler King on California.* Gideon & Co. Washington DC. 1850.

Kipling, Rudyard. *Rudyard Kipling's Letters From San Francisco.* Colt Press. San Francisco. 1949. Written when the 25 year old Kipling visited and sent these reports back to newspapers in India in 1889.

Klein, Alice. "Biggest ever die-off of ocean forests triggered by warming seas." *New Scientist.* July 7, 2016. https://www.newscientist.com/article/2096458-biggest-ever-die-off-of-ocean-forests-triggered-by-warming-seas/

Knight, Ronald L., Michael K. Rust. "The Urban Ants of California With Distribution of Imported Species." *"Southwestern Entomologist,"* Vol. 15, No. 2. Dallas. June, 1990.

Konkel, Lindsey. "DDT Linked to Fourfold Increase in Breast Cancer Risk." *National Geographic.* Washington D.C. June 16, 2015.

Kowaleski, Michael (ed). *Gold Rush. A Literary Exploration.* Heyday Books. Berkeley. 1997.

Kozloff, Eugene and Linda Beidleman. *Plants of the San Francisco Bay Region. Mendocino to Monterey.* Sagen Press. Pacific Grove, CA. 1994.

Kunkel, Benjamin. "The Capitolocene." *"London Review of Books."* Pages. 22-28. London. March 2, 2017.

Lagos, Marisa. "Hazardous Yosemite Slough in S.F. finally getting cleaned up." *SF Gate*. San Francisco. April 6, 2014. http://www.sfgate.com/politics/article/Hazardous-Yosemite-Slough-in-S-F-finally-getting-5376301.php

Langley, Henry G. *San Francisco Directory*. Britton & Rey (lithographers). San Francisco. 1870. The maps for this directory can be seen online at: http://www.davidrumsey.com/home

Langsdorff, G.H Von. *Voyages and Travels in Various Parts of the World During the Years 1803, 1804, 1805, 1806 and 1807*. Henry Colburn. London. 1813. Langsdorff's full name was Georg Heinrich von Langsdorff, Baron de Langsdorff (April 8, 1774 – June 9, 1852). Educated in science in his native Germany he long served the tsar. He lived and explored in Brazil, 1813-1830.

Langsdorff, G.H. Von. *Langsdorff's Narrative of the Rezanov Voyage to Nueva California in 1806*. Thomas Russell (trans). Thomas Russell Private Press. San Francisco. 1927.

Lewis, J.C., K.L. Sallee, and R.T. Golightly Jr. "Introduced red fox in California." *California Department of Fish and Game Nongame Bird and Mammal Section Report 93-10*. Sacramento. 1993.

Lindert, Peter H., Jeffrey G. Williamson. "American Incomes 1774-1860." *National Bureau of Economic Research*. Working Paper No. 18396. Cambridge, MA. September 2012 http://www.nber.org/papers/w18396?ie=UTF8&tag=hardwaresoftw-20&LinkCode=asn&CreativeASIN=

Lockwood, Charles. *Suddenly San Francisco. The Early Years of an Instant City*. San Francisco Examiner. San Francisco. 1978.

Ludlow, Fitz Hugh. *The Heart of the Continent*. Hurd & Hougton, Boston. 1870. Book first published in 1860, a new edition is available from Nabu Press, Charleston, South Carolina.

Lyons, Kathleen and Mary Beth Cooney-Lazaneo. *Plants of the Coast Redwood Region.* Looking Press. Boulder Creek, CA. 1988.

Madhani, Aamer. "Rats! Several big U.S. cities seeing surge in rodent complaints." USAToday. McLean, VA. April 21, 2016. http://www.usatoday.com/story/news/2016/04/21/rats-several-big-us-cities-seeing-surge-rodent-complaints/83328068/

Maillaird, Joseph. *The Birds of Golden Gate Park, San Francisco.* California Academy of Sciences. San Francisco. 1930.

Mapes, Linda, and Hal Benton. "Please Go Fishing, Washington State Says." *Seattle Times.* Aug.4, 2017. http://www.seattletimes.com/seattle-news/environment/oops-after-accidental-release-of-atlantic-salmon-fisherman-being-told-catch-as-many-as-you-want/

Mapes, Linda V. "Scientists now link massive starfish die-off, warming ocean." *SeattleTimes.*Seattle.Feb.12,2016.http://www.seattletimes.com/seattle-news/environment/scientists-now-link-massive-starfish-die-off-warming-ocean/

Margolin, Malcolm. *The Ohlone Way.* Heyday Books. Berkeley. 1978.

Marryat, Frank. *Mountains and Molehills Or, Recollections of a Burnt Journal.* Stanford University Press. Stanford. 1952. Reprint of 1855 edition.

Martinez-Solano, Inigo and Robin Lawson. "Escape to Alcatraz; Evolutionary History of Slender Salamanders On the Islands of San Francisco Bay." *BMC Evolutionary Biology.* 9:38 doi: 10.1186/1471-2148-9-38. 2009. Online at: www.biomedical.com/14712-2148/9/38.
"How Big Volcanic Eruptions Cause Mass Extinctions." Bigvolcanicblog.com. http://big-volcanic.com/flood-basalt-extinctions/

McAdie, Alexander. *The Clouds and Fogs of San Francisco.* A.M. Robertson. San Francisco. 1912. Includes many contemporary photos.

McClintock, Elizabeth. *The Trees of Golden Gate Park and San Francisco*. Heyday Books. Berkeley. 2001.

McLaren Park. Restoration recommendations. San Francisco Recreation and Park Department. San Francisco. February, 2006. This final report includes some fine maps of the current habitat and what the future goals could be.

Menzies, Archibald and Alice Eastwood. "Archibald Menzies' Journal of the Vancouver Expedition." *California Historical Society Quarterly*. Vol. 2, No. 4, pp. 265-340. Jan., 1924.

Menzies, Archibald. *Menzies' Journal of Vancouver Voyage, April to October, 1792*. C.F. Newcombe (ed). Archives of British Columbia. Victoria, BC, Canada. 1923.

Meyers, Tayla. "Scores of Birds, Sea Lions Suffering Likely Domoic Acid Poisoning." *Independent*. London. April 25, 2017. http://www.independent.com/news/2017/apr/25/scores-birds-sea-lions-suffering-likely-domoic-aci

"Microplastic Fact Sheet." San Francisco Estuary Institute. Berkeley. December 8, 2015

"Microplastic Pollution Study." San Francisco Estuary Institute. Berkeley. 2017. http://www.sfei.org/news/new-microplastic-pollution-study-launch-san-francisco-bay-and-adjacent-ocean-waters#sthash.MCO8Pcjr.dpbs

Miller, Joaquin. *True Bear Stories*. Yolla Bolly Press. Covelo, CA. 1985. Stories first published in 1900.

Mission blue butterfly. Golden Gate Parks Conservancy. San Francisco. http://www.parksconservancy.org/conservation/plants-animals/endangered-species/mission-blue-butterfly.html?

Moore, S.S., N.E. Seavy, and M. Gerhart. *Scenario planning for climate change adaptation: A guidance for resource managers.* Point Blue Conservation Science and California Coastal Conservancy. Petaluma, CA. 2013.

Muir, John. *Nature Writings.* Library of America. New York. 1997.

Munz, Phillip and David Keck. *A California Flora.* University of California. Berkeley. 1973.

Newts, California. Californiaherps.com. http://www.californiaherps.com/salamanders/pages/t.t.torosa.html#description

Nolte, Carl. "Ships Under San Francisco." *San Francisco Chronicle.* March 14, 1999.

Nuzzo, Victoria A., John C. MAERZ, Bernd Blossey. "Earthworm Invasion as the Driving Force Behind Plant Invasion and Community Changer in Northeastern North American Forests." *Conservation Biology.* 23(4):966-74. doi: 10.1111/j.1523-1739.2009.01168.x. August, 2009.

Ocean Beach Master Plan. San Francisco Bay Area Planning and Urban Research Association. San Francisco. 2012.

"Oil Upon the Waters." *The Gull.* Audubon Association of the Pacific. San Francisco. April, 1919. There was also a follow-up article in the June, 1919, issue of *The Gull.*

O'Reilly, James (ed) et al. *Travellers' Tales, San Francisco.* O'Reilly & Associates. Sebastopol, CA. 1966.

"Oyster reef ecology." National Oceanic and Atmospheric Administraion. Washington D. C. http://www.habitat.noaa.gov/pdf/ecology_of_oysters.pdf

Paddison, Joshua (ed). *A World Transformed. First hand accounts of California before the Gold Rush.* Heyday Books. Berkeley. 1999. Rich trove of stories of the boom town experiences.

Peard, George. *To the Pacific and Arctic With Beechey. The Journal of Lt. George Peard of "HMS Blossom" 1825-1828.* Benny Gough (ed). Cambridge University Press. 1973.

Perkowski, Mateusz. "Crazy Snake Worm Unearthed in Oregon." *Capital Press.* August 9, 2016http://www.capitalpress.com/Oregon/20160809/ crazy-snake-worm-unearthed-in-oregon. .

La Perouse, Jean Francois Galoup de. *A voyage round the world in the years 1785, 1786, 1787 and 1788 by J.F.G. de La Perouse*: published conformably to the decree of the National Assembly, of the 22d of April, 1791, and edited by L.A. Milet-Mureau, brigadier general in the Corps of engineers, director of the fortifications, ex-constituent, and member of several literary societies at Paris. In three volumes. Translated from the French. J. Muir. London. 1798.
Now online at: http://trove.nla.gov.au/work/5766697?q&sort=holdings+de sc&_=1477182940425&versionId=209747060

La Perouse, Jean Francois Galoup de. *Life in a California Mission. Monterey in 1786.* Heyday Books. Berkeley. 1989.

Phelps, William D. *Fore and Aft: or, Leaves From the Life of an Old Soldier.* by "Webfoot" [pseud.]. Phillips, Samson & Co. Boston. 1871. Reprinted by Kessinger Legacy Reprints. Whitefish, Montana. 2010.

Pickart, Andrea. "Restoring the Grasslands of Northern California's Coastal Dunes." *Grasslands.* Vol. XVIII, No.1. California Native Grasslands Association. Davis, CA. Winter, 2008.

Potts, D.C. "Persistence and Extinction of Local Populations of the Garden Snail *Helix aspersa* in Unfavorable Environments" *Oceologia.* Vol. 21, Issue 4. Springer-Verlag. 1975.

Presidio Geology: http://www.ohranger.com/presidio-san-francisco/geology

Presidio Rare Plants. National Park Service. San Francisco. https://www.nps. gov/prsf/learn/nature/rare-and-endangered-plants.htm

Radish,Californiawild.EnvironmentalProtectionAgency.WashingtonD.C.https:// cfpub.epa.gov/ncer_abstracts/index.cfm/fuseaction/display.highlight/ abstract/7715

Ray, Milton. *The Farallones The Painted World and Other Poems of California*. John Henry Nash. San Francisco. 1934. Includes history of use and settlement on the islands to the point of publication.

Red fox in Sierra Nevada. California Department of Fish and Wildlife. Sacramento. https://www.wildlife.ca.gov/Conservation/Mammals/ Sierra-Nevada-Red-Fox

Revere, Lt. Joseph Warren. *A Tour of Duty in California; Including a Description of the Gold Region*. C.S. Francis. New York. 1849. This memoir includes a map of the Bay Area. Revere was in California in 1847 and briefly commanded all U.S. forces there as a Navy Lieutenant. He first raised the U.S. flag in Sonoma. He was grandson of Paul Revere.

Roquefeuil, Camille de. *A Voyage Round the World, Between the Years 1816-1819*. British Library. London. 2011.

Rose. Evelyn. "A Foresting We Will Go." Tramps of San Francisco. San Francisco. http://www.trampsofsanfrancisco.com/a-foresting-we-will-go-a-history- of-trees-in-san-francisco/

Sanchez, Nellie Van de Griff. *Spanish Arcadia*. Powell Publishing. Los Angeles. 1929.

San Francisco's Amphibians & Reptiles. The San Francisco Preservation Society, San Francisco. http://sfpsociety.org/SFherps.htm

Schoenherr, Allan A. *A Natural History of California*. University of California Press. Berkeley. 1992. Comprehensive but now over two decades old and does not include any mention of climate change.

Sea lions, California. Pier 39. San Francisco. https://www.pier39.com/the-sea-lion-story/

Shah, Sonia. "As Pharmaceutical Use Soars, Drugs Taint Water and Wildlife." *Yale Envrionment 360*. New Haven. April 15, 2010.

Sharpsteen, William. "Vanished Waters of Southeastern San Francisco" *California Historical Quarterly*. San Francisco. June, 1941.

Shimuzu, Yu. *Geology of Lake Merced*. San Francisco State University. San Francisco. http://online.sfsu.edu/bholzman/LakeMerced/geology.htm

Simpson, Sir George. *Narrative of a Journey Round the World During the Years 1841 and 1842*. Two volumes. Henry Colburn Publishing. London. 1847. Simpson (1792?-1860) was Governor-in-Chief of the Hudson's Bay Company when he visited California.

Snail, brown garden. Division of Agriculture and Natural Resources, University of California. Berkeley. 2017. http://ucanr.edu/sites/CalSnailsandSlugs/Californias_Pest_Snails_and_Slugs/Brown_Garden_Snail/

Solnit, Rebecca and Mona Caron. *A California Bestiary*. Heyday Books. Berkeley. 2010.

Soule, Frank, John Gihon and James Nisbet. *The Annals of San Francisco*. Berkeley Hills Books. Berkeley. 1999. Reprint of the original published in 1855 and a thorough documentary accounting of San Francisco's beginning decades. Written by three newspapermen this book has become a standard reference on the early years of American San Francisco. It is rife with stunning details, racism and boosterism. On the fact of the inevitable next earthquake: "though even such lamentable event as the total destruction of half the place, like another Quito or Caracas, would speedily be remedied by the indomitable energy and persevering industry of the American character." Pretty accurate prediction fifty years before the 1906 quake.

Standiford, Richard B., Justin Vreeland, Bill Tietje. "Earthworm Ecology in California." Division of Agriculture and Natural Resources, University of California. Berkeley. http://ucanr.edu/sites/oak_range/Oak_Articles_On_Line/Oak_Woodland_Ecology_and_Monitoring/Earthworm_Ecology_in_California/

Starks, Edwin C. *A History of California Shore Whaling. Fish Bulletin No. 6.* California Fish & Game Commission. Sacramento. 1923. http://content.cdlib.org/view?docId=kt7t1nb2f7&&doc.view=entire_text

Starthistle. U. S. Forest Service. Washington D. C. Complete scientific summary with numerous references to specific publications on this species. https://www.fs.fed.us/database/feis/plants/forb/censol/all.html

Stevenson, Robert Louis. *From Scotland to Silverado.* James D. Hart (ed). Harvard University Press. Cambridge. 1966.

Stevenson, Robert Louis. *Selected Letters of Robert Louis Stevenson.* Ernest Mehew (ed). Yale University Press. New Haven. 1997.

Stewart, Robert and M. F. Stewart. *Adolph Sutro: A Biography.* Howell-North. Berkeley. 1962. One-time mayor and major landowner, Sutro once owned 12% of all the land in San Francisco, most of it west of Van Ness before the earthquake.

Stillson, Richard Thomas. *Spreading the Word: A History of Information in the California Gold Rush.* University of Nebraska. Lincoln. 2006.

Striped bass history in California. California Department of Fish and Wildlife. Sacramento. https://www.wildlife.ca.gov/Fishing/Inland/Striped-Bass# 35540374-history

Sullivan, Michael. *Trees of San Francisco*. Wilderness Press. 2013.

Sydeman, William, Jarrod Santora, Saran Ann Thompson, et al. "Increasing variance in North Pacific climate relates to unprecedented ecosystem variability off California." *Global Change Biology*.Wiley Online Library.Hoboken, NJ. Vol. 19. 2013.

Tarmy, James and Kartikay Mehrotra. "The Millennium Tower is still sinking, and residents might be stuck paying for the fixes themselves." *Bloomberg News*. New York. Feb. 2, 2017. https://www.bloomberg.com/news/articles/2017-02-01/ who-will-pay-for-san-francisco-s-tilting-sinking-millennium-tower

Taylor, Bayard. *Eldorado, or Adventures in the Path of Empire*. University of Nebraska. Lincoln. 1988. First published by Putnam in 1850. A journalist born in Pennsylvania, Taylor (1825-1878) was hired by Horace Greeley to report on the Gold Rush in 1848. Taylor was a prodigious traveler and writer as well as diplomat.

Taylor, Harry R. "A Trip to the Farallon Islands." Page 42-3, *"Ornithologist and Oologist."* Vol. XII, No. 3. Boston. March, 1887.

Thomes, William H. *On Land and Sea*. Donnelley, Loyd & Co. Chicago. 1883. Another prodigious traveler, this memoir was written years after Thomes was in California.

Venegas, Miguel. *A Natural and Civil History of California*. Readex Microprint. 1966. Originally published in English in London. 1759. First Spanish edition published in Madrid, 1758. Venegas was a Jesuit in Mexico who never saw California first hand.

Watson, Douglas. *An Hour's Walk Through Yerba Buena*. Lawton Kennedy for *E Clampus Vitus*. San Francisco. 1932.

Welch, Craig. "Heat Wave." Pp. 54-75. *"National Geographic."* Washington D.C. September, 2016. Superb summary of the Pacific Ocean heating in Northern Hemisphere during 2013-2015. Accompanied by excellent illustrative insert. http://www.nationalgeographic.com/magazine/2016/09/warm-water-pacific-coast-algae-nino/

West Nile Virus deaths. California Dept. of Public Health, et al. Sacramento. Updated annually. So far records show 2004 was worst year for birds and horses; 2014 was worst year for human infections of the disease in California. http://www.westnile.ca.gov/

Wilkes, Captain Charles. *U.S Exploring Expedition During the 4 Years 1838, 1839, 1840, 1841, 1842. Under the command of Captain Charles Wilkes, U. S. N. C.* Sherman & Sons. Philadelphia. 1844-1874. Volume XX on herpetology published in 1858. Volume XXIII on hydrography published in 1861.

Wilkey, Robin. "San Francisco Coyotes: Pups Spotted In Golden Gate Park." *Huffington Post.* June 22, 2013. http://www.huffingtonpost.com/2013/06/20/san-francisco-coyotes_n_3474123.html

Wilson, Katherine. *Golden Gate. The Park of a Thousand Vistas*. Caxton Printers. Caldwell, Idaho. 1950.

Wirtschafter, Eli. "Scientists and Fishermen Scramble to Save Northern California's Kelp Forests." *KQED*. San Francisco. Jan. 30, 2017. https://ww2.kqed.org/science/2017/01/30/scientists-and-fishermen-scramble-to-save-northern-californias-kelp-forests/

Wood, Hulton B., Samuel W. James. "Native and Introduced Earthworms From Selected Chaparral, Woodland, and Riparian Zones in Southern California."

General Tech. Report PSW-GTR-142. *Pacific Southwest Research Station, U.S. Forest Service.* Albany, CA. 1993.

Wood, Michael. "The Treasure of Yerba Buena Island." *California Coast & Ocean.* Vol. 22, No. 4. Coastal Conservancy. Oakland. 2007.

Wores, Theodore. *"Sand Dunes and Lake Merced" Painting ID: LA-2874-KA.*

Yosemite Slough Wetlands Restoration Project. California Department of Parks and Recreation. Sacramento. https://www.parks.ca.gov/?page_id=28024

MAPS:

"The Ecology and Natural History of San Francisco: Wild in the City." By Nancy Morita. San Anselmo, CA. 1992.

"Historical View of Central Bay Subregion, ca. 1770-1820" San Francisco Estuary Institute. Richmond, CA. 1997.

"The Natural Presidio" National Park Service. 2007.

"Nature in the City" San Francisco Recreation and Parks, Presidio Trust, Nature in the City.

"San Francisco. Rand-McNally Vest Pocket Map" Rand McNally. San Francisco. 1925.

Tunison's Atlas Map of San Francisco. 1902.

U.S. Geological Survey maps of San Francisco.

Vioget's map of Yerba Buena. 1839.

INDEX

escargot 72

Eschscholtz, Dr. Johann von 23

eucalyptus xix, xxvii, 38, 51, 64, 67-71, 95, 106, 128, 133, 139, 142, 152. 162

Eurasian Collared-Dove 74, 107

Eureka 106

European green crab 66, 140, 171

Starling xiii, 106, 152, 169

Europeans xii, 2, 3, 20, 31, 32

Evermann, Dr. Barton 123

Fages, Pedro xvii

falcon 4, 35

Peregrine 39, 86, 109, 110, 167, 169

Prairie 86

fan palm 105

Farnham, Thomas 43

Farallon Islands xvii, 31, 42, 75, 76, 84, 121, 122, 125, 126, 155, 169

Farallones xvii, xix, xx, 31, 42, 43, 48, 76, 77, 86, 117-127, 138, 161, 169

Institute 145

National Marine Sanctuary xx, 125

Wilderness Area 125

feather xxvi, 33, 44, 75, 87, 102, 167

fennel 57, 67, 68

Ferry Building 149

filaree 66

Financial District 24, 64

finch 4, 39, 103, 109, 168

adobe 103

House 101, 103, 128, 152

Fine Arts, Palace of 10, 93

fire xx, xxi, 3, 5, 21, 30, 33, 34, 50, 61, 65, 67, 69, 89, 97, 145, 159

firewood 22, 60, 62, 69

fish xxiii, xxvii, 2, 4, 5, 6, 10, 33, 41, 46, 49, 61, 72, 73, 79, 109, 111, 118, 122, 124-127, 140, 145, 146, 150, 151, 158-160, 162, 167, 168

Fisherman's Wharf 93, 95, 97, 149

fishing 5, 14, 42, 59, 73, 83-85, 109, 110, 117, 123, 124, 158, 162

fleas 46, 50, 88, 89, 116

Florida 74, 107

fly, fruit 66

spotted wing vinegar 66

flycatcher 2

Pacific-slope 100

fog xi, xxiv, xxv, 19, 25, 37, 47, 50, 89, 95, 119, 130, 131, 135, 137, 141, 146, 154, 157, 172

forbs 28

Forster's Tern xxvi

Fort Funston 1, 69, 101, 111, 112, 149

Mason xx, 7, 10, 25, 69, 149

Montgomery 90

Point 7, 10, 17, 26, 95

Ross xviii, 42, 76, 77, 120

fox 36, 38, 39, 42, 85, 115

red 114, 115

squirrel 115, 116

French broom 68

hollyhock 68

hollyleaf cherry 11, 61, 63

honeybee mite 73

Hooded Oriole 104, 105, 107

horn-owls 4

Horned Lark 37, 101

horse-chestnut 21, 22

horse(s) 3, 4, 17, 24, 44, 53, 54, 56-58,
  94, 95, 113, 130, 133, 152

horsetail, giant 24, 27, 128

House Finch 101, 103, 128, 152

House Sparrow 106, 124

huckleberry 70

Hudson's Bay Company xix, 42, 56

Humboldt Bay 80

Hummingbird, Anna's 39-41, 128

Hunters Point 12, 26, 37, 96, 112, 161,
  168

hunting xi, xviii, xxvii, 3, 5, 36, 38,
  40, 42, 53, 56, 58, 59, 61, 69,
  73, 76-79, 82-84, 91, 100,
  114, 120, 169, 170

Huntley, Henry Vere 63

Hutton's Vireo 106, 136

hybridization 146

hydraulic mining 83, 84

ice age 1

iceplant 68, 70

icterids 38

Idaho 66

India Basin 96

Indians [Native Americans] xii, xviii,
  xx, xxvii, 1, 2, 5, 6, 10, 19-21,
  28-34, 36, 42, 49, 50, 53, 54,

58, 60, 61, 72, 84, 120, 128,
  155

influenza 32

Inspiration Point xxi, 26, 141, 142,
  168

introduced [non-native species] 32,
  48, 50, 65-74, 85, 100, 101,
  106, 107, 114-116, 128, 131,
  136, 140, 143, 140, 143, 144,
  152, 154, 168

Inuit xii

invasive xv, xxvii, 1, 3, 26, 47, 51, 53,
  65-74, 120, 129, 140, 141, 166

Invasive Species Council, California
  74

invertebrates 50, 51, 58, 71, 120, 141

iron 26

irrigation 3, 30, 68, 94, 100, 106, 131,
  135, 166

Ishi xiii

islay [hollyleaf cherry] 63, 70,

Islais Creek 11, 12, 63, 70, 96

Island Creek 12

ivy 72

  Cape 68

  English 68, 69

  German 68

jackals 43

jackrabbit 38

Japan 66, 67, 78, 80

Japanese beetle 73

  Tea Garden xix, 135

jasper 17

jaumea, fleshy 25

reptile 46, 115, 171

Revere, Lt. Joseph Warren 82

Rezanov, Count Nikolai xviii, 22, 36

Rhinoceros Auklets 122, 124, 126

rhododendron 133, 134

ribes xxvii

Richardson, Steve 41

Richardson, William xviii

Richmond 93, 157

    District 25

Rincon Hill 15, 92

    Point 1, 14, 15, 45, 91

    Post Office 17

river otter 30, 42

Robin, American xx, 104, 105, 152

Rock Gulch 12

    Pigeon 74, 103, 106, 169

    Wren 124

Roof, James 5

Roquefeuil, Camille de xviii, 76

rose xi, 5, 24, 133

    California 23

Ross, Fort xviii, 42, 76, 77, 120

Ruddy Duck 84

rush, scouring 24, 27

Russian-American Company 42, 76, 120

Russian Hill xii, 1, 13, 14, 45

    hunters [sealers] 42, 76, 120, 169

    olive 152

Rutte, Theophile de 91

rye 57

Sacramento 106

    River xix, xxiv, 3, 41

Valley xix, xxiv, 115

sagebrush 24

sagewort, beach 25, 140

salamander 48

    arboreal 48

    California slender 48

salmon 41-43, 46, 49, 66, 79, 83, 84, 146

    Atlantic 66, 79

    coho 3

    king 79

salmonberry 24

salt grass 27

samphire 20

San Andreas Fault 18

San Benito County 3

San Bruno 159

    elfin butterfly 51

    Mountain 47, 91, 112, 142,

Sanchez, Nellie Van der Grift 52

sand dunes 19, 23, 27, 47, 68, 92, 104, 132, 141, 142, 162

Sandhill Crane 3, 78, 84, 85

sand-lark 35

sandpiper 31, 37, 39

    Least 111

    Western 111

San Francisco Bay xvii, xviii, xxvii, 2, 7, 8, 14, 17, 19, 23, 30-32, 37, 55, 62, 66, 79-81, 108, 115, 123, 125, 127, 140, 150, 157

    Bay National Wildlife Refuge Complex 71

    Botanical Garden 28, 102, 136

    Call 70

Nuttall's 100
Wores, Theodore 70, 141
wren 37, 38
    Bewick's 100, 101
    Marsh 112
    Rock 124
Wrentit 70, 100, 106, 142
Xerces blue butterfly 13, 47
Xerces Society 47, 70, 71
Yahi xiii
yarrow 70
yedra [poison oak] 22, 23, 34, 118
yellow-eyed grass 142

Yellowthroat, Common 101, 106
yerba buena (plant) 5, 19, 23, 128
Yerba Buena xix, xviii, 8, 14, 22, 24, 32,
    40, 41, 43, 44, 56-58, 62, 89,
    91, 92
    Cove 50, 54, 92
    Island xix, 9, 28, 48, 57, 128
Yosemite Creek 12, 17
    National Park 106
Yount, George 41
Yukon 119
zika virus 152

50136562R00146

Made in the USA
Middletown, DE
23 June 2019